ENCYCLOPEDIA OF
FAMILY HEALTH

ENCYCLOPEDIA OF

FAMILY HEALTH

CONSULTANT
DAVID B. JACOBY, MD
JOHNS HOPKINS SCHOOL OF MEDICINE

VOLUME
15

SYMPTOMS—TWITCHES AND TICS

MARSHALL CAVENDISH
NEW YORK · LONDON · TORONTO · SYDNEY

Marshall Cavendish Corporation

99 White Plains Road

Tarrytown, New York 10591-9001

© Marshall Cavendish Corporation, 1998

© Marshall Cavendish Limited 1998, 1991, 1988, 1986, 1983, 1982, 1971

Update by Brown Partworks

The material in this set was first published in the English language by
Marshall Cavendish Limited of 119 Wardour Street, London W1V 3TD, England.

Printed and bound in Italy

Library of Congress Cataloging-in-Publication Data

Encyclopedia of family health
17v. cm.
Includes index
1. Medicine, Popular-Encyclopedias. 2. Health-Encyclopedias. I. Marshall Cavendish Corporation.
RC81.A2M336 1998   96-49537
610'. 3-dc21   CIP
ISBN 0-7614-0625-5 (set)
ISBN 0-7614-0640-9 (v.15)

INTRODUCTION

We Americans live under a constant bombardment of information (and misinformation) about the latest supposed threats to our health. We are taught to believe that disease is the result of not taking care of ourselves. Death becomes optional. Preventive medicine becomes a moral crusade, illness the punishment for the foolish excesses of the American lifestyle. It is not the intent of the authors of this encyclopedia to contribute to this atmosphere. While it is undoubtedly true that Americans could improve their health by smoking less, exercising more, and controlling their weight, this is already widely understood.

As Mencken put it, "It is not the aim of medicine to make men virtuous. The physician should not preach salvation, he should offer absolution." The aims of this encyclopedia are to present a summary of human biology, anatomy, and physiology, to outline the more common diseases, and to discuss, in a general way, the diagnosis and treatment of these diseases. This is not a do-it-yourself book. It will not be possible to treat most conditions based on the information presented here. But it will be possible to understand most diseases and their treatments. Informed in this way, you will be able to discuss your condition and its treatment with your physician. It is also hoped that this will alleviate some of the fears associated with diseases, doctors, and hospitals.

The authors of this encyclopedia have also attempted to present, in an open-minded way, alternative therapies. There is undoubtedly value to some of these. However, when dealing with serious diseases, they should not be viewed as a substitute for conventional treatment. The reason that conventional treatment is accepted is that it has been systematically tested, and because scientific evidence backs it up. It would be a tragedy to miss the opportunity for effective treatment while pursuing an ineffective alternative therapy.

Finally, it should be remembered that the word *doctor* is originally from the Latin word for "teacher." Applied to medicine, this should remind us that the doctor's duty is not only to diagnose and treat disease, but to help the patient to understand. If this encyclopedia can aid in this process, its authors will be gratified.

DAVID B. JACOBY, MD
JOHNS HOPKINS SCHOOL OF MEDICINE

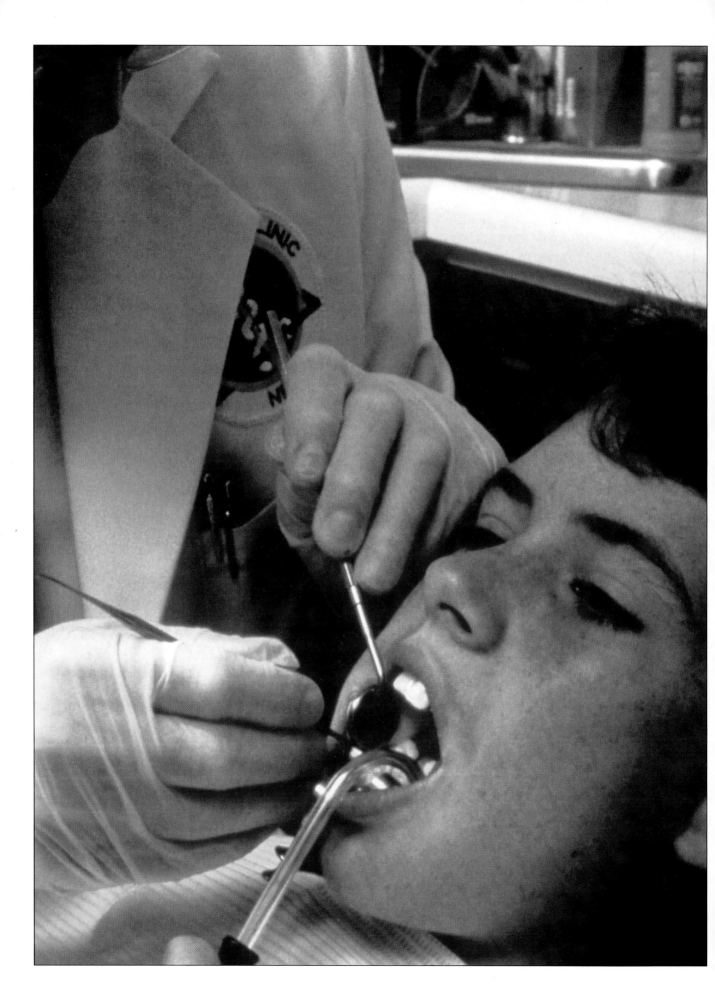

CONTENTS

Symptoms

Q Are there special problems involved in being able to tell when babies are sick? After all, they cannot talk about their symptoms like older children.

A Babies do show obvious signs of illness like diarrhea and vomiting, but often doctors rely upon the intuition of the mother, who just knows that the baby is not well. Sometimes there are obvious upsets in a baby's behavior: crying, not eating, and sleeplessness, for instance. But at other times the mother might suspect that the baby is sick even if there is nothing really evident. Doctors always try and find out from the mother as much as they can, since a mother is most aware of how her baby is feeling. The doctor will then make a diagnosis from this and from an examination.

Q Do all serious illnesses give rise to symptoms?

A No, and this is both a good and a bad thing. On the one hand, it is obviously a good thing that people don't necessarily have to suffer unpleasant symptoms such as pain as a result of the development of something like a blockage in one of the coronary arteries (main blood vessels to the heart). On the other hand, some diseases that might be treatable in their early stages can go unnoticed until it is too late. So symptoms can be both unpleasant and a valuable early warning at the same time.

Q I keep getting a severe pain in my teeth, yet my dentist says that there is nothing wrong with my teeth and the trouble is in my sinuses. Why is this?

A There are many different conditions and diseases that can cause pain at a place away from the center of the trouble. This is called the radiation of pain. Doctors can gain a great deal of useful information by finding out where different sorts of pain radiate to. Heart pain, for example, may be felt in the chest but often spreads to the arms, shoulders, and jaw. Sometimes it is only felt in these apparently unconnected places.

To the doctor, symptoms are the primary means of discovering what is wrong with a patient. To the unlucky people with symptoms, they are the spurs that drive them to seek help from a doctor.

Unpleasant or persistent symptoms are usually what make us see the doctor in the hope of having them relieved. But to a doctor the symptom being complained about is often just one of the clues he or she has in making a diagnosis upon which any treatment that is prescribed will eventually be based (see Diagnosis).

What are symptoms?

Many people get confused about what symptoms really are. In effect, a symptom is any change in the body or its functions that intrudes sufficiently upon a person's awareness to cause him or her to associate it with something not being right. These physical or mental sensations can range all the way from a pain in the stomach after eating, to amnesia after an accident. The range of symptoms is enormous, and people suffering from the same underlying illness can experience and describe the way they feel in vastly different ways. This sometimes makes it hard for the doctor to interpret, from the patient's own words, what they are actually experiencing. But this description of symptoms is, of course, the doctor's primary means of diagnosis.

It is during the discussion between the doctor and patient that the doctor establishes what direction to pursue in tracking down the nature of the patient's illness. By taking what is called a history—asking diverse questions about the patient's life and general health—other symptoms often come to light. These are often things that the patient thought were unconnected with whatever they may be suffering from. For instance, someone who goes to the doctor complaining of weight loss might be asked whether he or she likes hot or cold weather. This might seem to be irrelevant to the patient, but weight loss and intolerance of heat are two clear symptoms of an overactive thyroid gland (see Thyroid).

There are other symptoms that the doctor spots when examining a patient and these are called signs. These are things that the patient might not have noticed and they range anywhere from lumps and bumps under the skin to sounds heard through a stethoscope. Other signs that the doctor can find may be discovered by asking questions; questions about a person's life, for instance, will test the memory and can reveal defects in the brain (see Brain).

Timing of symptoms

Something that is very important to the doctor and his or her diagnosis is when any symptoms might have occurred, so it is a very good idea to try and remember when any symptom that is being com-

Referred pain

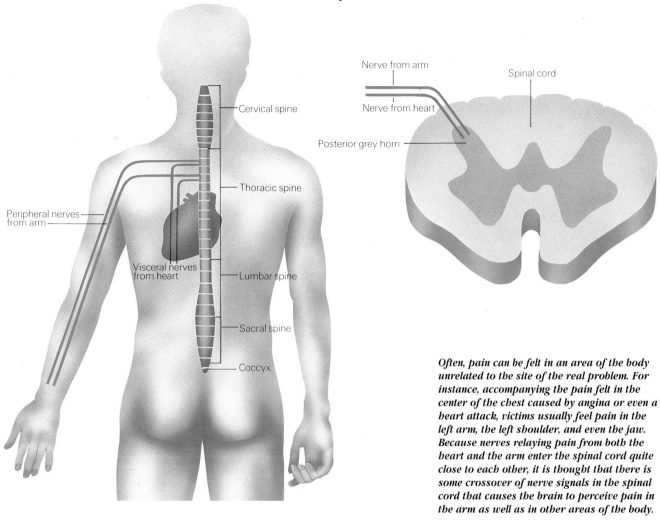

Cervical spine

Thoracic spine

Peripheral nerves from arm

Visceral nerves from heart

Lumbar spine

Sacral spine

Coccyx

Nerve from arm

Nerve from heart

Spinal cord

Posterior grey horn

Often, pain can be felt in an area of the body unrelated to the site of the real problem. For instance, accompanying the pain felt in the center of the chest caused by angina or even a heart attack, victims usually feel pain in the left arm, the left shoulder, and even the jaw. Because nerves relaying pain from both the heart and the arm enter the spinal cord quite close to each other, it is thought that there is some crossover of nerve signals in the spinal cord that causes the brain to perceive pain in the arm as well as in other areas of the body.

It is usually quite safe and normal to treat minor symptoms with simple remedies at home (below left). But persistent problems should be attended to by a doctor.

A vital part of any medical examination involves the doctor listening to the patient's description of his or her symptoms (below). This gives clues to diagnosis.

Bearing in mind the symptoms, the doctor then goes on to the physical side of the examination (below). Here the doctor is looking for signs of the illness.

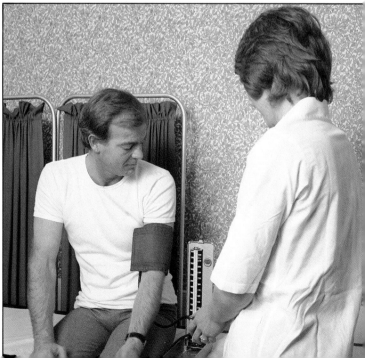

Some common symptoms and what they mean

The list of symptoms, causes, treatment, and dangers shown here is only a representative collection and is by no means intended to serve as a home diagnosis guide. However, it does give some idea of the vast range and diversity of symptoms, where the symptoms occur, and what they can reveal to a doctor.

Symptom	Causes	Treatment and dangers
General and psychiatric		
Tiredness and weakness	Anemia	Determine the cause of the anemia and treat. Iron deficiency is treated with iron. Untreated anemia can be fatal
	Depression: the most common cause of this complaint	Sometimes this diagnosis is quite clear, with obvious unhappiness, and sleep disturbance. At other times physical symptoms can appear. Suicide is a risk
	Convalescence	Tiredness and weakness are to be expected after any serious illness. Sometimes people are surprised at how long it takes to get over a simple viral infection
	Uremia (raised level of breakdown products in the blood, particularly urea): indicates failure of the kidneys Addison's disease (lack of steroid hormone)	The work of the kidneys has to be taken over. This is either done by dialysis—normally using a kidney machine—or by transplantation. Without treatment kidney failure can prove fatal Replacement of the steroid hormones. The disease is easy to diagnose once suspected
Hallucinations (hearing voices)	Schizophrenia	There are many symptoms of schizophrenia, but hearing voices and paranoia—the conviction that people are out to get you—are among the most common. Treatment with drugs controls these symptoms in most cases
	Toxic confusional state	Symptoms of confusion, plus additional features like hallucinations, can occur in any serious illness, particularly in the elderly, and people with a high fever
Anxiety	As well as being a symptom this is a disease in its own right	Treatment is by many different means, including behavior therapy, psychotherapy, and drugs. Long-lasting anxiety can be very difficult to conquer, despite all the different sorts of treatment available
	Thyrotoxicosis (overactive thyroid gland)	Can be almost indistinguishable from pure anxiety, but blood tests make the diagnosis. Treatment is by pills, surgery, or a radioactive iodine drink
Fever	Usually caused by any sort of infection, but can be caused by tumors or dead tissue	An attempt to identify the organism causing the infection is made, and antibiotic drugs are used if they are effective against the organism concerned
Head and nervous system		
Headache	Migraine: in migraine the headache is characteristically on just one side of the head	This is one of the most common conditions and may affect up to 20 percent of the population. Most episodes are irritating but not serious and subside with painkillers and rest
	Tension headache: headache without obvious cause	Painkillers alone help this common problem; it is not dangerous
	Brain tumor	Although there is no denying that brain tumors can cause headaches, it is very uncommon for them to cause headache with no other problem, and they can only contribute to a minute fraction of headaches
	Sinusitis: the ache is more in the face and the teeth, along cheeks	Quitting smoking is essential. Antibiotics and decongestants help
	Temporal arteritis: pain and irritation in the head and scalp	This odd disease is caused by inflammation of the arteries and responds dramatically to treatment with steroids. If untreated, blindness can result
Weakness or complete or partial paralysis	Trauma or diseases that destroy nerves from the brain, through the spinal cord, down to individual nerves or muscles. Common causes are strokes and multiple sclerosis	There is little in the way of curative treatment, but much can be done with physical therapy to reeducate and rehabilitate the parts of the body that are unaffected

Symptom	Causes	Treatment and dangers
Lungs, heart, and chest		
Chest pain	Angina or a heart attack, depending on duration and severity. Typically, the pain feels crushing and is in the center of the chest, often spreading to the arms and neck	Pills reduce the severity and frequency of angina attacks, and surgery may be performed to provide an improved blood supply to the heart. The treatment of a heart attack is to observe the patient carefully and treat problems as they arise
	Pleurisy. A pain felt anywhere in the chest on breathing	May be a complication of pneumonia, in which case antibiotics are appropriate, or it may just occur on its own accord; in which case painkillers are used
Lungs, chest, and heart		
Breathlessness	Heart failure. This is where the heart fails to pump adequately so fluid collects in the lungs	The basis of treatment is with water pills (diuretics) which reduce the load on the heart by clearing fluid and salt from the circulation. Although heart failure can be very serious, patients can have a minor degree of heart failure for years
	Acute bronchitis: with a cough and pneumonia	Infection in the chest both blocks off the bronchial tubes and causes inflammation of the lung tissue. Antibiotics are the usual treatment
	Chronic bronchitis with or without emphysema	A long-term disease causing breathlessness by inflammation of the tubes with excessive phlegm production (chronic bronchitis), or destruction of lung tissue (emphysema). No curative treatment in most cases. Usually caused by smoking
	Asthma: wheezing is characteristic	There are now many effective drugs that reduce the frequency, duration, and severity of attacks
Hemoptysis: coughing up of blood	Cancer of the lung, tuberculosis, bronchitis, and bronchiectasis (destruction of bronchi walls)	Because there are serious causes it is essential to see your doctor and have this symptom investigated
Abdomen and gastrointestinal system		
Dyspepsia: upper abdominal pain	Gastric and duodenal ulceration	Treatment is to reduce the effect of stomach acid which causes the ulcers. Alternatively, the production of acid can be stopped by drugs or surgery. Ulcers can bleed internally and emergency surgery may be needed
	Cholecystitis: gallstones	Removal of the gallbladder
	Esophagitis and hiatus hernia	Treatment with drugs
Acute abdominal pain, severe pain of sudden origin with a hard, tender abdomen	Many causes: especially anything that inflames the peritoneum (membrane lining the inside of the abdomen), such as appendicitis or spillage of intestinal contents through a perforation (burst ulcer)	This is known as an acute abdomen and the treatment of such problems occupies a lot of the time that surgeons spend on emergency duty. If you develop an acute abdominal pain, seek medical help as early as possible
Constipation	Many causes	A high fiber diet is the best treatment, with laxatives only needed rarely
Diarrhea	Gastroenteritis: associated with vomiting	The infection will settle spontaneously. Keep taking as much fluid as possible
	Colitis, where there is also blood and mucus in the feces	Ulcerative colitis is a common type of colitis which usually responds well to drug treatment. The similar Crohn's disease produces colitis as well
Appetite and weight		
Thirst	Diabetes, where there is also weight loss, and copious urine is passed	Insulin in the younger diabetic, while pills alone may be sufficient for many older diabetics. The urine should always be tested for sugar in anyone (even a baby) who is losing weight, with excessive thirst, and passing a large volume of urine
Obesity	Constitutional: related to an excess food intake for that particular person	The only treatment is dieting, which may be combined with an exercise program. Dangers: probably an increased risk of heart attack in younger people, and an increased risk of diabetes
	Cushing's syndrome: overactive adrenal glands causing obesity (with other symptoms)	This is a rare disease that is easy to recognize and accounts for many people thinking they can blame obesity on glands.
Loss of appetite and weight loss	There are many causes, including most of the serious diseases such as cancer	Although there are serious causes, it is rare for a cancer to show up as weight loss with no other symptoms or signs. When people who have isolated weight loss are investigated, mild depression is often the cause

Q Can a doctor tell what is wrong just by talking about my symptoms, or is a physical always needed?

A Doctors have to build up a complete picture of an illness and, although the symptoms are usually the most important feature, the signs the doctor picks up on examination and even the results of tests are often essential for an overall assessment. However, there are some conditions that have such characteristic symptoms that the diagnosis can be made as soon as the patient has told his or her story. Tight pain in the chest that spreads to the neck and occurs on exercise, and which is relieved after a minute or so of rest, is almost certain to be angina.

Q I've heard doctors talking about signs in connection with certain diseases. What is the difference between a sign and a symptom?

A A sign is something that the doctor can either see, feel, or hear when examining a patient, while a symptom is something that a person complains about to a doctor. When a doctor is examining a patient, it's the physical signs that he or she is looking for. Sometimes a sign may be a symptom as well.

Q Is it true that you could have lung cancer without any symptoms? I'm a smoker and I have always been terrified at the thought of cancer.

A Cancer of any tissue must always start with just one abnormal cell. This divides and eventually gives rise to a tumor consisting of abnormal cells. This process can start years before the tumor is finally detected. Tumors in the lung do not give rise to symptoms as fast as some other types of cancers, so they can remain undetected for some time. As a smoker, you are right to be worried. The chances of a smoker having cancer of the lung are much greater. However, if you quit smoking now, in five years your chances of getting lung cancer will revert to being nearly as low as someone who has never smoked.

plained of first occurred, how long it lasted, and how often it happened.

If you were to go to your doctor with a fever, for example, it would be essential to be able to tell him or her when it started and whether it developed suddenly or whether it was preceded by something like a runny nose. The relationship between the various symptoms and the order in which they occur is extremely important in helping the doctor make up his or her mind about all sorts of different diseases, especially infections.

Overall, with any symptom, the doctor is going to want to know not only when it started, but also if it is a pain that comes in attacks, how long each attack lasts, and how often they occur.

What brings them on?

As well as knowing the precise timing of symptoms, the doctor will want to know what, if anything, brings the symptoms on. Sometimes food, or certain types of food, can bring on a burning pain in the upper abdomen. Milk or antacid pills may make the pain go away, and this makes the diagnosis of indigestion virtually certain (see Indigestion).

Some symptoms may be brought on by exertion and relieved by rest, and others by one particular action or movement.

Our symptoms are a two-edged sword: on the one hand they cause the suffering associated with the disease, but on the other, they are the most important means the doctor has in reaching a diagnosis. Diagnosis depends on an accurate assessment of every aspect of the symptoms.

Treatment of symptoms

These days there are all sorts of powerful pain-relieving drugs, and on the face of it there seems to be no reason why patients shouldn't just have their pain relieved

without having to go through the often time-consuming business of a diagnosis being made, during which time the pain might be allowed to continue.

So why not simply give people a mighty dose of painkiller and wait for them to get better? The answer is obvious: if the pain were due to some condition that became progressively worse or needed urgent treatment, the patient, although not in pain, could be killed by it. This is the main reason why diagnosis must be made, in most cases, before treatment of the symptoms can begin.

If someone with severe pain in the abdomen were given a shot of morphine, the doctor would not have any idea about what might be going on. If the pain were due to an inflamed appendix, matters in the abdomen would get worse, without the patient caring, until the appendix ruptured (see Appendicitis). If surgery were then not performed, possibly the patient would die.

But there are some symptoms that it is safe to treat, even when the doctor is not entirely sure what is wrong. For instance, it is safe to take an aspirin for a minor headache. There are many other times when treatment is given to relieve a particular symptom even though the medicine has no effect on the cause of the trouble. Such treatment is often called symptomatic treatment. The use of simple painkillers or cough medicines are good examples of symptomatic treatments. One of the main skills involved in a doctor's job is to know when this kind of simple treatment is safe and appropriate.

These urine samples all show something different. From the left they show the red discoloration of kidney damage, the cloudiness of infection, the clarity of health, and the darkness of liver damage.

Syphilis

Q Why do people regard syphilis with so much fear?

A For three main reasons. First, because it is potentially the most serious of the sexually transmitted diseases; it may lead to death in 5 to 10 percent of untreated patients, or to permanent disability. Second, because it is very difficult to identify in the early stages except by a doctor, and this is the only time at which a cure can be certain. Third, because if it does escape detection the patient has what is virtually a life sentence of uncertainty and worry about if, when, and where the condition may strike since it is able to affect almost all the systems in the body, especially the heart and the brain.

Q Why is it so difficult to diagnose syphilis?

A Established syphilis isn't very difficult to diagnose, but by that time it is usually too late to do anything more with treatment than halting its progress. Only some of the damage—late skin lesions and brain injury—can be reversed by treatment. However, no cure is possible for the lesions of the cardiovascular system.

In its early stages syphilis can be very difficult for patients to recognize, but this is precisely the time at which it must be diagnosed if a cure is going to be effective. The difficulty in detecting the condition in the early stages is due to several different factors.

First, the sore that characterizes early syphilis often takes a long time to develop, sometimes as long as three months, so that people are likely not to associate it with the event that caused it. In many cases, possibly as many as a third, no sore occurs and the first stage is silent.

Another problem is that the sore or ulcer is painless and, furthermore, it heals by itself, without any treatment, in the course of a few days. It is therefore understandable that all these factors tend to make the patient think that he or she doesn't have anything very serious, and consequently no medical advice is sought about the situation.

Of all the sexually transmitted diseases, syphilis is the most dangerous, for if it goes undetected it may eventually cause disablement or death. It is therefore imperative to seek immediate medical attention if the disease is suspected.

Syphilis is not the most common sexually transmitted disease (STD), but it is potentially the most serious if it is not treated within the first few years (see Sexually transmitted diseases). If it remains undiagnosed it continues—like a life sentence—through three progressively more serious stages. However, in a proportion of untreated patients it seems to clear up spontaneously; the reason for this is still unknown.

In the primary and secondary stages, syphilis is an infectious disease of the sex

Notorious Chicago gangster Al Capone still smiling as he is escorted to begin an 11-year prison sentence. Capone had syphilis, from which he later died.

Popperfoto

Q Is it possible to tell whether or not you've got syphilis just by doing a blood test?

A Unfortunately no—something about which there is a great deal of misunderstanding. In established cases the blood tests are certainly positive. But the important thing to remember is that these tests do not become positive until the disease has become established, usually about six weeks or so after sexual contact. Cure is certain in the presence of a positive blood test providing treatment is given within a year or two of infection. However, early treatment is vital to prevent infection of sexual partners.

Q I read somewhere that there is something called latent syphilis. What is this?

A This is the stage in which the disease is inactive. It follows the secondary stage, in which the disease is often virulent, and may lead to the last stage, which is when the really unpleasant consequences of syphilis occur. In the dormant, or latent, stage, the patient has no indication of illness, and the only evidence that he or she has the disease will be the discovery, usually at a prenatal examination or when donating blood, that the blood tests are positive, or when blood tests are performed because of suspected contact with the infection. There is no risk of passing the disease on to anybody else through sexual intercourse during the latent stage, but women can unwittingly pass the condition on to their fetuses if they become pregnant. This is why all pregnant women are tested for syphilis. Should the test turn out to be positive, it is possible to give the mother treatment during the pregnancy which, if given early enough, will prevent the baby from being born with syphilis.

Q Can you recover from syphilis without treatment?

A Yes. In fact 60 percent of those with syphilis clear spontaneously, but this is certainly no reason not to seek treatment!

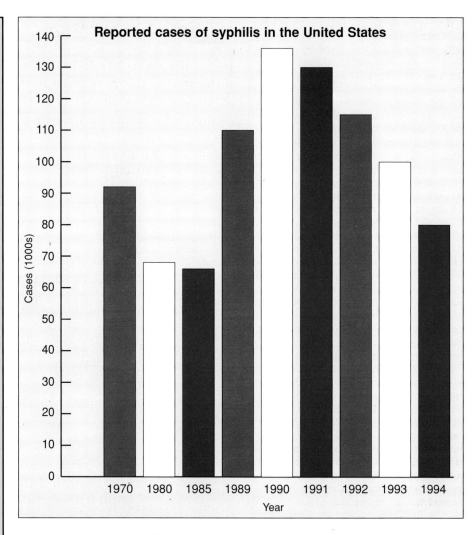

Reported cases of syphilis in the United States

organs and sometimes of the skin and lining of the mouth. It later passes into a dormant, or latent, stage, when no signs of the disease can be seen and the patient has no symptoms of illness. This stage may last from five to as many as 50 years, and it is only after all that time that some of those infected enter into the third stage. In these people, syphilis is often a chronic, crippling, and, for some, a killing disease. Indeed, in the United States alone, hundreds die from it every year.

Progress of the disease

The syphilis germ, shaped like a tiny corkscrew, called *Treponema pallidum*, is a spirochete. About a thousand of these may be acquired during intercourse with an infected person. Every 30 hours or so each germ grows and divides into two, each two into four, each four into eight, and so on. When the first sign of the disease appears, many millions of germs are already present in the victim's body.

The first stage: In the first or primary stage, the disease usually shows itself by the appearance of an ulcer or sore on or in the sex organs. This ulcer is complete-

ly painless and is often neglected for this reason. Occasionally, the primary sore may appear on other parts of the body, for example, in or around the mouth or on the fingers. In homosexual men, the sore may appear on or at the opening of the anus. Primary sores (there may be several) appear about 21 days after the infecting intercourse, but this incubation period may be as short as 9 days or, rarely, as long as 90 days. In some patients there is nothing to be seen; in a few, the sore may only be a small crack in the skin.

A week or two after the sore appears, painless lumps (enlarged glands) can be found in the groin. These swellings show that the body's defenses are working to try to kill off the invading germs. In some women with syphilis, the primary ulcer or sore is internal, and therefore may pass unnoticed. After days or weeks the ulcer, even if untreated, heals. This gives those who have not been treated the impression that all is well. Unfortunately this is not so. If the disease is not treated the germs may invade almost any organ of the body, something that occurs in about 40 percent of patients.

The second stage: This stage shows itself as a generalized rash. This rash is not itchy and may appear anywhere on the body. It can be so slight and faint that it is often ignored. There may also be sores in the mouth or in the throat, or around the sex organs. Headache, fever, and aches in the bones may occur, and there is often enlargement of the glands in the neck and elsewhere. These symptoms of secondary syphilis come and go if the disease is not treated.

The dormant, or latent, stage: If the infection is not diagnosed, or not treated properly, the rash and other symptoms wax and wane and eventually disappear. The disease then enters the dormant, or latent, stage: this can last from 5 to 50 years and will be wholly symptom-free. The disease is no longer infectious and will not be transmitted through sexual intercourse, but women who have undetected syphilis can pass on the condition to their fetus if they become pregnant even several years later. This may result in a baby being born dead, deformed, or diseased.

The third stage: About a third of those who have undetected syphilis suffer sooner or later from skin ulcers, syphilitic heart disease, syphilitic paralysis, insanity, blindness, or deafness. In this stage so much damage has often been done by the germs over many years that treatment can only halt the progress of the disease; but in some the mechanical damage progresses, even though the infection can be cleared. In the earlier stages, syphilis can be cured completely and permanently.

Detection and treatment

In the primary and secondary stages of syphilis the disease can be diagnosed by scraping the primary sore, or one of the parts of the rash, taking some of the fluid which then oozes out, and finding the tiny corkscrew bacterium in it under the microscope. Six weeks after infection, substances that show the body's defenses are working can be detected by a blood test, but before that time the blood test will be negative. In the latent stage, only a blood test will detect syphilis. This test is given to all people attending a genitourinary clinic (see Screening).

All pregnant women attending prenatal clinics have a blood test for syphilis as a matter of course. If the disease is detected, they are treated immediately and usually go on to have perfectly healthy children (see Prenatal care). Every donation of blood for transfusion is, by law, tested for syphilis before it can be given to another person (see Blood donor). Blood tests are also done selectively for patients who are under investigation in the hospital because syphilis may actually imitate other illnesses.

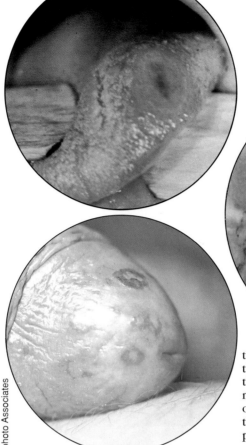

The cause of syphilis is the **Treponema pallidum** *spirochete (below). In the primary stage, the tongue becomes ulcerated (left); in the secondary stage, a rash and sores appear on the sex organs (below left).*

Biophoto Associates

Mary Evans Picture Library

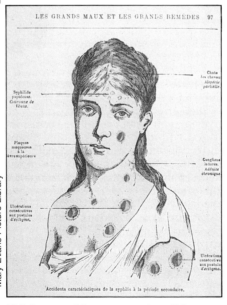

This is a graphic representation of the sort of symptoms that are associated with the secondary stage of syphilis.

At all stages penicillin is the chosen treatment (see Penicillin). It is given as a course of daily injections; the patient attends after working hours if possible. Then every treated person is asked to attend for two years at monthly, and later

three-monthly, intervals for an examination and a blood test. Only in this way can the doctor guarantee that the cure is permanent. Treatment given in the first year of the latent stage is curative, but after that all that may be done is to halt the progress of the disease.

Warning

Syphilis is a great cheater. It is curable, but only with certainty if it is recognized in the first few years of what may be its 50-year course. The problem is that it is often extremely difficult to detect at this stage since blood tests are often negative and thus misleading. The symptoms may sometimes take three months to develop and the victim may not associate a sore developing in March with a casual sexual encounter at Christmas. Probably as many as a third of all people who develop syphilis have no sore and can pass through the primary stage with nothing to show, and thus be completely unaware that they have the disease. A number don't have a proper sore, but only a rather insignificant crack in the skin, which may be difficult to find and may require a doctor to diagnose. Also the sore is quite painless, and patients tend not to go to a doctor with things that don't hurt; moreover, the sore goes away by itself, even if no treatment is given.

So if you think that there is even the slightest chance that you may have been with somebody who has syphilis, go to a genitourinary clinic and find out for sure; it's much too dangerous and insidious a disease to be in any doubt about it. Clinics exist in most cities throughout the United States, and you can usually go without having to make an appointment.

Syringing

Deafness and irritation could mean that your ears need syringing. A doctor can soon remove the cause—hard earwax—by gently squirting water into the ears.

Q My ears seem to make a lot of wax. Will they need syringing every so often to clear out the wax?

A Wax is a natural substance secreted into the ear canal and it acts as a cleanser. It picks up dust from the canal and passes out toward the edge of the ear. You can then wipe it away without poking anything into the canal. Your ears certainly do not need syringing unless the wax becomes hard and builds up in the canal, causing irritation, infection, or deafness.

Q My four-year-old son had a runny ear last winter, which I thought was due to excess wax. I took him to the doctor and he was given antibiotics for infection. Why was this?

A You certainly did the right thing in taking your son to have his ears checked. Sometimes a runny ear is due to wax, but often it is caused by an infection in the middle ear breaking through the eardrum, causing a hole or perforation in the drum to let the pus leak out. This may be apparently painless, or the ear may be painful until the drum is perforated, when the ache caused by the pressure is released. A doctor is always pleased to find that a runny ear is due simply to wax and not to perforation, which can lead to later deafness unless treated quickly. The perforation itself causes some deafness, which disappears when the hole in the drum heals.

Q I had my right ear syringed recently. Why did my doctor ask me to tell him if I felt dizzy during syringing?

A If the water is squirted too forcibly on the eardrum, you may feel dizzy because the inner ear structures that help in balancing are affected. These lie very near the drum and are also affected if the water used to syringe is too warm or too cold. Sometimes a patient may react so strongly to a high or low water temperature that he or she may lose balance completely and fall onto the floor.

Usually ears are syringed to rid the outer canal of wax. This wax may build up and then harden, impairing hearing. The basic process involves water being squirted gently into the ear to soften the wax and to help dislodge it (see Wax in ear).

Conditions requiring syringing

Wax, or cerumen, is the normal secretion of the ceruminous glands that are found in the outer part of the external ear canal. Mixed with this wax is keratin, a horny material from the surface of the skin that is normally rubbed off in tiny quantities, and sebum, the greasy lubricant of the skin. Dust and other materials also find their way into the external ear passage, especially in occupations such as coal mining. The amount and texture of the wax secreted varies considerably. Most people form a small amount of soft wax that works its way, unnoticed, out of the ears. It is only likely to be produced in large amounts, and to become harder, in the middle and later years of life.

Children are rarely affected by hard wax, but they sometimes put things into their ears, such as beads, pips, seeds, and small stones. Never poke anything in the ear to try to remove the object, since this can often cause rupture of the eardrum. Cotton-covered sticks are dangerous; they will only push the object in farther. Instead, go to the doctor. He or she will try to flush the object out with water using a syringe, while looking frequently into the ear. Alternatively, he or she might use a small hook or probe and look through an auriscope (a special instrument used for looking into ears). If a young child is involved, or if the object is deeply embedded, then general anesthesia will be necessary.

Insects also sometimes get into the ear, particularly the common fly, which causes terrible irritation with its whirring wings. The best treatment is to drop warm olive oil into the ear, which can be done safely at home. This kills the fly so a doctor can easily syringe it out later.

Wax buildup

When hard wax fills the ear canal it causes deafness (see Deafness). In an elderly person whose hearing is already poor, or in anyone who has diminished hearing, excess wax may make a huge difference. The wax may cause irritation, noises in the ear by pressing on the eardrum, and, occasionally, feelings of unsteadiness.

Procedure

After your doctor has prescribed syringing, you will be told to use a few drops of warm olive or almond oil once or twice a day for seven to fourteen days in order to soften the wax before your treatment. The instrument used for the treatment is

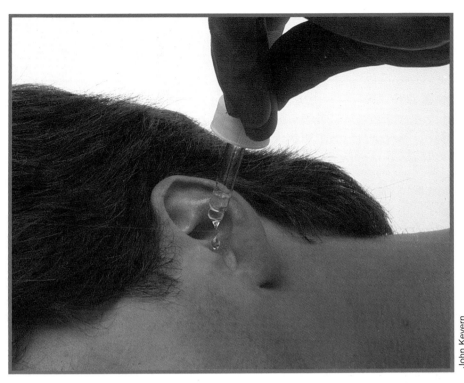

is usually warm water, but sodium bicarbonate or saline solutions may be used. The temperature of the water is vital: it should be no hotter or colder than body temperature, 98.6°F (37°C). The external ear is usually drawn upward and back in order to straighten the ear canal. The syringe nozzle is kept away from the eardrum and the water is directed at the sides and ceiling of the ear canal; there should be no pain. If the wax remains, the patient is sent away with further advice to soften it with oil, and the syringing is then repeated a week later. Excess fluid should be mopped up from the ear canal; stagnant fluid may result in an infection (otitis externa; see Otitis).

Dangers and outlook

Damaging the eardrum is the main danger. If a perforation should result, then infection can enter the middle ear, resulting in deafness, and may spread to the sensitive organs of balance in the inner ear. Syringing while there is a perforation can spread infection and force bacteria into the blood vessels and bone as well as the inner ear. Occasionally the skin of the external ear canal is damaged and may bleed or become infected. This usually heals quickly and can be helped with antibiotic and steroid drops.

Prior to syringing, the doctor will tell you to drop oil into your ear for a week or so to soften the wax (above). The doctor then squirts warm (body temperature) water into the ear to remove wax deposits (left). A doctor uses an auriscope to inspect for wax buildup in the outer ear (below).

usually a large metal syringe with a rounded nozzle, although some operators prefer a rubber syringe. The patient is protected with towels and plastic sheeting, and is usually asked to hold a kidney-shaped dish beneath the ear to catch the water and any bits of wax. The fluid used

John Kevern

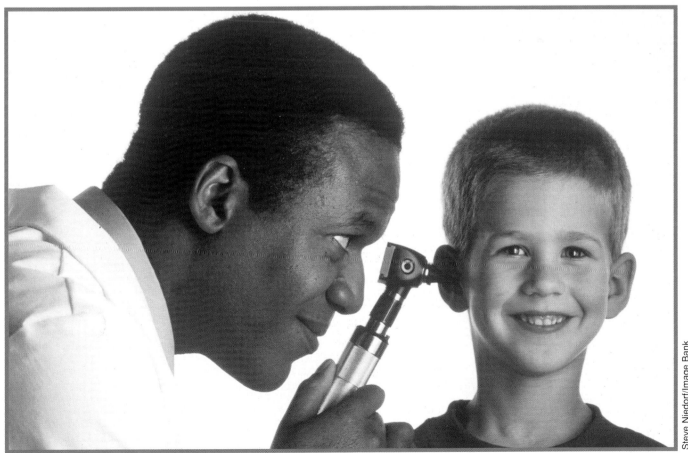

Steve Niedorf/Image Bank

Systemic lupus erythematosus

Q My aunt suffers from SLE and I'm afraid I will inherit it. Recently my fingers and wrists have been aching. Could this be the first sign of its onset?

A There is a small chance of inheriting lupus, but it is by no means a foregone conclusion. The ache in your hands could be the symptom of a great many disorders besides SLE, from rheumatoid arthritis to tenosynovitis: swelling in the protective membranes around the tendon caused by overuse, for example from using a computer keyboard. Your doctor will be able to put these symptoms in context and carry out tests to determine whether SLE is present.

Q My doctor diagnosed a scaly rash on my face as discoid lupus erythematosus (DLE). He gave me some cream and a drug called Plaquenil. He said my condition isn't serious, but isn't Plaquenil given for systemic lupus erythematosus?

A DLE can go on to affect the internal organs and develop into SLE, but this is rare. Plaquenil, or hydroxychloroquine, is helpful in treating skin disorders associated with both forms of lupus, and may act against the development of more serious complications.

Q As an SLE sufferer I was told not to get pregnant, but I want children. Is there really a risk of passing on the condition?

A The risk of passing it on to the fetus in the form of neonatal lupus is minimal. Some studies have shown that symptoms can flare up in pregnancy, but these are unproven. However, some dangers in pregnancy are increased with lupus, including a greater chance of miscarriage or an illness called preeclampsia. Drugs for lupus may have side effects that could affect the mother or fetus, and you may have to suspend treatment while you are pregnant. Certain drugs, or kidney disorders arising from SLE, may also make conception difficult. None of this rules out your having children, but take medical advice.

Systemic lupus erythematosus, a disease of the autoimmune system, involves inflammation of the skin, internal organs, blood vessels, and joints. Often painful, it can result in serious complications such as kidney or heart disorders.

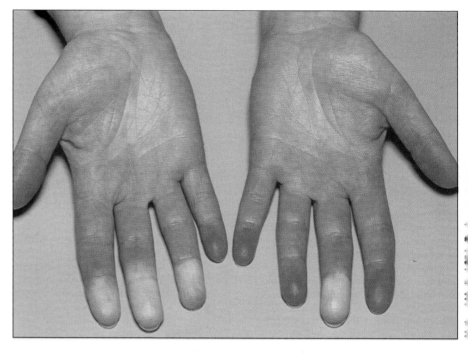

An SLE sufferer with just one of many typical symptoms, Raynaud's phenomenon, in which the fingers become numb and begin to turn blue when exposed to cold.

Systemic lupus erythematosus (SLE), usually called lupus, derives its name from a typical symptom of a butterfly-shaped rash across the nose and cheeks that can produce a wolflike appearance (*lupus* is Latin for wolf). It is one of many autoimmune disorders that occur when the body makes antibodies that attack its own tissues rather than harmful viruses.

About 20 to 30 percent of sufferers experience a mild form of SLE, but for the remainder, lupus is likely to lead to potentially dangerous kidney disorders; a small proportion can have fatal complications. However, some sufferers recover completely. A less serious type of lupus, discoid lupus erythematosus (DLE), characterized by disklike patches of scaling skin on the face, and sometimes on the body, may develop into full SLE.

Symptoms

Because SLE involves a general assault on the body's tissues by its own antibodies, the symptoms are widespread and varied. The joints, especially the knuckles and wrists, may be swollen and painful, with symptoms resembling rheumatoid arthritis. The fingers may also become blue and numb in cold weather, a condition called Raynaud's phenomenon. The butterfly-shaped rash over the face is a common symptom, and may be exacerbated by ultraviolet light or sunlight. The sun may also stimulate fever, rashes, or patches of skin that turn lighter or darker in color. Sufferers may experience sores in the mouth or vagina, and loss of hair.

Coughing and chest or abdominal pain may result if lupus inflames the tissues around the heart, lungs, and abdomen. Or the tissues of the central nervous system may become inflamed, giving rise to seizures or fits, fatigue, migraines, and problems with concentration and memory. Blood disorders are another potential problem, with an imbalance in the number of red or white cells or platelets in the blood producing the same symptoms as diseases such as anemia (see Anemia).

For up to 70 percent of sufferers, lupus results in some form of kidney disorder (see Kidneys and kidney diseases). The kidneys filter waste materials from the blood and control the fluid balance in the body; chronic kidney failure caused by lupus is incurable, leading to severe or fatal illness if not controlled. Rarely, lupus can lead to mental problems, including depression or psychosis (see Depression). Depression may also result from symptoms such as hair loss, skin rashes, and patchy skin coloration, which can damage self-confidence, or simply from the stress of living with a painful long-term disease.

SLE and pregnancy

The symptoms of SLE tend to occur in cycles, with periods of remission. Some research suggests that pregnancy can lead to an attack in existing sufferers, or cause symptoms to appear for the first time. Pregnant women with SLE are more likely to develop preeclampsia, a complication that involves high blood pressure, fluid retention, high protein levels in the urine, and sometimes headaches and visual disturbances (see Pre-eclampsia, and Pregnancy). Untreated, pre-eclampsia develops into eclampsia, which can be fatal. Pregnant SLE sufferers are also more prone to miscarry or to give birth prematurely. Rarely, the fetus may have neonatal lupus, perhaps involving a slow or irregular heartbeat (see Fetus).

A woman with SLE who becomes pregnant has to consider whether to continue or vary any drug treatment in consultation with her doctor. She must be carefully monitored throughout the pregnancy, including tests for neonatal lupus.

Who is at risk?

The causes of SLE are unknown, although it may have a hereditary factor since it is more common among some ethnic groups than others, and may be more likely if a family member is a sufferer. SLE affects eight to ten times as many women as men. In the United States, Native American women are about twice as likely to suffer from SLE as Caucasian women, while there are almost three times as many African American women sufferers; the latter are also more likely to experience serious disorders as part of the disease.

The symptoms of SLE can also appear following the use of certain drugs, including some tranquilizers and other medication used in the treatment of hypertension, arrhythmia, and tuberculosis. Some studies suggest that postmenopausal women taking hormone replacement therapy, and those taking oral contraceptives, may be more at risk of developing SLE (see Hormone replacement therapy).

Diagnosis and treatment

When lupus is suspected, the range of symptoms is compared with those of other disorders that produce similar effects. Lupus can be confused with diseases such as polymyositis, polymyalgia rheumatica, and rheumatoid arthritis, all of which involve inflammation of the connective tissues and are believed to be caused by an autoimmune disorder; however, their overall pattern of symptoms vary slightly (see Rheumatoid arthritis).

Blood tests will be conducted to detect antinuclear antibodies, a type of protein present in the blood of most SLE sufferers; some also have other proteins, called antiphospholipid antibodies, which may be present where there is a risk of stroke or heart attack from blood clotting. Blood tests may also show kidney damage. If this is indicated, a tissue sample may be taken from the kidneys (see Blood).

Sufferers with mild or no symptoms are given hydroxychloroquine, an antimalarial drug, to help prevent any long-term damage. Antiinflammatory drugs such as aspirin may be given for minor

Another symptom common to SLE sufferers; a butterfly-shaped rash across the face that creates a wolflike appearance. It occurs when antibodies attack the body's own cells.

symptoms, while corticosteroid creams can help combat rashes (see Rashes).

Oral corticosteroids and other drugs that suppress the immune system are likely to be prescribed for more serious symptoms affecting the central nervous system or kidneys. These must be used under careful medical supervision since they can cause unpleasant side effects, including osteoporosis (brittle bones; see Osteoporosis), hypertension, and depression, as well as depressing the immune system and thus laying the body open to other infection (see Immune system). Treatment specific to the symptom is prescribed, such as a combination of special drugs used to treat kidney disorders.

SLE sufferers should avoid sunlight and other ultraviolet light, or wear high-protection sunscreens where this is unavoidable. Women patients should also avoid taking estrogen in contraceptive pills or hormone replacement therapy, since this may make symptoms worse. Gentle exercise combined with plenty of rest may help if fatigue is a symptom.

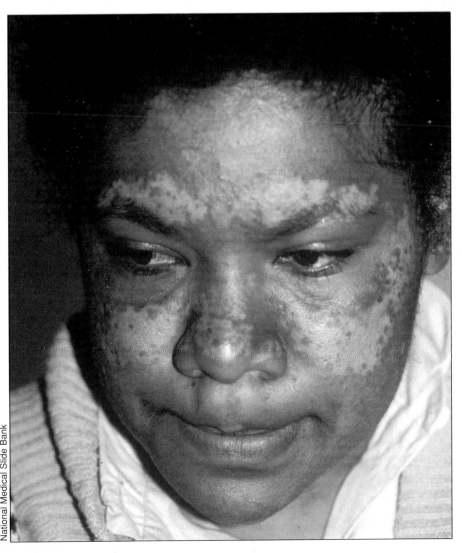

Tai chi

Tai chi is a type of Chinese martial art that was developed several hundred years ago. It is valued for improving fitness, health, and longevity, and is now one of the most popular ways to exercise both the body and the mind.

Q Tai chi seems a relaxing way to exercise. How does slow movement help to maintain the body's physique?

A The aim of tai chi, which is a series of slow body movements, is to relax both the body and the mind so that the person is prepared for an effective defense against illness and psychological disorders. Some of the more obvious physical benefits that can be derived from tai chi are greater flexibility, improved circulation, better balance, and also an enhanced sense of well-being.

Q Is tai chi similar in any way to yoga?

A Only in the sense that it relaxes both the body and the mind. The main physical activity of tai chi is different from yoga in that it is carried out standing up, using balletlike movements of the legs and the arms. Yoga is a system of exercises, postures, meditation, breathing, and relaxation, which is performed standing up, in a sitting position, or lying down. The final effect is similar—a balance of the body and the mind.

Q Do you need to be strong to practice tai chi?

A Not necessarily. Physical strength is not needed for the fluid, balletlike movements. Obviously, a certain degree of strength is required because you have to be able to hold a position before moving with ease to the next one. What is necessary, however, is to have strength of mind for concentration.

Q Can anybody practice tai chi?

A Yes. Age and sex are not barriers to the art of tai chi. Many people take it up for the first time in their middle or later years in order to try to find peace of mind and also to restore a balance in their working and private lives. The best thing about tai chi is that you can practice it anywhere—in your living room, the garden, or even the office.

Nik Wheeler/Corbis

The Chinese call this ancient martial art tàijíquán, but Westerners refer to it colloquially as tai chi chuan or tai chi. Over 10 million people carry out this elegant form of exercise every day in China, and its popularity has spread from Asia during the past 30 years to countries such as Japan, Australia, the United States, Canada, and many European countries.

The philosophy of tai chi

Tai chi promotes complete body and mind relaxation. There are five main styles, each of them based on similar principles. The name *tai chi chuan* means "supreme ultimate fist," and is taken for the concept and philosophy of tai chi, which is symbolized in the ancient symbols of yin and yang—the inviolable duality. The light and the dark of the yin-yang symbol represent the two central forces in the universe around us. The two symbols are linked by a smaller circle within the center of each, representing its opposite.

The movement in tai chi is characterized by a yielding element, and by a continuous flow of energy. It is a play of opposites. Every movement is circular and as a result of each movement, the opposite is revealed. You sink before you rise up, pull back before reaching out, and move left in order to swing right. Such are the opposites.

Over 10 million people practice some kind of tai chi daily in China. Its popularity has spread, and it is now widely practiced in many Western countries.

The form, or solo practice, is a precisely choreographed sequence of movements lasting for anything between five and 60 minutes, depending on which version or style you practice. Every movement is carried out in slow motion and is accompanied by regular breathing. Movements are coordinated with the breathing so that everything is in harmony.

The aim of the serious practitioner, or player, as they are referred to in China, is to harmonize the various individual parts of the body, the emotions, and the spirit, while at the same time becoming aware of states of inner conflict, such as tension and relaxation, that exist in the body and the mind.

Tai chi can also include exercising with weapons, self-defense stances, and perhaps contact sparring. It can also involve standing in a particular posture for as little as a few minutes or as long as an hour. This discipline creates a state of spiritual peace, inner strength, and centers the body.

Among the guiding principles that underlie the concept of tai chi are: relaxation, coordination, slow and continuous movement, cultivation of a calm psychological state and a clear spirit, and finding the center of energy that each of us has, or sinking as it is called in this form of martial art.

Relaxation

Relaxation is the most important aim of tai chi. It is achieved by being loose and extending the arms, legs, and torso to loosen the joints.

It is essential for the body to be relaxed so that the back and shoulders, the arms and legs, and the hips are all correctly aligned. Correct alignment allows an ease of movement.

Coordination

Every movement of the sequence should be coordinated properly so that the whole body is connected. Each movement involves enticing the energy up through the legs, hips, back, and shoulders, and out into the air through the arms and hands.

Slow and continuous movement

There should be no pausing or stopping in the sequence of movements. The speed of the movement can vary depending on the style of the individual. However, there must not be even a slight pause between movements.

Calm state and clear spirit

The process of achieving calmness and a clear spirit should be sought from the first day you begin to study tai chi.

The theory is that the daily practice of the art helps to build up the sense of calm. This sense of calmness also promotes a sense of well-being in all other areas of the practitioner's life.

Sinking

This term refers to sending the essential energy, the Qi (chi), to the lower abdomen (dantian) where it can gather together more energy and become the force behind all of the movements.

The benefits

Many people join tai chi classes to improve their health and spiritual state. However, it also offers an element of self-protection, since the world is understood as a changing interplay of various forces. Each of us, the theory is, must realize our nature, and endure. The prescription for life survival is integrity gained through persistence. The form of tai chi helps to train the body to be free, to learn a keen awareness of sensation and an intimate knowledge of a life force.

In pursuit of power, the tai chi practitioner learns to yield rather than resist.

All forms of tai chi are designed to tap into the energy that runs throughout the body along the pathways called meridians. The points on these meridians are sometimes used by players as focal points through which energy can be directed, making the tai chi exponent extremely strong in will as well as body.

Research group results indicate that players of advanced ages who have been involved with tai chi all their lives show fewer signs of aging. It is ideal for older people because the movements are carried out in a slow and smooth manner.

The movements

In tai chi, the sequence of movements is learned and memorized. The form is specific in terms of direction and the shape of the body, and the placement of each part of the body. The sequences must be practiced daily until they are almost a natural habit.

The body is always upright, unlike the other Eastern relaxation technique, yoga. You have to imagine your body's skeleton hanging from the crown of your head,

Tai chi can be practiced in almost any environment, either alone or in a group. In China it is common for large groups of people to gather for daily practice.

Tai chi chuan

Chinese physical culture begins before history. A legendary philosopher of the 46th century BC, who is believed to have created the original eight trigrams of the I Ching, ordered the performance of a Great Dance to help to cure his people of illness. This ancient combination of exercise with therapeutic and preventive medicine predates the beginning of the martial arts. As early as AD 190 a series of exercises based on the posture of animals was taught, and many of the steps of tai chi take their names from animals, both real and mythical. The expressions "carry the tiger to the mountain," "repulse the monkey," and "dance of the dragon" are a few of the names given to movements.

The person given credit for creating tai chi was a 14th-century Taoist monk by the name of Chang San-Feng, who recast the original elements of an exercise called Shao-Lin Ch'uan. He placed more of an emphasis on breathing and inner control. The tale has it that tai chi was revealed to Chang during a midday meditation session. When he glanced out of a window he saw a magpie trying to attack a snake. The snake teased the bird, moving to be out of reach, curling around in spirals as is the natural way for a snake to behave. In this spiraling snake the essential spirit of tai chi was perceived and adopted. The earliest work is attributed to Chang. He states: "Ultimately, everything depends on one's will or mind and not on the external appearance of the movements." This leads us to assume that specific movements and the order of the sequence are not the most important things.

Another name associated with its origins is that of Wang Chung-yueh, who lived in the 17th century. Wang is credited with having linked the 13 postures to create the continuous movement sequence. Two classic theoretical works are attributed to Wang Yang Lu-chu'an, an ambitious servant who became a well-known teacher in Peking.

Tai chi is divided into different styles, identified by family names. The style called Yang, named after Yang Lu-chan, is now the most popular.

Ten main points of Yang Ching-Pu (grandson of the founder of the Yang school)

1. Suspend the head from above and keep it up straight.
This will enable your inner strength to reach the crown and your spirit will soar free. Keep your neck relaxed—a stiff neck becomes an obstacle to achieving this.

2. Depress the chest and raise the upper back.
This way, you can sink the energy into your "tan-tien" and this, in turn, enables you to bring inner strength to your vertebrae.

3. Loosen the waist.
A key point of the body, loosening your waist allows you to anchor your feet and make the body secure.

4. Distinguish between solidness and emptiness.
Once you have learned this, through moving weight from the left leg to the right and back again, your movements will be light-footed.

5. Droop the shoulders and sink the elbows.
Loosening the shoulder joints allows energy to flow freely.

6. Apply will and not force.
Completely relax the body while practicing tai chi. Awkward tensions in the body hinder the flow of energy.

7. Coordinate upper and lower body movements.
Inner strength is centered in the feet, developed in the thighs, controlled by the waist, and expressed through the fingers.

8. Unify internal and external movements.
Working on the theory that the spirit is the master and the body is the servant, the individual practitioner must seek to move body and spirit as an integrated unit.

9. There must be certainty in the movements.
Will, as opposed to force, is applied to guide all body movements, making them continuous.

10. Seek serenity in activity.
The perfect state to achieve is that of inner serenity and outer activity.

Benefits
- better sense of balance
- greater flexibility of movement
- improved circulation
- an improved sense of well-being
- can lower blood pressure

Studies reveal that older people who have practiced tai chi enjoy better health than other people of the same age. Their breathing, cardiovascular functions, bone conditions, and general metabolism are all in far better condition than those who did not practice tai chi.

The slow movements exercise the muscle fiber of the bones and improve the elasticity of the smooth vascular wall. This increases the circulation of the blood and stabilizes the vascular motor nerve.

completely relaxed through each of the joints. The weight of the body sinks downward through the legs and the feet, in a physical sense, placing roots in the ground. Stillness is at the center of tai chi. All movements start from this stillness.

Learning tai chi

The art of tai chi is not easy to learn. It may look simple when you see an experienced player going through the motions. However, it takes time and concentration to learn the sequences of movement and to become relaxed and completely coordinated while you are doing them. It is generally recognized that even if you have learned all of the exterior movements and become a tai chi master, you will continue to gain an internal spiritual knowledge.

Regular practice

Choose the place where you feel happy to go through the sequences, and then insure that you practice each day, preferably at the same time, so that you do not allow other less important activities to prevent you from doing it.

The study is a long-term investment and the results you gain are directly related to the amount of time and effort that you put into it.

The movements in tai chi are slow, continuous, and graceful. Sometimes a player may stand in a particular posture for up to an hour (above). As in many other martial arts, swords are often part of the ceremonial art of tai chi. Here a woman with a wooden sword leads tai chi exercises in Victoria Park, Hong Kong.

Nik Wheeler/Corbis

Initially the gains may be small, but gradually over the months and years, if you practice regularly and seriously, you will notice the benefits.

You may like to add to your learning by reading about the principles and philosophy of tai chi. It is always a good idea to check the author's credentials, since there are many books on this subject and not all of them are authentic and useful.

You may also want to branch out and explore some of the other Eastern answers to Western stresses (see Acupuncture, Massage, Shiatsu, Yoga).

Finding a teacher

One of the best ways to find a teacher is to contact the local martial arts school and ask for the name of a reputable teacher. Many community centers advertise the services of teachers.

It is important that you are satisfied with the way the teacher approaches the subject and his or her professional relationship with you. If you feel in any way uncomfortable, then this will be a barrier to learning.

Insure also that the methods used conform to accepted tai chi principles. Before you sign up for a class, ask if you can go along as an observer so that you can get some experience of the teacher.

Taste

It is ironic that the word taste *stands for discernment when you consider that this is the crudest of our five senses. We are capable of distinguishing only four basic taste sensations from our food and drink.*

Q I recently had a bad head injury, fracturing my skull. I seem to have recovered completely now but am troubled by a nearly complete loss of my sense of taste. Does this mean that the nerves from the tongue have been damaged?

A Probably not. It is much more likely that you sustained damage to the two olfactory nerves in the front of your brain. The loss of smell may not be obvious and may only surface as what you presume to be a loss of taste. You can test this by seeing whether you can taste a small piece of salt placed directly on your tongue. If it is your sense of smell that is missing the salt will be tasted normally.

Q I have noticed that since I quit smoking I can taste food much better than before. Does this mean that smoking affects the taste buds?

A Smoking probably does alter the taste buds' ability to discriminate tastes to some extent, but most of your increased sense of taste probably comes from the fact that your smell receptors have recovered from the smoke as well.

Q Do animals have a sophisticated sense of taste and, in particular, can they really tell the difference between the various foods offered to them?

A Animals do have a good sense of taste, though it is probably not of the gourmet type often suggested by some animal food manufacturers. But some animals, deprived of certain vitamins or minerals, use their sense of taste to seek out and eat foods selectively with those substances in them.

Q Does one's sense of taste improve with age?

A The sense of taste, measured scientifically, becomes poorer as we get older, and by middle age is rather inept. However, greater experience as we get older means that we are able to get more pleasure from a wider range of tastes and smells.

The sense of taste is the crudest of our five senses. It is limited in both range and versatility and presents us with less information concerning the world about us than any other sense. In fact, this sense's exclusive role is that of selector and appreciator of food and drink, a role that is considerably aided by the more sensitive sense of smell. This sense adds color to the four basic tastes that our taste buds can recognize. Consequently, the loss of the sense of taste, for whatever reason, is less of a problem than the loss of the sense of smell (see Smell).

How do we taste things?

Like smell, the taste mechanism is triggered by the chemical content of substances in food and drink. Chemical particles are registered in the mouth and converted into nerve impulses that are then sent to the brain and interpreted.

The taste buds are at the heart of this system. Studding the surface of the tongue (see Tongue) are many small projections called papillae. Inside these are the taste buds. An adult has about 9,000 taste buds, mainly on the tongue's upper surface, but also on the palate, and even the throat (see Palate, and Throat).

Each taste bud consists of groups of receptor cells, and each of these has fine hairlike projections called microvilli, which stick out into the surface of the tongue through fine pores in the surface of the papilla. At the opposite end to this, the receptor cells link up with a network of nerve fibers. The design of this network is complex, since there is a great deal of interlinking between nerve fibers and receptor cells. Two different nerve bundles, which make up the facial nerve and the glossopharyngeal nerve, carry the impulses to the brain.

The taste buds respond to only four basic tastes: sweet, sour, salty, and bitter; and the receptor sites for these tastes are located on different parts of the tongue. The buds that respond to sweet are at the tip of the tongue, while those specializing in salty, sour, and bitter are located progressively farther back.

How the taste buds respond to the chemicals in the food and initiate the nerve impulses to the brain is not fully understood, but in order to be tasted, the chemicals must be in liquid form. Dry

The sense of taste

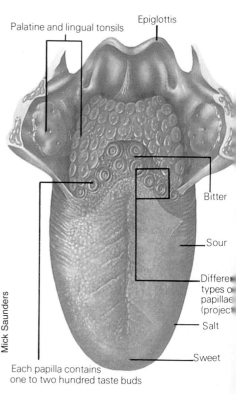

Palatine and lingual tonsils

Epiglottis

Bitter

Sour

Different types of papillae (project

Salt

Sweet

Mick Saunders

Each papilla contains one to two hundred taste buds

The papillae on the tongue increase the area in contact with food and, except for those in the center, they contain numerous taste buds. These, in turn, contain taste receptors that are distributed so that different parts of the tongue are sensitive to different tastes: sweet, salty, sour, or bitter.

food gives little immediate sensation of taste, and only acquires its taste after being dissolved in saliva (see Saliva).

It is believed that the chemicals in food alter the electrical charge on the surface of the receptor cells, which in turn cause a nerve impulse to be generated in the nerve fibers (see Nervous system).

The analysis of taste by the brain

The two nerves carrying taste impulses from the tongue (the facial nerve or the glossopharyngeal nerve) first pass to specialized cells in the brain stem. This area of the brain stem also acts as the first stop for other sensations coming from the mouth. After initial processing in this

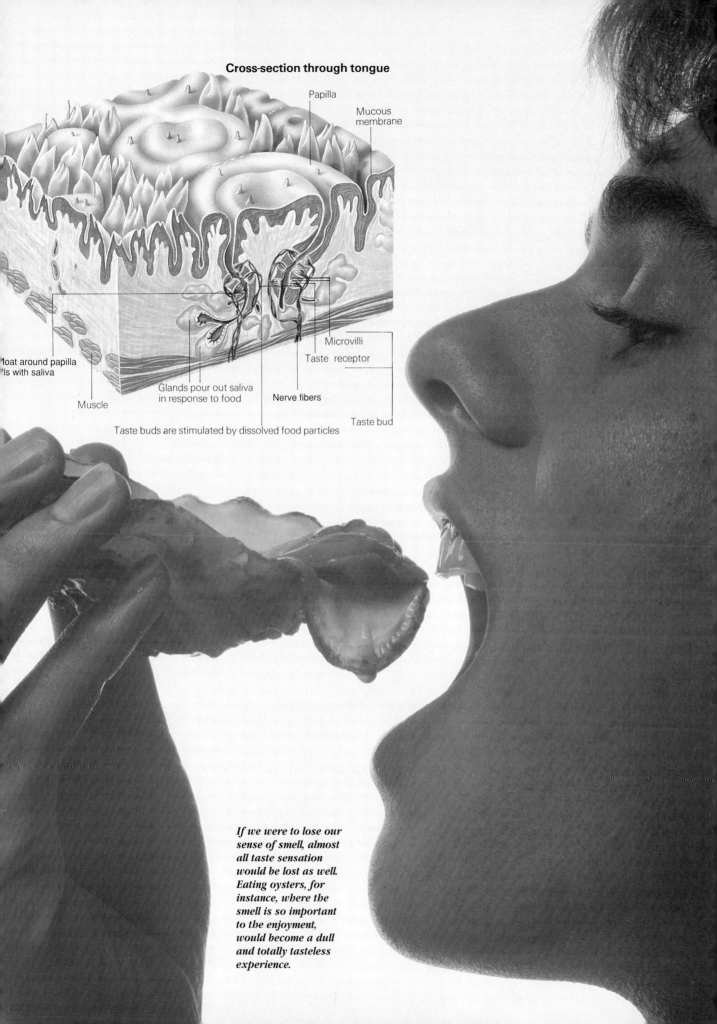

Cross-section through tongue

Papilla

Mucous membrane

Moat around papilla lls with saliva

Muscle

Glands pour out saliva in response to food

Nerve fibers

Microvilli

Taste receptor

Taste bud

Taste buds are stimulated by dissolved food particles

If we were to lose our sense of smell, almost all taste sensation would be lost as well. Eating oysters, for instance, where the smell is so important to the enjoyment, would become a dull and totally tasteless experience.

John Kevern

occurs just before the facial nerve passes near the eardrum. When frequent ear infections were common and operations had to be performed (before antibiotics were available) for mastoiditis, the nerve was often damaged (see Mastoiditis).

However, even when the nerve on one side of the face is severely affected, the other side will continue to send taste information to the brain. If the nerve that connects to the back third of the tongue is also damaged there may be considerable taste loss.

Taste may also be affected in the much more common Bell's palsy, where the facial nerve becomes inactive quite suddenly and for reasons that are not known. It is very rare for all taste nerves to be affected at the same time; complete taste loss is very rare.

It is much more common for people who have lost their sense of smell on both sides (for example, as the result of a head injury) to complain of loss or reduction in their sense of taste. This is because without this sense of smell, much of the subtler refinements of taste are lost.

Unpleasant alterations in taste

It is common for people suffering from depression to complain of unpleasant tastes in their mouths. The cause of this is not clear, but it may be related to the close relationship of taste and smell. Smell-analyzing centers of the brain have close connections with the emotional circuitry of the limbic system, and it has been suggested that certain moods can conjure up tastes and smells (see Brain). Another type of unpleasant taste occurs in some people as the aura or warning sensation before an epileptic fit. This usually means that the abnormal electrical activity causing the fit is centered either low in the parietal lobe or in the neighboring temporal lobe (see Epilepsy).

---

brain stem center, the taste impulses are transferred via a second set of fibers to the other side of the brain stem and ascend to the thalamus. Here there is another relay, where further analysis of the taste impulses is carried out before information is passed to the part of the cerebral cortex participating in the actual conscious perception of taste.

The cortex also deals with other sensations, like texture and temperature, coming from the tongue. These sensations probably are mixed with the basic taste sensations from the tongue, and so produce the subtle sensations with which we are familiar when we eat.

This analysis, carried out in the lower part of the parietal lobe in the cortex, is further influenced by smell information being analyzed in the nearby temporal lobe. Much of the refinements of taste sensation are due to smell sensations.

How sensitive are the taste buds?

Compared to other sensations (in particular smell) our taste sense is not very sensitive. It has been estimated that a person needs 25,000 times as much of a substance in the mouth to taste it as is needed by the smell receptors to smell it. However, despite this, the combination of the four types of taste buds responding to the basic tastes of salty, sour, bitter, or sweet enable a wide range of sensations to be determined as the brain analyzes the relative strength of the basic flavors. Some of the stronger tastes, such as the hot flavor of spicy food, come about through stimulation of pain-sensitive nerve endings in the tongue.

The stickier and the more colorful the better! Children are irresistibly drawn to sweet foods that may have little appeal to the adult palate.

What can go wrong?

Loss of taste itself usually comes about from trouble in the facial nerve. This nerve is connected to the muscles of the face, but a small branch carries the taste fibers from the front two-thirds of the tongue. For the taste part of the nerve to become affected, the nerve must be damaged before the branch. This branch

The world's great culinary masters, like Robert Carrier, bring a wide range of skills to their art, not the least of which is a well-developed sense of taste.

Daily Telegraph Colour Library

Tattooing

A spur of the moment decision to have a tattoo can have a lifelong effect, with remorse being every bit as common as pride. Its removal is never entirely satisfactory, and may be both painful and expensive to achieve.

Q Can you get blood poisoning from a tattoo?

A Not if the tattooing has been done by a professional who took antiseptic precautions. However, there is a risk of hepatitis leading to jaundice if inadequate sterilizing methods are used. It is standard procedure in some hospitals to ask if you have had a recent tattoo so that your blood can be checked for the hepatitis virus before any surgery.

Q Why do tattoos become less distinct with time?

A The black pigment used in tattooing is relatively indelible, but the yellow, green, and red pigments are not permanent and gradually fade. The permanence also depends on the method used. The older, hand-pricked designs went deeper into the skin and therefore lasted longer than the modern ones applied with an electrical instrument.

Q Is it true that tattooing can cause dermatitis?

A Modern tattoo pigments are virtually nontoxic and should not cause any skin reaction. Older pigments, however, which are still occasionally used, may give rise to allergies. This is particularly true of the red and yellow pigments, which contain cadmium and cinnabar. The allergic reaction takes the form of a rash in that part of the tattoo, and it may even spread to other parts of the body. To avoid any recurrence, the affected part of the tattoo would have to be removed.

Q I was tattooed as a teenager. Can I have the tattoo removed?

A It is usually possible to have a tattoo removed if it is not too large, but it is a costly and time-consuming business. For small tattoos the simplest method of removal is to have the area cut out. Larger tattoos can sometimes be removed by the procedure known as dermabrasion (the high-speed sanding of the skin) or by laser treatment.

The history of tattooing is a very ancient one. However, the origins of the modern Western practice of tattooing began in the British navy in the late 18th century, when sailors adopted it from South Sea islanders. In the 20th century, tattooing has continued to be popular among the military, and has been adopted not only by such minority groups as Hell's Angels and punks, as a kind of mark of tribal status, but by street culture in general.

Owing to the increased sophistication of the tools used and the strict regulation of tattooists, the health risks of tattooing are now minimal. The risks of blood poisoning (see Blood poisoning) and of syphilis (see Syphilis), which used to be common complications, are now very small provided aseptic precautions are taken. However, there still seems to be a slight but significant risk of hepatitis (see Hepatitis) following the procedure.

How tattooing is done

Techniques used to vary considerably but are now becoming standardized. Most tattooists first draw an outline of the design on the skin using transfers or stencils. The design is then tattooed into the skin in black, and the colors filled in after this. The electrical tool used consists of a number of vibrating needles lying parallel inside a metal tube. Ink is inserted into the lower layer of skin (the dermis) by the pricking action of the needles. If it were introduced into the surface layer of the skin, where cells are constantly being shed, it would soon disappear.

The discomfort of the procedure depends on the sensitivity of the area being tattooed. The skin over bony areas and the chest and belly is particularly

Ancient body arts such as tattooing and piercing have been adopted by street culture.

Tom Hanley

sensitive. The sensation also varies with the individual: to some it feels like a tickle, while to others it is a painful scratch. The initial outlining of an image is usually more painful than the filling in.

Aseptic precautions are necessary to prevent the complications of infection. The skin is cleansed with antiseptic and, if necessary, the area is shaved. The needles are sterilized after each client, and all the instruments are stored in sterile conditions (see Sterilization).

After the tattoo is finished, it is fairly tender and sensitive. It is bandaged for a couple of days, during which a scab may form. This falls off to reveal the tattoo. The amount of bleeding should be minimal, but does vary to a certain extent, possibly in relation to the bluntness of the needles used.

Removal of tattoos

Today the removal of tattoos is usually done by dermatologists or plastic surgeons. There are various methods of removal, but none is entirely satisfactory.

The simplest method, if the tattoo is small enough, is to cut out the tattooed area and to stitch the gap in the skin. Larger areas may also be cut out, but skin grafting may be necessary to close the wound (see Grafting). This method is time-consuming and may require a long period off work.

Another type of treatment is dermabrasion, which involves rubbing the area with an abrasive instrument to create a deep graze. This is fairly painful, and takes several months to complete. When the pigment in the skin has been removed, the body's cells finish the job by a process of inflammation and healing (see Inflammation, and Healing).

Laser treatment is a newer method of tattoo removal, and has the advantage of being painless. The pigment in the skin absorbs the energy of the laser beam and is vaporized by it while the normal skin remains unaffected (see Lasers).

Finally, a tattooist may be willing to alter a design to make it more acceptable, although tattooists are traditionally reluctant to offer their services for the removal of tattoos.

Complications

Today the only serious risk of being tattooed is that of catching hepatitis, and this is minimal where there is careful attention to aseptic techniques, though cases do still occur. Infection due to ordinary bacteria is less of a problem since most of these infections can be treated with antibiotics (see Antibiotics).

Many native peoples, the Polynesians among them, have long traditions of tattooing.

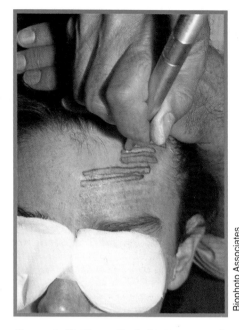

The most effective method of tattoo removal is laser treatment. The pigment is painlessly vaporized by the laser energy, and the slow process of healing is thereby avoided.

Biophoto Associates

A less common problem is allergy to the colored pigments, particularly the red and yellow ones (see Allergies). Red pigments are often based on mercury, which can cause severe allergies even after many years. If this happens the tattoo may have to be removed. Modern pigments are less likely to cause this problem, but tattooists often use the old, well-tried kinds.

Some skin diseases show a preference for tattooed skin, and may appear or worsen after tattooing (see Skin and skin diseases). Psoriasis and warts are examples of this (see Psoriasis, and Warts).

Medical uses of tattoos

Tattoos may be used in the treatment of certain medical conditions. For example, after reconstructive surgery to the lips following an injury, normal lip color can be simulated by tattooing ordinary skin. Similarly, the pigmented area around the nipples can be imitated when breast reconstruction has been performed.

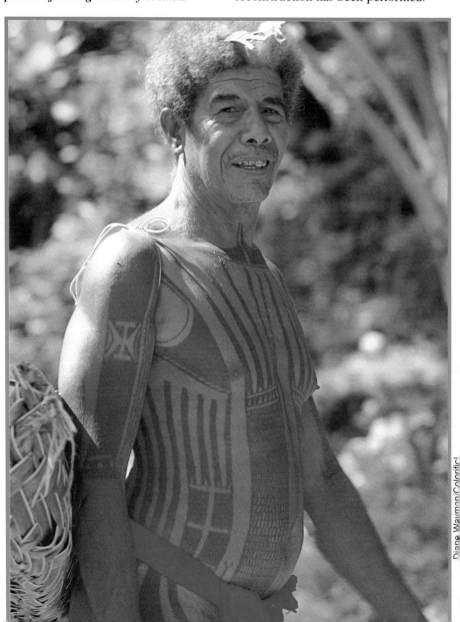

Diane Wayman/Colorific

Teeth and teething

Q Why do some people have crooked teeth but others don't?

A The development of the teeth and jaws is mainly controlled by genetic factors inherited from the parents. Each individual, however, has a unique assortment of genes and it is possible, for example, for a child to inherit large teeth from one parent and small jaws from the other, leading to overcrowding. However, teeth in irregular positions can usually be aligned and made to bite together by using orthodontic appliances.

Q Does an impacted wisdom tooth always have to be removed?

A An impacted wisdom tooth is one that is unable to grow properly because its path is blocked, usually by the tooth in front. Some impacted wisdom teeth are highly prone to infection, especially those that are only partially through the gum. Such teeth are best removed to avoid infection recurring. However, very deeply placed wisdom teeth may be best left alone if their removal requires the loss of an excessive amount of bone. Some impacted wisdom teeth, when developing, may contribute to overcrowding of the incisors and should therefore be removed. Your orthodontist will decide which is the appropriate course of action.

Q My sister's baby was born with a tooth that had to be removed. Does this mean that there will be one missing when the teeth finally erupt?

A About one in 5000 babies are born with one or two teeth already present in the mouth—Julius Caesar and Napoleon, for example, are both reputed to have had this distinction. It sometimes runs in families. These teeth are not fully formed and will fall out; occasionally, however, they present a danger of choking the baby, and so it is better to have them removed. The teeth will develop normally later on.

The day that a baby sprouts a tiny tooth is a memorable moment, but it is also the prelude to the development of teeth, which have the function of tearing and grinding food so that it can be easily swallowed and digested.

Ron Sutherland

The teeth are hard, bonelike structures implanted in the sockets of the jaws. Two successive sets occur in a lifetime.

Anatomy

Each tooth consists of two parts: the crown, which is the portion visible within the mouth, and the root, which is the part embedded within the jawbone. The roots of the teeth are usually longer than the crowns. Front teeth have only one root, while those placed further back generally have two or three roots.

The major structural element of a tooth is composed of a calcified tissue known as dentine. Dentine is a hard, bonelike material that contains living cells. It is a sensitive tissue and gives the sensation of pain when stimulated either thermally or

Would that we all had such a perfect set of teeth! Heredity is crucial, but we can all take care of what we have.

by chemical means. The dentine of the crown is covered by a protective layer of enamel, an extremely hard, cell-free and insensitive tissue. The root is covered with a layer of cementum, a substance somewhat similar to dentine, which helps anchor the tooth in its socket.

The center of the tooth is in the form of a hollow chamber filled with a sensitive connective tissue known as dental pulp. This extends from within the crown right down to the end of the root, which is open at its deepest part. Through this opening, minute blood vessels and nerves run into the pulp chamber.

TEETH AND TEETHING

Support of teeth

Each tooth is attached by its root to the jawbone; the part of the jaw that supports the teeth is known as the alveolar process. The mode of attachment is complex; teeth are attached to the jaw by fibers known as the periodontal ligament. This consists of a series of tough collagen fibers that run from the cementum covering the root to the adjacent alveolar bone. These fibers are interspersed with connective tissue, which also contains blood vessels and nerve fibers (see Blood, Mouth, and Nervous system).

The mode of attachment of the teeth allows a very small degree of natural mobility. This serves as a kind of buffer that may protect the teeth and bone from damage when biting.

A zone of crucial importance in this system is at the neck of the tooth where the crown and root merge. In this area a cuff of gum bonded tight to the tooth protects the underlying supporting tissues from infection and other harmful influences (see Gums and gum diseases).

Types of teeth

There are two series of human teeth. Deciduous teeth are those present during childhood and are all usually shed. Deciduous teeth can be divided into three categories: incisors, canines, and molars. The permanent teeth are those that replace and also extend the initial series. These teeth can be divided into the same types as the deciduous teeth, and in addition there is a further category known as the premolars, which are intermediate,

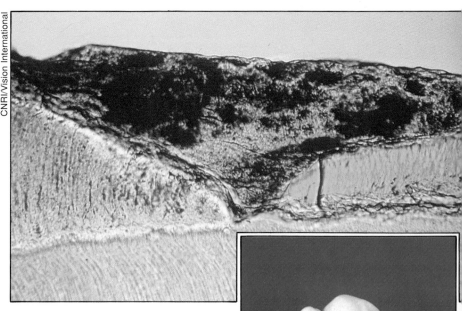

CNRI/Vision International

Each tooth consists of several layers: a stout shell of dentine (colored blue and yellow); cement covering the root (blue); and the crown's protective layer of enamel (yellow). The brown is plaque.

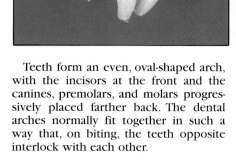

both in form and position, between canines (eyeteeth) and molars.

Incisors are characterized by a narrow, bladelike incised edge. The incisors in opposite jaws work by shearing past each other like scissor blades. Canines and pointed teeth are well adapted for a tearing action, while molars and premolars are effective at grinding food rather than cutting it.

Teeth form an even, oval-shaped arch, with the incisors at the front and the canines, premolars, and molars progressively placed farther back. The dental arches normally fit together in such a way that, on biting, the teeth opposite interlock with each other.

Dental decay can occur in all parts of a tooth and a mouthful of fillings will be the eventual result. So be sure you take care of your teeth and visit a dentist regularly.

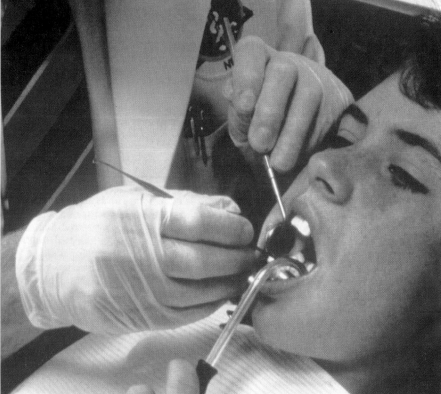

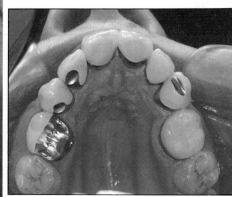

U.S. National Institute of Health/Science Photo Library

Elaine Keenan

Q I broke my front teeth in a car accident. Can they be repaired?

A If only a small piece of enamel is broken off, then the sharp edges can be smoothed. Where much of the tooth is missing, the tooth can be repaired by using a filling material bonded to the rest of the tooth, or a crown can be fitted. Where the root of the tooth has been fractured, usually the only treatment is to extract the tooth and replace it.

Q When milk teeth decay, why are they filled if they are going to fall out anyway?

A If teeth do decay, it is usually preferable to fill them rather than take them out since the early loss of milk teeth may result in the permanent teeth drifting into incorrect positions. Also, removal of teeth at the first signs of dental disease may make a child think that tooth loss is inevitable, and hence he or she won't take good care of his or her teeth.

Q My son had a convulsion and started running a high temperature. I thought this was because he was teething, but my doctor sent him to the hospital. Was this necessary?

A Teething does not cause high temperatures or any serious illnesses, although a child may be teething at the same time as he or she develops an illness. Your doctor was aware of this and how important it was to make sure that there was no other cause for your son's temperature and convulsion.

Q Should I give my baby fluoride tablets, which I've heard prevent tooth decay?

A There is substantial evidence that the addition of fluoride to toothpaste and to water that contains a low level of natural fluoride helps prevent tooth decay, particularly in children. It may be a good idea to give your baby tablets if you live in an area where there is no extra fluoride in the water supply, but talk to your dentist about this before going ahead.

Deciduous (baby) and permanent teeth

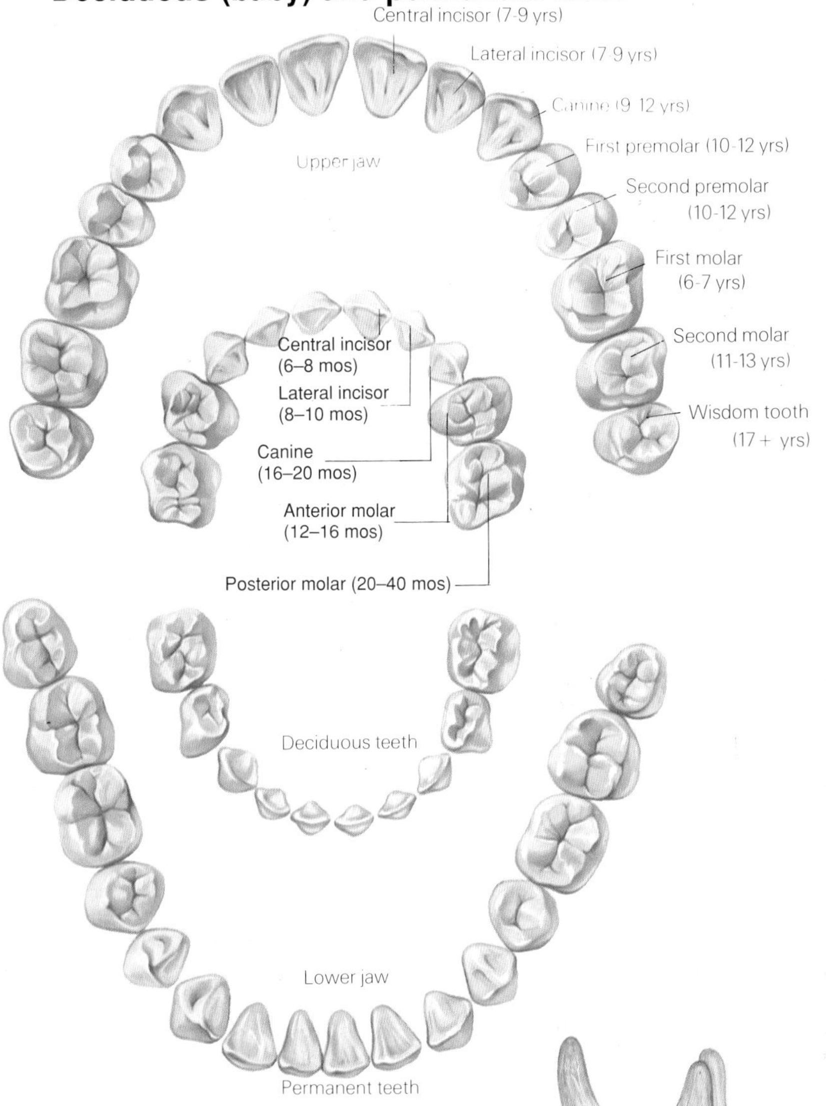

Central incisor (7-9 yrs)
Lateral incisor (7-9 yrs)
Canine (9-12 yrs)
First premolar (10-12 yrs)
Second premolar (10-12 yrs)
First molar (6-7 yrs)
Second molar (11-13 yrs)
Wisdom tooth (17+ yrs)

Upper jaw

Central incisor (6–8 mos)
Lateral incisor (8–10 mos)
Canine (16–20 mos)
Anterior molar (12–16 mos)
Posterior molar (20–40 mos)

Deciduous teeth

Lower jaw

Permanent teeth

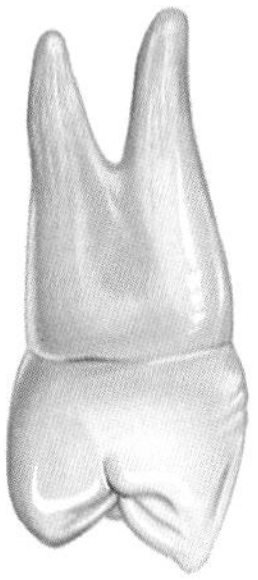

Premolar

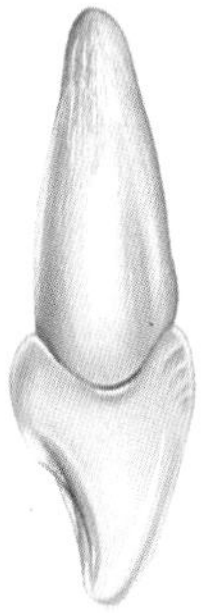

Incisor

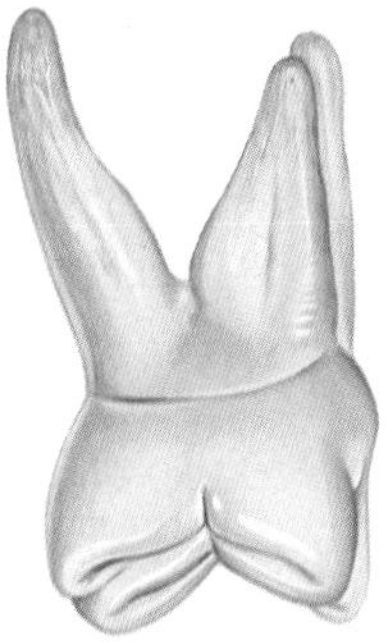

Molar

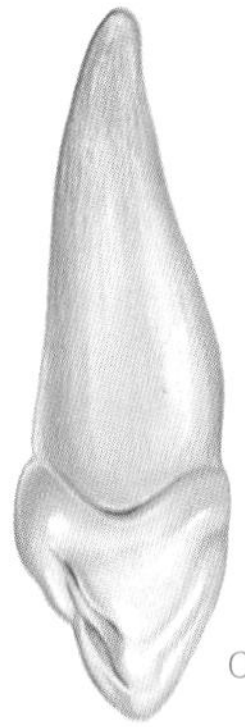

Canine

In theory we all have 32 permanent teeth. The arrangement of these is exactly the same in the upper and lower jaws. In each jaw there are 4 incisors, 2 canines, 4 premolars, and 6 molars—16 in total. Babies and young children have only 20 deciduous teeth. Again, in each jaw there are 4 incisors, 2 canines, and 4 molars—10 in all. Incisors cut food; canines tear it; and molars and premolars grind it. As human beings have evolved, teeth have changed; canines have become far less pointed, and many people never develop any wisdom teeth.

The deciduous teeth begin to erupt about halfway through the first year of life, a painful process for many babies (left). These are the central incisors. The first permanent teeth to erupt are molars, around the age of 6. By the early twenties, everyone normally has a full set.

Camilla Zessel

Development of teeth

The first sign of the development of the teeth occurs when the fetus is only six weeks old (see Fetus). At this stage the epithelial (lining) cells of the primitive mouth increase in number and form a thick band that has the shape of the dental arch. At a series of points corresponding to individual teeth, this band produces budlike ingrowths into the tissue that the epithelium covers. These buds then become bell-shaped and gradually grow in such a way as to map out the shape of the eventual junction between the enamel and dentine. Certain cells then go on to form the dentine, while others give rise to the enamel itself.

The edges of the bell continue to grow deeper and eventually map out the entire roots of the teeth, although this process is not complete until about one year after the deciduous teeth have emerged. At birth the only sign of the occlusion is provided by gum pads, which are thickened bands of gum tissue. Around the age of six months, the first of the lower incisors begins to push through the gum, a process known as dental eruption. The age at which this occurs is variable: a few babies have teeth at birth, while in others they may not emerge until age one.

After the lower incisors have emerged, the upper incisors begin to erupt, and these are followed by the canines and molars, although the precise sequence may vary. Teething problems may be associated with any of the deciduous teeth.

By age two and a half to three, the child will usually have a complete set of 20 milk teeth. Ideally they should be spaced in such a way that provides room for the larger permanent teeth.

Subsequently, after age six, lower then upper deciduous incisors become loose and are replaced by the permanent teeth. The permanent molars develop not in the place of the deciduous molars but behind them. The first permanent molars come through at age six, the second molars at age 12, and the third molars, or wisdom teeth, around age 18. There is, however, considerable variation in the timing of the emergence of all the teeth. About 25 percent of people never develop one or more wisdom teeth. The reason for this may be an evolutionary one: as the jaw has gotten smaller, the number of teeth has decreased. Some wisdom teeth may never erupt through the gum and if they become impacted (wedged closely together under the gum) they may need to be removed. This happens in 50 percent of people.

Cross section of a molar

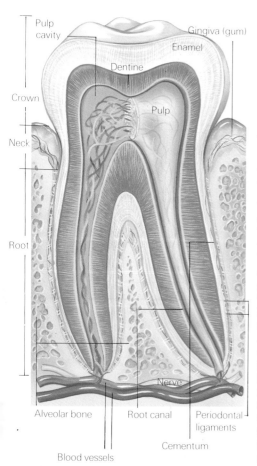

Pulp cavity
Gingiva (gum)
Enamel
Dentine
Crown
Pulp
Neck
Root
Alveolar bone
Root canal
Periodontal ligaments
Cementum
Nerve
Blood vessels

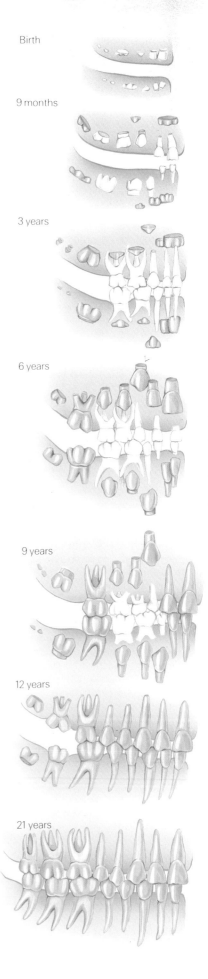

Birth

9 months

3 years

6 years

9 years

12 years

21 years

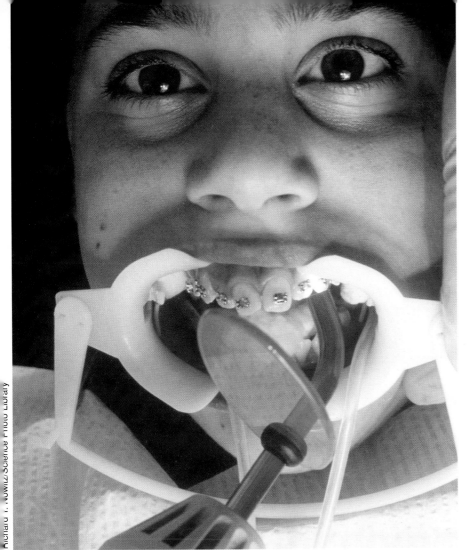

Richard T. Nowitz/Science Photo Library

ed. Because the teething infant will occasionally suck or bite frantically on anything within reach, you can give him or her a teething ring or hard pacifier or, alternatively, a piece of raw carrot or a teething biscuit. Never give a baby candy to suck; this will not do much to relieve discomfort and will almost certainly be detrimental to the developing teeth. In some cases it may be advisable to apply creams that have the effect of a local anesthetic on the child's sore gum, but bear in mind that they wear off rather quickly because the teething baby tends to salivate and drool so much.

Other problems

Not all teeth develop perfectly, and some babies may have problems. Sometimes a bluish swelling, called an eruption cyst, appears over a molar tooth before it erupts. This disappears once the tooth emerges and does not require treatment.

Changes in teeth arrangement

The part of the jaw that supports the milk teeth increases very little in size from the age when all the milk teeth have erupted. Milk teeth tend to be smaller than their permanent replacements, and only when the large permanent incisors have erupted does the final form of the dental arches become apparent. The upper permanent incisors often appear out of proportion to the child's face when they first come through, but this naturally becomes less apparent as the face grows while the teeth remain the same size. Any tendency for the upper incisor teeth to protrude usually only becomes obvious when the milk teeth are replaced; the larger permanent teeth will exaggerate any discrepancy in their position. Similarly, crowding often only becomes clear when the permanent teeth have erupted.

During the six years or so that it takes for the milk teeth to be entirely replaced by their 32 permanent successors, it is common for a gap to appear between the upper incisors. This gap usually closes when the permanent canines erupt and push the incisors together. However, discrepancies either in the alignment or in

The lessons of good dental care should begin early. Teething babies should be given carrots to relieve discomfort, not tooth-decaying candy, and toddlers should be taught to brush their teeth (right). If teeth are crooked, spaced, or protruding, orthodontic appliances can be fitted (above).

the bite of the teeth may require orthodontic treatment to bring the teeth into line (see Orthodontics).

Tooth eruption and teething

Tooth eruption is a normal developmental process and can be quite painless, but many babies appear to suffer from a lot of discomfort, particularly as each new tooth breaks through.

Sometimes a baby whose new tooth is hurting develops a red, inflamed patch on his or her cheek, and the gum may also become red. There is often excessive drooling, rubbing of the mouth, and crying; the cheeks may appear pinker than usual. Symptoms such as fever or diarrhea are unlikely to be due to teething as is commonly supposed, and if they persist, medical advice should be sought.

Where teething causes the baby distress, a number of measures can be adopt-

Anodontia, which is the total absence of teeth, is extremely rare, although the absence of individual teeth is a phenomenon that commonly occurs in roughly 5 percent of people.

Occasionally teeth development will be delayed. This can occur in a number of diseases affecting growth; for example, rickets (see Rickets). Children with Down's syndrome may also have delayed teeth (see Down's syndrome). However, it should be stressed that this is rare. Many babies teeth erupt as late as 18 months.

There is a wide variation in the color of teeth that appear in a baby's mouth, ranging from glistening brown to deep cream. If a pregnant woman or a baby is given tetracycline antibiotics, the drug may combine with the calcium to cause a brown discoloration (see Antibiotics).

Twinning occurs when two of the baby's teeth become joined together, often the incisor milk teeth. The second incisors usually develop normally.

Temperature

The body's sophisticated temperature control mechanism is one of the major features that sets us aside from lower forms of life. The way that heat is produced and lost depends on a series of complex bodily functions.

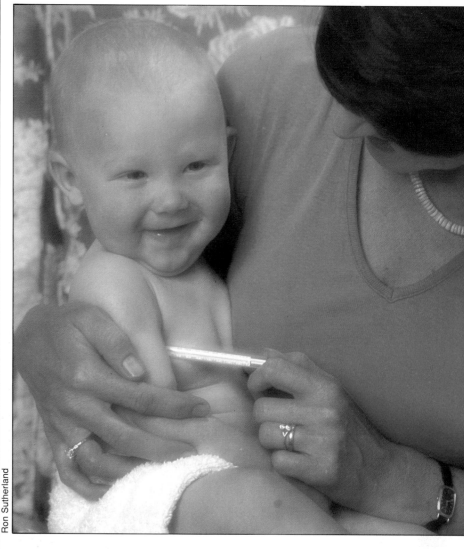

Ron Sutherland

Those of us who live in temperate climates often take very little notice of the temperature of our surroundings. However, the environmental temperature is one of the most important factors in determining how we live.

The temperature of the outside world is very important in the way it affects our so-called internal environment. In a very advanced animal like the human being, there are several sophisticated mechanisms that are designed to keep the internal environment balanced, despite any change in the external conditions. The maintenance of constant temperature, constant levels of salt and water in the tissues (see Salt), constant supplies of oxy-

A young child's temperature can be taken by placing the thermometer under the arm and holding it there for two minutes. This method avoids the risk of the thermometer being bitten off in the mouth.

gen (see Oxygen), and a constant balance of the amount of acid and alkali in the body is a process called homeostasis. Temperature control is perhaps the most important element of the homeostatic mechanism. If, for instance, our temperature regulating mechanism were to break down or to start to work inefficiently, then a number of potentially fatal disorders could result (see Heat and heat disorders, and Hypothermia).

Temperature control

All forms of life depend on chemical reactions and the enzymes that regulate their reaction rate (see Enzymes). It is the temperature at which these reactions take place that determines their speed and whether or not they happen quickly enough to be of use to the body. An internal temperature that is fixed within narrow limits insures that chemical systems work efficiently.

It is only the higher forms of life such as warm-blooded mammals or birds that can keep their internal temperatures constant within a very small range. This allows them an existence that is very much less controlled by external circumstances than are the lives of cold-blooded reptiles, whose less efficient chemical systems have to work over a much wider range of temperature.

How temperature control works

To enable the body to maintain a constant internal temperature during heat loss, the balance will be regained by the production of an equivalent amount of heat. If, on the other hand, you are basking in hot sunshine, then heat is being

Paolo Koch/Vision International

Even Russia's frozen winters can't deter these swimmers from taking the plunge. Exercise raises body temperature and will help keep them warm (above). This basketball player (left) is sweating profusely after a strenuous game.

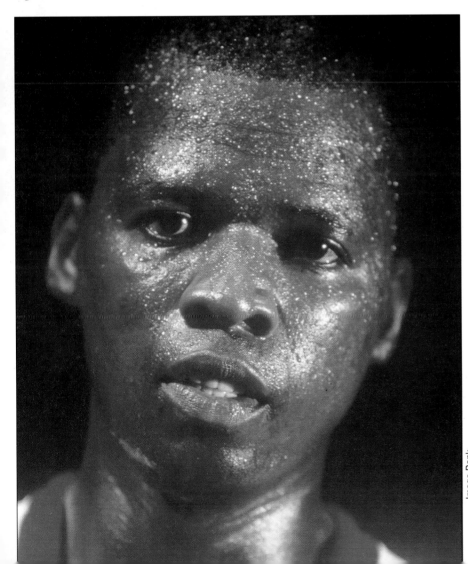

Image Bank

absorbed by the body rather than being lost from it. In these circumstances, the body has to have an efficient way of losing heat. The system of temperature control is one that determines that heat lost from the body must be made up, while heat gained must be reduced in order to maintain a stable temperature.

The overall control of this temperature system is managed by the hypothalamus, the area at the base of the brain that controls so many of the body's vital functions (see Hypothalamus).

Heat production

When the body temperature starts to fall, there are a number of processes that the body can set in motion to produce more heat. However, certain mechanisms in the body already constantly produce heat, since every one of the body's many chemical reactions liberates some heat as it takes place. This is called the heat of metabolism, and the general rate at which these reactions take place is called the metabolic rate (see Metabolism). Although it cannot be controlled entirely by one organ, the metabolic rate is very closely related to the activity of the thyroid gland. An overactive thyroid will lead to a high metabolic rate, while an underactive thyroid causes a low metabolic rate.

This close relationship between thyroid function and heat production explains why people with overactive thyroids are very intolerant of hot weather, and those who have underactive thyroids feel the cold and so may be more prone to suffer from hypothermia (see Thyroid).

If the heat of metabolism is insufficient to meet the demands of the homeostatic control system, then the hypothalamus will increase the activity of the muscles by working particularly on the main postural muscles up and down the spine.

The first thing that happens is an increase in the tone of the postural spinal muscles, so more energy is used by each muscle fiber, and more heat is generated. We are not aware of the hypothalamus making these subtle alterations in the tone of the main postural muscles, but they are the most important way of making extra heat (see Muscles).

If the hypothalamic alterations in the amount of tone in the postural muscles fail to produce enough heat, another familiar and obvious mechanism comes into play: shivering. Shivering works by setting up alternate contraction and relaxation in many muscles in the body. This action uses up energy and so starts to heat the body.

Heat loss

Just as the main way of gaining heat is not really obvious to us, so the main mechanisms by which heat is lost function without our being aware of them.

The body has a certain amount of heat that it cannot avoid losing. Food and drink may have to be warmed by the body to its own temperature, and in cold conditions we have to warm the air we breathe. As we breathe there is also some unavoidable loss of water, in the form of vapor, from the lungs (see Breathing). This vaporization or evaporation of water uses up heat the same way as heat is used up in steam from boiling water.

Apart from the heat that is lost in these various ways in the gut and the lungs, the rest of the heat loss happens through the skin. There are two main ways of heat loss through the skin: convection and radiation. Convection is the system in which a fluid or gas moves from colder to warmer areas, carrying heat with it. In the case of the skin, it is usually cool air that moves across the surface of the skin and, as it does so, takes heat from the surface and carries it away from the body, becoming warmer air in the process.

Radiation, on the other hand, is the way in which an electric fire produces heat, by pushing it out directly into the environment. In a cold climate a person will radiate quite a lot of heat; but when the same person is standing in the hot sun, then heat will be radiating into him or her rather than the reverse.

If the amount of blood, and therefore the amount of heat, that flows through the skin is increased, then the amount of heat lost by both convection and radiation will also increase. This variation in the skin's blood flow is in fact the main way in which the hypothalamus controls heat loss from the body.

Following an increase in the flow of blood to the skin in order to lose heat, there will of course be an increase in the amount of sweating (see Perspiration). The sweat glands work by liberating sweat onto the surface of the skin, which is then evaporated with a consumption of heat in the same way that the evaporation of water from the lungs loses heat.

Most sweating takes place at a low level so that we never notice any liquid on our skins. However, when the system becomes overworked, and is therefore not working efficiently, sweat is clearly visible on the surface of the skin.

The efficiency of the sweating system also depends on the humidity of the air. Humidity is the amount of water already present in the air in the form of water vapor. If we sweat profusely when there is a lot of humidity, then the sweat will not easily evaporate. This causes the body to be less efficient at losing heat than it should be (see Humidifiers).

perature, will not immediately fall back to room temperature when taken from the mouth. So, when you have finished using a thermometer always shake the column back down and rinse the thermometer in cold water or alcohol, since hot water may cause the mercury to expand and this will break the thermometer.

Apart from looking for fevers there are other reasons for taking a temperature, such as wishing to know if and when ovulation has occurred.

Intensive care units use a special temperature measuring instrument called a thermistor to see whether the heart is working hard enough, or whether it is failing to pump enough blood around the body. The temperature of the central part of the body is measured simultaneously with that of the big toe. A minor difference in temperature indicates a relative lack of blood being supplied to the peripheral areas.

Measuring temperature

The main reason why most of us want to measure body temperature is to see if we have a fever (see Fevers). The standard way of measuring temperature is with a thermometer.

In all older children and adults the way of taking a temperature is to place the thermometer under the tongue for about 90 seconds, and then to remove it and read it. In very small children or babies, where there is a possibility of the thermometer being bitten off in the mouth, the temperature can be taken under the armpit or in the rectum. To take an axillary (armpit) temperature, put the ther-

mometer up into the armpit and keep it there, with the arm pressed against the side, for about two minutes. The temperature will read slightly lower than an oral temperature. In a baby, the rectal temperature is best taken with the baby face downward on your knee. Hold the thermometer gently between your fingers, with its tip in the rectum and your hand flat on the buttocks. The reading will be slightly higher than an oral reading.

Medical thermometers have a special mechanism in them so that the column of mercury, which shows the tem-

Cold-blooded reptiles like crocodiles (above left) have to live in a climate that remains sufficiently hot so that their essential chemical functions are not switched off by the cold. Warm-blooded animals like these emperor penguins (below) can live happily in the freezing conditions of Antarctica.

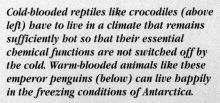

Tendons

Q Is it possible for tendons to be dislocated?

A This is an unusual occurrence, but it can happen. Normally it is brought about by a sudden wrenching movement sufficiently powerful to jolt the tendon out of the groove over a bone in which it normally runs. Treatment consists of manipulating the tendon back into its proper position.

Q My boyfriend had an accident in which he cut through one of his wrist tendons. Will he be able to use his hand normally after the tendon has healed completely?

A The eventual outcome depends on the exact circumstances, but in most cases it is possible to sew the cut ends of the tendon together again. This is usually successful in restoring full movement to the affected muscle on recovery. But the tendon may not seem as strong as it was before and its use may give rise to discomfort.

Q Do severed tendons ever heal naturally?

A If the tendon is nicked or only partially severed, scar tissue will probably form to fill in the gap. If the tendon is completely severed, the two ends are likely either to spring apart because they are under tension, or to separate when the muscle tries to move. Unless they are carefully identified and deliberately sewn firmly together, healing is unlikely.

Q What activities are most likely to cause actual damage to the tendons?

A Two different sorts. Sudden sharp strains or twisting pressures on a tendon are likely to tear some of the tendon fibers away from the bone to which they were anchored. Alternatively, repetition of a movement over a long period of time may use up all the lubricating fluid in the tendon sheath and thus give rise to the friction and inflammation of tenosynovitis.

Although very simple and apparently humble pieces of the body's equipment, tendons play a crucial role in transmitting muscular power and enabling movement.

Ann Kelley

Tendons, or sinews, play an important part in a wide variety of movements. A tendon is a very strong and tough band of fibrous connective tissue that joins the active section or body of a muscle to the part, usually a bone, which it is intended to move. The force of the contracting muscle fibers is concentrated in and transmitted through the tendon, achieving traction on the part concerned and thus making it move (see Body structure, Bones, and Muscles).

Tendons and muscles

Tendons are specialized extensions or prolongations of muscles. They are formed by the connective tissue, which binds the bundles of muscle fibers together, joining and extending beyond the muscles as a very tough, inelastic cord. They have very few nerve endings and, being essentially inactive tissues, little in the way of a blood supply. At one end they are formed from the belly of the

Should he miss with his mallet, he could damage a tendon. In addition, regular use of certain muscles can cause tenosynovitis.

muscle, and at the other they are very firmly tethered to the target bone, some of their fibers being actually embedded in the bone structure.

Location

Several tendons are located just beneath the surface of the skin, and so can be felt easily. For instance, the hamstring tendons, which control knee bending, are at the back of the knee. Because they take up much less space than meaty muscles, tendons are also often found where there are a large number of joints to be moved in a relatively small space. Therefore both the backs and the fronts of the feet and the hands contain a whole array of different tendons (see Feet, and Hand). The muscles that make these tendons work are sited in the arms and legs.

An unusual tendon is found in connection with the muscle tissue that forms the wall of the heart and brings about its pumping action. Here strips of thickened, fibrous connective tissue form tough strips within the heart muscle, which both give it a firmer structure and form firm supporting rings at the points where the great blood vessels join the heart.

Tenosynovitis

In order that they can move smoothly and without friction or the danger of abrasion, tendons are enclosed in sheaths at the points where they cross or are in close contact with other structures. The tendon sheath is a double-walled sleeve designed to isolate, protect, and lubricate the tendon so that the possibility of damage from pressure or friction is reduced to a minimum. The space between the two layers of the tendon sheath contains

Tendons take fierce punishment during physical exertion (above right). The membranes surrounding the muscles and muscle fibers (the endomysium, the perimysium, and the epimysium) join at the end of a muscle to form the tendon (inset below). Sheaths protect tendons from rubbing against other structures (below right).

Rex Features

fluid so that when the muscle is in action the two layers slide over each other like the parts of a well-oiled machine.

But the human body cannot sustain repeated movements of the same sort without sustaining damage in the form of inflammation. So rest periods are necessary for the lubricating fluid to be replenished. If this does not happen, and the system is run without adequate lubrication, the two layers of the tendon sheath begin to rub against each other and chafe. Continued movement will then be painful and cause a creaking sound called crepitus. This is the basis of the condition called tenosynovitis—inflammation of the tendon sheath. Any tendon sheath can be afflicted by this annoying and painful condition, which is particularly common in keyboard operators, athletes, dancers, and others who use one particular set of muscles repeatedly. Sudden, unaccustomed use of a particular set of muscles is especially likely to cause tenosynovitis.

Injury

Virtually all the disorders of tendons are due to injury of one sort or another. A deep cut near the foot, ankle, hand, or wrist may sever one of the tendons that lie quite close to the surface. It is usually possible to sew the two severed ends together, but there always remains the possibility of pain or some weakness of the muscle on using it for any length of time. Extreme tension, overstretching, or sudden jerking on a tendon may damage it in a variety of ways. What happens is that some of the fibers of the tendon anchoring it to the bone get torn away from their moorings. The tendon itself is not really stretched, and only very rarely ruptured or snapped, since the force required to do this would already have pulled it away from the bone.

Treatment of such injuries is with ice packs and rest, with the support of an elasticized bandage. A gradual return to normal use is the best way to regain full use of the limb involved in the injury.

Tendons and tendon sheaths

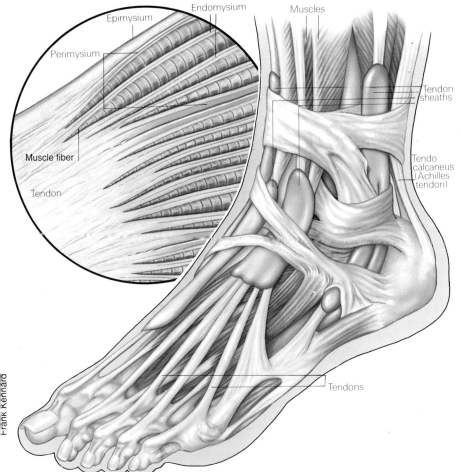

Frank Kennard

Tennis elbow

This painful muscle condition deserves its graphic name. Although athletes suffer from it, it can also be brought on by mundane activities such as wringing out wet clothing.

Q If I had tennis elbow, how would I recognize it?

A You would have a dull ache around the elbow area and upper side of the forearm, with a particular tender spot on or near the bump that can be felt on the upper side of the elbow when the forearm is placed across the chest. Activities such as typing, using a squash or tennis racquet, or even picking up heavy objects may be painful.

Q How soon can one resume playing tennis after suffering from tennis elbow?

A That depends on how serious the injury was; you should seek your doctor's advice. The symptoms vary considerably from person to person. In mild cases, you may only have to wait for a few days until the pain and stiffness subside, and then resume the sport gradually. More serious cases may necessitate a longer layoff. But if you find that the tenderness returns whenever you play, then consult your doctor as soon as possible.

Q I am taking part in a two-week tennis tournament, but have developed a painful tennis elbow on the first day. I don't want to withdraw from the tournament, so what can I do?

A You should ask your doctor for a painkilling injection, but he or she may not be willing to give it. The danger is that you could seriously aggravate the injury and delay full healing for several weeks or even months. As an alternative wear an elasticized bandage around the affected forearm. This will provide some relief and reduce the chance of aggravating the injury. Ideally you should rest the arm for a few days.

Q Do you only get tennis elbow from playing tennis?

A No. The injury is common in many sports, especially racquet sports, and also occurs as a result of doing other repetitive tasks, such as those involved in carpentry.

Tennis elbow is a common arm injury. Although it often develops during a hard game of tennis, it can also occur in a wide variety of other sports, and even as a result of nonsporting activities. The injury

Allsport

is not actually to the elbow itself, but is an inflammation of the tendon that attaches the muscles of the forearm to the bones of the upper arm (see Tendons). These muscles control movements of the wrist and fingers, which is why it is such a common injury among racquet players.

Causes
The elbow joint forms a pivot between the humerus bone in the upper arm and the two bones in the forearm. At the

lower end of the humerus are two projections (called epicondyles) to which a number of forearm muscles are attached. The actual pain of tennis elbow is due to small tears where the muscles join the lateral epicondyle.

The cause of the injury is vigorous or prolonged use of the forearm muscles, especially during sports such as tennis, squash, racquetball, and athletic throwing events. It can also be caused while wringing out wet clothing or using a carpentry tool such as a screwdriver.

Symptoms
The pain of tennis elbow comes on gradually rather than suddenly, and is made worse by activities that involve gripping something or picking up a heavy object such as a full kettle. A very tender spot can usually be felt at the site of the injury where the forearm muscles are attached to the lateral epicondyle, but pain and stiffness may sometimes extend over the whole of the upper side of the forearm.

Treatment
Rest and a pain-relieving drug are usually sufficient to permit use of the affected arm within a few days. More persistent tennis elbow may be treated with a corticosteroid injection containing an anesthetic to reduce pain and tenderness during healing. Where the injury is severe and persistent, heat treatment and physical therapy are used. Some have found acupuncture helpful (see Acupuncture).

The flamboyant tennis star Venus Williams demonstrates her fluid service action, which requires healthy muscles (left). A case of tennis elbow (below).

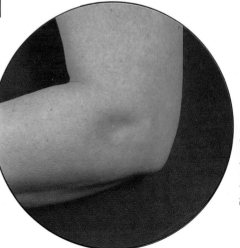

Tension

Q Is tension always a destructive force?

A Not at all. It is generally a constructive force stimulating resourcefulness and inventiveness, and biologically designed to promote survival. We would soon lose motivation without tension in our lives; and we would probably not survive for very long without it to stimulate us. Stress is often destructive, but tension is not.

Q Is there any specific type of tension that is particularly insidious today?

A Yes there is. And poisonous (rather than insidious) is the right word for it, because it is almost certainly responsible for more deaths than many a more obvious cause. One of the most serious features of life today is that it has become almost impossible to achieve ordinary things like traveling to work, getting the groceries, driving the car, taking a bus or train (the list is endless) without becoming unwillingly involved in a nightmarish web of hassles every day of our lives. These completely nonproductive conflicts give rise to high levels of tension for which, unless we are prepared to lose our temper 20 times a day, there is no outlet, and which are very potent progenitors of potentially damaging levels of stress.

Q What defenses do people have against the buildup of tension?

A Fortunately several. First, the example and encouragement of having handled problems successfully in the past, allied to the skills of one's particular trade. Second, the confidence that one is able to succeed, and an interest in doing so. Third, the defenses of avoidance, adaptability, and escape in leisure pursuits. All of these must be utilized to the full whenever the going gets rough! Finally, there is the support of somebody close to us, not only in lending a sympathetic ear but also in helping to keep things in perspective and in giving advice.

As an insidious component of modern life, tension can occur during even the most mundane everyday activities. Prolonged tension can lead to stress, an all too potent cause of serious physical and psychiatric illness.

Tension and strain, in the emotional or mental sense rather than in the mechanical or physical, are often spoken of as though they were indistinguishable from stress. Not only are they quite distinct, but the differences between them are very important. Tension and strain are things that happen to all of us, usually every day. They are the load, the pressure, the effect that is imposed on us by the inevitable confrontations that sometimes occur between us and our environment in terms of the things, the people, and the circumstances around us. Stress, however, is a disease that occurs when the tension or strain becomes more than we can cope with and some sort of breakdown in health results (see Stress).

Causes of tension

Tensions occur for a variety of reasons and in a variety of ways. The most basic and intense result from situations where the

Worry beads are very popular with many different cultures. There is a traditional thought that "having something to do with your hands" can reduce tension.

Q Do all people respond to tension in the same way?

A No they do not. One of the fascinating things about tension is the way in which its effects vary so widely. A challenge or conflict that turns out to be the stimulus that is the making of one person may spell doom, disaster, and breakdown to another. In general, response to an episode of tension depends both on its intensity and duration, and on the personality and outlook of the person concerned.

Q What happens if a person is subjected to more tension than they can cope with?

A If the tension proves to be too much for the person's coping mechanisms, a situation of stress will develop. This will lead to some form of stress illness or disorder, such as raised blood pressure, heart attack, peptic ulcer, depression, addiction, or a nervous breakdown.

Q How does everyday tension turn into stress?

A Simply when there is more of it than an individual can cope with. Tension or arousal is intended to lead to, and have its natural outlet in, some form of action. If that does not happen, perhaps because the action is blocked in some way, or because the amount of tension is greater than the opportunity for activities in which it can be either utilized or worked off, then it will build up, like steam in a pan, until the lid blows off. This may result in something as serious as a coronary thrombosis, stroke, or suicide. But the solution can be simple: a full recovery can soon be made just by resting and changing to a more relaxed attitude. Otherwise a vicious circle can rapidly build up in which, as a person's ability to cope with tension becomes inadequate, they push themselves harder to try and achieve results that they cannot attain. Often the person who is most in need of taking a rest, the workaholic, finds it hardest to slow down and take a calm look at the problems facing him or her.

expression of our instincts is inhibited. The universal, primary instincts are concerned with self-protection and preservation of life, obtaining food and drink, and reproduction. These are regarded as the primary instincts, since without them and the driving force that they supply, both we as individuals and humankind as a species would perish. These are the things that in most of us are inborn as driving forces that override all else.

The secondary instincts are not quite so demanding as the primary, and are not so vital to man's survival. But for most people they are vital to happiness. The first of them is the power instinct, which

All too often the apparently simple events of daily life can lead to an excessive build up in tension that nobody needs (right). The tension inherent in playing a skilled game for very high stakes shows up only too clearly on the face of the brilliant chess player Garry Kasparov (left).

drives people to be competitive and ambitious, and to try to gain positions of superiority over others in terms of achievement, wealth, position, or title. The second is the herd instinct, which leads people to think and act in groups and communities. Finally, denied by some psychologists, is the spiritual instinct that urges people toward goals that are nonselfish, idealistic, and, at least materially, unrewarding.

These primary and secondary instincts constitute the major basic driving forces in most people's lives; satisfying them without conflict or restraint gives people a sense of security and emotional happiness and contentment.

If, on the other hand, the following of their demands is made impossible or difficult, mental tension and pain result. And this tension, if it is severe enough, will lead to some form of mental or physical stress illness. The likelihood of this occurring depends on the extent to which the instinct concerned has been frustrated, the mental strength and capacity for adapting to a heavy tension load of the person involved, and whether or not an alternative area of satisfaction is available.

Many feelings that appear as tension are related to particular instincts. Fear, for example, is associated with concerns about self-preservation and security; anger with the need for confrontation and combat; loneliness with the desire for company and protection of the herd; appetite and hunger with the need for regular nourishment; sexual desire with the need to reproduce future generations. Therefore the satisfaction of instincts is associated with and results in pleasurable, happy feelings, while their frustration generally results in tension and unpleasant, painful feelings.

Conflict

However, the frustration of instincts and other desires leads not only to feelings of tension and unhappiness but also to something that frequently accompanies tension—conflict. Tension and conflict, though born of frustration and dissatisfaction, are nevertheless the fundamental mainsprings of human endeavor and progress. They occur whenever what we want to do is not immediately possible, and can result from a wide variety of circumstances. What we want to do may involve us in a collision course with anoth-

er person after the same goal. Or it may be incompatible with the interests of the herd or the rules of the community in which we live. Or it may represent a struggle with some limitation imposed by our own bodies, such as illness or disability, or with an obstacle in the world around us, such as drought or flood. Or the tension may be the result of the demands of rival instincts and emotions that are competing with each other for domination within ourselves.

There are four possible outcomes to a situation of tension conflict: we may be successful and victorious; we may decide to submit; we may try to escape; or the tension may continue and interfere with the stability of our lives, in the form of stress, indefinitely. Submission normally occurs when we realize that to continue the conflict is no longer in our interests. It may be total or partial, with an element of compromise. For instance, most members of the community agree to, or submit easily to, the rules of the herd and never get into any trouble, but some are always at odds and in difficulties with it. Generally, however, it is those who do not submit easily who are responsible for new ideas and progress. These people are driven by tension to experiment and explore new possibilities.

Reactions to tension

In all these reactions to tension there are three classes of response: those that we can accept as normal; those that seem excessive or exaggerated; and those that are definitely not normal and represent

some form of psychiatric illness. The difference between them, however, is really only one of degree. The response that occurs depends partly on the importance and intensity of the conflict and partly on the personality and mentality of the person concerned.

Thus it is not regarded as abnormal for us generally to submit to the conventions of our community with regard to acceptable behavior. But we would regard persistent feelings of inferiority, unworthiness, groveling, or guilt over small matters as inappropriately excessive.

However, manifestations of persistent depression, prolonged melancholy or feelings of persecution are viewed as being definitely abnormal. In the realm of escape as a response to tension we regard jokes, hobbies, vacations, and fantasy as in plays and films as acceptable; we find heavy drinking, drug taking, and outbursts of temperamental behavior excessive; and we consider alcoholism, permanent running away, and suicide attempts as definitely abnormal.

The kinds of situation that are most likely to give rise to abnormal tension in our lives today are quite different to the much more basic and immediate threats of hunger, thirst, cold, lack of shelter, fight for food, and rivalry for partners to mate with that were the prime sources of emotional and physical conflict in our distant ancestors' time. However, 20th-century tensions operate and affect us in very much the same way, and we need to be able to cope with them no less effectively if we are going to survive.

Testes

The testes are the twin organs that govern male fertility and the production of the sex hormone. Moreover, it is the importance of these functions that makes prompt treatment of any problems so essential.

The normal human male has two testes that develop in the embryo from a ridge of tissue at the back of the abdomen. When the testes have formed, they gradually move down inside the abdomen so that, at the time of birth, each testis has arrived in its final position, usually within the scrotum.

Function and structure

The function of the testes is twofold. First, they provide the site where sperm is manufactured; each sperm contains all the genetic information for that particular male. Second, the testes contain cells that produce the male sex hormone testosterone (see Testosterone), and con-

Structure of the testes

The testes consist of seminiferous tubules, where sperm are made, and interstitial cells, which produce the male hormone testosterone. Sperm is stored in the

epididymis before passing along the vas deferens to be ejaculated. One disorder is hydrocele, an abnormal accumulation of fluid around the testes (below right).

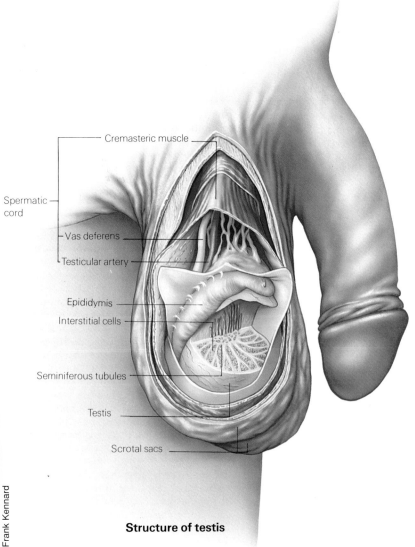

Cremasteric muscle

Spermatic cord

Vas deferens

Testicular artery

Epididymis

Interstitial cells

Seminiferous tubules

Testis

Scrotal sacs

Frank Kennard

Structure of testis

sequently the masculine characteristics, such as the deep voice, male hair distribution, and typical distribution of fat. These two functions are carried out by separate sets of cells within each of the testes; one function can fail without the other one necessarily doing so.

The testes are oval structures. Attached to the back of each one is a smaller structure shaped like a long comma. This is called the epididymis. The epididymis consists of a series of microscopically tiny tubes that collect sperm from the testis. These tubes connect together to form one tube, called the vas deferens, which transfers the sperm toward the base of the bladder. All these structures, with the exception of the vas deferens, are microscopic in size.

Each testis is suspended in the scrotum by the spermatic cord, which consists of the vas deferens, the testicular artery, and the testicular vein. These three structures are surrounded by a tube of muscle called

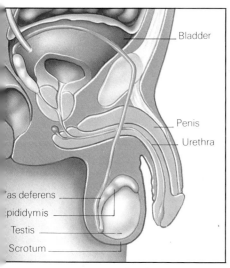

Connection of testis with penis

Hydrocele

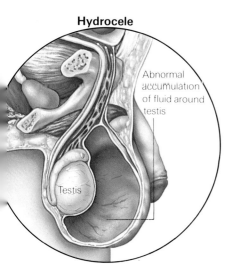

Abnormal accumulation of fluid around testis

Testis

the cremasteric muscle. The spermatic cord, therefore, serves two purposes: first, to provide a blood supply to the testis; and, second, to conduct the sperm away from the testis.

What can go wrong?

For the vast majority of males, the testes carry out their vital and complex role without problems. But sometimes structural or functional difficulties do occur which, fortunately, can usually be treated. **Undescended testes:** In order for sperm to be manufactured the testes have to be at a slightly lower temperature than the normal body temperature. This is why the testes are suspended outside the abdominal cavity, in the scrotum.

At birth, however, it may be noted that one testis is not in the scrotum. It may be in the groin, having got stuck on the way, or it may have failed to get as far as the groin. An undescended testis can have several effects: it will be unable to produce sperm; it may be damaged in the groin and be more prone to twisting, or torsion; there is also an increased risk of developing a tumor in an undescended testis (see Tumors).

It is important to distinguish between an undescended testis and one that is retractile. The latter means that the cremasteric muscle is overactive and has pulled the testis up into the groin. A retractile testis will probably descend into the scrotum at puberty; an undescended testis will not descend, and will require surgery (see Surgery).

The operation for an undescended testis, an orchiopexy, is usually performed at the age of three or four years. It consists of a small incision in the groin to find the testis, followed by stitching it into place in the scrotum. There is some evidence that, if the operation is delayed beyond this age, then irreversible damage to the testis may occur. However, even if a testis does not produce sperm because it has not descended, it still may be able to produce normal amounts of testosterone. One testis that is functioning normally should be perfectly adequate to produce sufficient sperm and testosterone (see Sperm).

Torsion: In some men there is an abnormality in the way in which the testis hangs in the scrotum. This abnormality is present at birth, and usually affects both testes. The abnormality is such that one of the testes can twist on its spermatic cord, leading to a sudden cutting off of the blood supply to the testis. The most common age for this to occur is in the teens, but it can also happen in younger children or young adults.

The usual symptom of a torsion of the testis is extreme tenderness and the

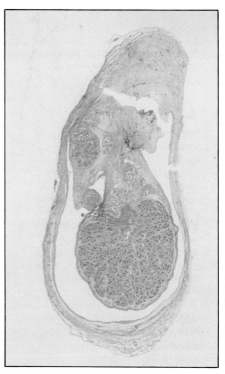

This cross section of the testes clearly shows the scrotum, the epididymis, the vas deferens, and the seminiferous tubules.

sudden onset of severe pain on one side of the scrotum. Untreated, the twisted testis swells and becomes inflamed, and eventually becomes gangrenous. Irreversible gangrene can occur within hours of the onset of the pain. Because of the swelling and inflammation there is a danger that a case of torsion could be mistaken for infection. Infection in the testis in a teenager is rare, and all cases of inflammation of the testis in this age group should be treated as torsion until proved otherwise.

Treatment involves surgical exploration, untwisting of the testis, and fixing it with stitches so that it cannot twist again. If it is gangrenous, it will have to be removed. Because the abnormality is present on both sides, a small operation is usually done on the other side to prevent torsion from occurring.

Infection and inflammation: Sometimes infection can pass from the bladder along the vas deferens, and then gain access to the epididymis.

This infection, called epididymitis, usually occurs in older men and may be related to prostate disease. The symptoms are pain and swelling in one side of the scrotum. Usually the urine is infected and, after treatment with the appropriate antibiotic, the infection clears up. There are normally no long-term effects, but the patient may be prone to repeated attacks. Inflammation of the testis itself is known

Q If the testes are damaged, does this lead to changes in secondary sex characteristics, such as facial hair or voice?

A If there is insufficient male hormone produced by the testes at puberty, then the secondary sex characteristics, such as facial hair and a deep voice, fail to develop. This results in what is known as eunuchism. Once the voice has deepened, then removal of, or damage to, the testes will have no effect. However, there will be a loss of sexual drive if both testes are removed in adulthood. If necessary, male hormones can be administered by injection.

Q My two-year-old son appears to have only one testis in his scrotum. Will the other one appear at puberty?

A It depends. You should take him to see your doctor. If the testis is retractile, that is, it has been pulled up into the groin by an overactive muscle, then it will come down at puberty. If, however, it never reached the scrotum, then he will need a small operation in a year or two to bring it down.

Q One of my husband's testes has become larger than the other. There is no pain. Should he have it checked?

A Yes. It is very important that he is seen by a doctor right away. The enlargement could be caused by a collection of fluid around the testis, or by a small tumor inside the testis. It should be immediately apparent to a doctor which of these it is. If it is a tumor, there is a good chance that it can be completely cured.

Q Is it possible to get an infection in the testis that makes it tender and swollen?

A Yes. But this is quite unusual in young men, and tenderness and swelling would be more likely to be caused by a twisting of the testis on the spermatic cord, cutting off its blood supply. In an older man, it may be related to infection in the urine as a result of an enlarged prostate gland.

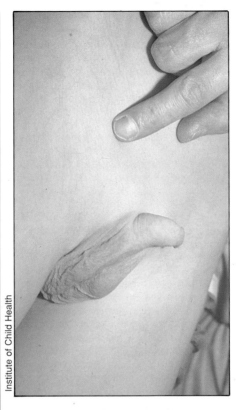
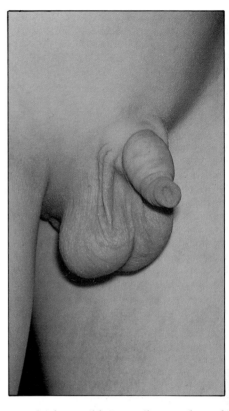

Institute of Child Health

When a male baby's testes are absent, it may be due either to their having become stuck in, or on their way down to, the groin (undescended), or to them having been pulled into the groin by overactive cremastic muscles (retractile). Retractile testes descend on their own at puberty. Undescended testicles (above left) are operated on when the baby is three or four years old to place them in position (above right).

as orchitis. Infection with the mumps virus can cause orchitis and, if both testes are affected, can lead to sterility (see Sterilization). Fortunately, however, this complication is rare (see Mumps).

Cysts: There are several different types of cyst that can occur in the testes. They are usually associated with some congenital abnormality, but may not become apparent until the patient is quite old. The first type is known as an epididymal cyst and shows itself as a lump attached to the testis; the testis can still be felt as a separate entity. Shining a strong light through the lump confirms that it is not solid, but is full of clear fluid.

The other type of cystic swelling is known as a hydrocele. This may be larger and is different in that the fluid-filled cavity surrounds the testis so that the testis cannot be felt separately. The former type of cyst is entirely harmless. The second type is usually harmless but occasionally may be associated with underlying inflammation in the testis or, more rarely, a tumor.

The treatment of these cysts is to remove them surgically, but only if they are causing symptoms (see Cyst).

Varicocele: This is a condition where the veins in the spermatic cord become enlarged and twisted, like varicose veins. The patient usually notices an aching sensation in the scrotum and may feel a lump just above the testis when he stands up. Because the lump is in fact the veins full of blood, it goes away when the patient lies down. Apart from a dragging, aching sensation, varicoceles are significant because they can cause a rise in the temperature of the tissues in the scrotum. This can lead to impairment of sperm production and infertility (see Infertility).

Treatment involves surgical removal of the large veins and this sometimes leads to a rise in the sperm count.

Tumors of the testis

Tumors of the testis are actually quite rare in comparison to the incidence of some other tumors. Many of them can be cured completely, even though they are, technically speaking, a form of cancer. These tumors generally occur in young men, between the ages of 18 and 40 years, although they can occur in other age groups.

The most common way in which they become apparent is by the patient noticing that one testis is bigger than the other. There may not be pain, but occasionally there is some tenderness.

Treatment involves removing the testis, followed by further investigations to see whether the tumor has spread. Even if there is spread, the results of treatment with X rays and special drugs are good.

Infertility

Infertility can be caused by many factors, but the fault may lie in the failure of the man to produce adequate sperm in the semen. There may be many reasons for this. First, there may be a blockage in the vas deferens so that the normal number of sperm produced in the testis cannot pass into the urethra during intercourse (see Intercourse). Second, the testes may for some reason be failing to produce sperm. This may or may not be associated with a failure to produce the male sex hormone, testosterone. The failure of

Fashion or display: tight jeans are worn by countless men. However, they may be responsible for lowering sperm production or even infertility because they increase the temperature in the testes.

sperm production may be inherent in the testes, or it may be caused by other factors. These include general illness, tiredness, increased heat in the testis caused by wearing underpants that are too tight and push the testes up into the groin, or the presence of a varicocele, which also raises the temperature of the testes.

Various measures can be taken to increase the sperm count, such as wearing loose pants, taking regular cold scrotal douches, and concentrating on good health. Special hormone tablets may be prescribed. If there is a complete absence of sperm, and a mechanical blockage is suspected, then surgery can sometimes be undertaken to bypass the blockage. This will be performed after a biopsy of the testes has shown normal production of sperm (see Biopsy).

If both testes are removed before puberty, facial hair and a deep voice will fail to develop; there will also be an absence of sexual drive. Altogether these shortcomings made eunuchs—castrated males—trustworthy servants in the harem.

Testosterone

Q **My son is 16 and does not yet show signs of puberty. Should he see the doctor?**

A Yes. In boys puberty normally starts around the age of 13, when they begin to grow more quickly. Their genitals enlarge; they develop facial, pubic, and general body hair; and their voices begin to deepen. If your son does not yet show any of these changes it could mean that he has a deficiency in the hormone that stimulates the production of testosterone. The doctor will examine your son and can arrange for his hormone level to be measured. Delayed puberty can be successfully treated with testosterone, and this treatment is often advised to prevent psychological problems.

Q **My sister has been diagnosed as having an ovarian cyst. Her doctor told her that the cyst is producing testosterone, and this is why she has grown some facial hair and her voice is getting deeper. Isn't testosterone a male hormone?**

A Testosterone is the most important male sex hormone, but it is also produced in small amounts in the ovaries. In women with healthy ovaries all the testosterone is converted into another substance called estradiol. If for some reason the ovaries produce so much testosterone that it cannot all be converted it begins to have a masculinizing effect. Once the cyst is removed the male characteristics should disappear.

Q **My baby son has undescended testes. Does this mean that he won't produce testosterone when he is older?**

A No. It is likely that your son's testes will descend during the next two or three years, and that he will develop normally and go through puberty at the usual age. However, if the testes have not descended by the time he is about five, he can have an operation called an orchiopexy to lower them into the normal position. Once the testes are descended he should develop normally.

Testosterone is the most important of the male sex hormones, and it is responsible for producing typical male characteristics of deep voice, beard growth, and increase in muscle bulk.

Paul Souders/Corbis

Adolescent boys gather in a huddle at a football game. At this age they develop muscle, become generally bigger and stronger, and have lots of forceful energy.

The glands of the body produce many different hormones (see Hormones)—substances that act as chemical messengers. They are made and released in one part of the body and then travel (mainly in the blood) to other body cells where they bring about their effects. One important group of hormones is the sex hormones. These are different in men and women, and they are responsible for controlling fertility and reproduction, and for producing distinctive physical characteristics, such as deep voice, beard growth, and increased muscle bulk in men, and breast growth in women.

The male sex hormones are called androgens, and the most important of the androgens is testosterone. Like all the sex hormones it is a steroid hormone (see Steroids).

How is testosterone produced?
Testosterone is produced in specialized cells (called Leydig cells) in the testes (see Testes). It is also produced in very small amounts in the ovaries of women.

Testosterone production begins when a boy reaches puberty (see Adolescence). A hormone called luteinizing hormone (LH) is secreted by the pituitary. LH is then carried in the blood to the testes, where it stimulates the Leydig cells to secrete the hormone called testosterone. During puberty, LH, and therefore testosterone, are only secreted at night, but later, as LH levels rise during the day, testosterone is secreted 24 hours a day.

In women the testosterone secreted by the ovaries is converted into the hormone estradiol, which plays an important role in ovulation and the menstrual cycle.

What does testosterone do?
The most noticeable effects of testosterone occur at puberty, when it is responsible for many of the physical changes in maturation that take place. There are changes in both the external and internal genitalia. The penis increases in length and width (see Penis), and the scrotum becomes pigmented. Internally, the seminal vesicles, which lie just behind the bladder, and the prostate gland, which

is tiny at birth, start to enlarge; the prostate to the size of a walnut. They both begin to secrete seminal fluid.

Testosterone causes the larynx to enlarge and the vocal cords to increase in length and thickness. These changes cause a boy's voice to break and become deeper. Around the same time the beard begins to appear, with the growth of chest, underarm, and pubic hair. The amount of body hair also increases over the whole body.

All androgens have what is called an anabolic effect, that is, they raise the rate of protein synthesis and lower the rate at which it is broken down. The effect of this is to increase muscle bulk, especially in the chest and shoulders, and to accelerate growth of the long bones (in the arms and legs), especially during early puberty. At the end of puberty testosterone stops the long bones growing.

The skin changes that often occur in adolescence are also caused by androgens. Androgens stimulate the sebaceous glands in the skin to secrete sebum. If the glands secrete too much sebum, this can lead to acne (see Acne).

Around this time sex drive begins to increase, and boys start to show an interest in girls, and also to produce sperm. Ejaculation sometimes occurs during the night. Testosterone also promotes a more aggressive attitude, which is a characteristically male trait.

The testes will produce testosterone throughout a man's life. After puberty testosterone maintains the male sex characteristics, and along with a hormone called follicle stimulating hormone (FSH) it is involved in the production of sperm in the seminiferous tubules of the testes.

Hereditary baldness in men is also linked to testosterone (see Baldness).

What can go wrong?

Excess testosterone, either secreted by the body or taken as a drug, causes problems in both males and females. In women, too much testosterone causes the development of masculine features such as an increase in body hair, deepening of the voice, and some hair loss. Facial spots may develop and testosterone can also lead to an increase in body weight. It is very rare for a woman to produce an excess of testosterone, but occasionally it may be the result of an androgen-secreting ovarian tumor, or an ovarian cyst.

In adult males the presence of excess testosterone accentuates male physical characteristics. It can also cause a condition called priapism, which is a painful persistent erection. It may be the result of a testicular tumor. Excess testosterone given to stimulate puberty may interfere

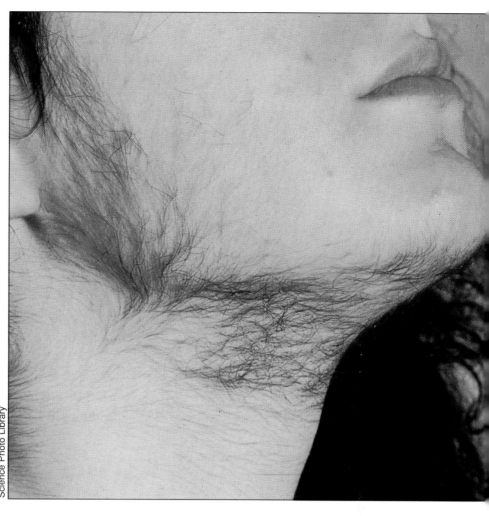

Science Photo Library

This young woman has developed excessive facial hair, called hirsutism. The cause is thought to be associated with an hormonal disturbance producing excess testosterone.

with normal growth or cause over-rapid sexual development. Initially the testosterone increases bone growth but adult height is reduced because the testosterone causes the long bones to stop growing too soon.

A deficiency of testosterone is far more common than an excess. This may occur if the testes are diseased, or if the pituitary gland does not secrete LH. The effects vary, depending on whether the deficiency develops before or after puberty. If it develops before puberty the boy's limbs continue to grow so that his final adult height will be increased, and he will have particularly long arms and legs. Other typical effects include decreased body hair and beard growth, smooth skin, a high-pitched voice, reduced sexual drive and performance, underdevelopment of the genitalia, and poor muscle development.

Teenage boys with delayed puberty are usually treated with testosterone. This boosts puberty artificially, and so avoids psychological problems (see Puberty). Testosterone may also be given to men who have become infertile because of a deficiency of pituitary hormones.

Testosterone can be given as a pellet that is implanted under the skin of the abdominal wall under local anesthesia, as an injection into the muscle, or it can be taken orally. All forms of treatment are effective and safe. Occasionally, if testosterone is given to an adult who has never been through puberty, testosterone can trigger aggression.

Menopausal women are sometimes given implants of testosterone in addition to hormone replacement therapy.

In the condition called female transsexualism, although the individuals have the appearance of femininity, they believe that they actually belong to the male sex. After discussing their condition with a doctor and psychiatrist, it may be decided that the best solution is for the transsexual to take regular doses of testosterone. This gradually deepens the voice, promotes hair growth on the face and chest, decreases feminine fat, and gives the external appearance of maleness.

Tetanus

A rusty nail, a clumsy step, and the resulting wound could be the ideal breeding ground for the virulent bacterium that causes tetanus. The disease can be fatal, so adequate immunization is of the utmost importance.

Q Can you be immunized against tetanus?

A Not only can you be immunized, you definitely should be. Children are given a vaccine against this serious disease with their first series of injections and then are given a booster dose as they start school. Older people may have escaped vaccination and should ask their doctor to give them one, since they will otherwise be at a much greater risk of infection.

If you have been vaccinated you should have a booster dose about every 10 years. When people go to the emergency room with wounds of various sorts they are often given a booster. The vaccination is actually against the toxin, or poison, rather than the bacteria that make it, since it is the toxin that causes all the trouble.

Q Can you only get tetanus in a wound made by a rusty, rather than a clean, object?

A No, tetanus spores are very common in our environment, and it is certainly possible to infect yourself, even with an object that is apparently clean. However, the highest concentration of spores is found in the soil and in manure. An object like a rusty nail is perhaps more likely to have been in contact with spores; therefore you may be a little more likely to get an infection from such an object.

Q Is it true that tetanus paralyzes you so that you can hear everything around you but you can't move or speak?

A No. Tetanus is caused by a toxin that acts directly on the nervous system. The effects of the toxin are to produce both a general rigidity of muscle, leading to lockjaw, a name sometimes given to the disease, and to produce spasms. These spasms can be exhausting and even fatal if they occur frequently. In order to prevent them, sedation is used. If this fails then the patient may be deliberately paralyzed with drugs and have his or her breathing taken over by a respirator.

Sally and Richard Greenhill

Tetanus is a frightening and dangerous disease that can be fatal, even with the best medical care. However, all the techniques of intensive care can be brought to bear on sufferers in developed countries, and there is no doubt that modern treatment does significantly reduce the number of deaths from this disease.

Cause

Tetanus is caused by a bacterium called *Clostridium tetani*. This organism is found freely in the soil, and is even more common in manured and cultivated soil since it is very common in animal dung. However, it is not confined to soil; street dust from the center of a town certainly contains the spores of the bacteria, and they can even be found inside buildings in large amounts (see Bacteria).

The bacterium has one very important characteristic that controls the way the disease behaves: it is killed by oxygen and only grows in oxygen-free surroundings. This is why the bacteria have to be introduced into the body via a wound of some sort, since the blood supply, and therefore the oxygen supply, are cut off as a result of the tissue damage. The deeper and more contaminated a wound, the higher the risk of tetanus (see Wounds).

The toxin that the bacterium makes is a deadly substance, exceeded in potency only by the toxin responsible for botulism (see Botulism). A tenth of a milligram is the fatal dose for an adult. From its site of production in the wound contaminated by the bacteria, the toxin passes into the spinal cord and the brain. It is thought that it travels through the nerves, although transmission via the blood could also be important. Once in the nervous system the toxin cannot be neutralized by antibodies either produced by the body after immunization, or given as antitoxin (see Nervous system).

It is not uncommon for tetanus to be picked up in cities. The bacterium makes spores that are resistant to the effects of drying and heat, and can survive for long periods in dust. These children, if not immunized, would therefore be at risk, simply because they are playing in a dusty area where they are exposed to injury.

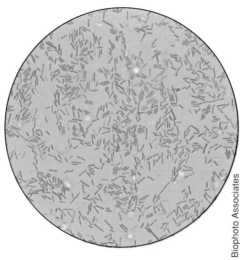

Once in the body, the bacterium may grow in an area with no blood supply, making it difficult for antibiotics to reach.

Symptoms

The incubation period is six to ten days as a rule, although in rare cases it may be several months. At the other extreme, symptoms can occur within a day.

There is a short vague illness with headache, general illness, and fever, but the important first signs are due to the generalized muscle rigidity that is one of the two classic symptoms of the disease. This especially affects the jaw muscles—giving rise to lockjaw, by which name the disease is sometimes known—the muscles of the abdomen, which are found to be firm on examination, and the muscles of the back. Eventually the back may be arched over and the neck bent back.

Spasms develop later and can be brought on by any stimulus. Minor spasms may simply affect the face, with contraction of the facial muscles into a ghastly grin, known by the chilling Latin title *risus sardonicus*, meaning sardonic smile. Breathing can be affected by these spasms and when they become more generalized they lead to even more exaggerated arching of the back and neck.

The difficulty in caring for tetanus patients really becomes marked when the disease interferes with the way that the brain controls vital functions. The heart may be affected, leading to abnormalities of rhythm and either very low or very high blood pressure. Sometimes the temperature may increase very rapidly.

Treatment

The aim of treatment is to maintain the patient over the period of his or her illness and prevent any possibly fatal problems from occurring. These problems include exhaustion due to spasm, asphyxia during spasm, pneumonia due to stomach contents entering the lungs, and death due to disorders of control of vital functions, such as the heartbeat and blood pressure.

In milder cases, simple sedation and the avoidance of all types of disturbance will prevent spasms, but in the more severe cases a tracheostomy is performed, and the patient is treated by total paralysis using curare (a paralyzing drug), while breathing is taken over by a respirator (see Tracheostomy).

The disease is likely to be most severe when the incubation period has been short and when there has been less than 48 hours between the first symptom and the first spasm.

Prevention

Immunization with tetanus toxoid is given with a baby's first immunization, and boosters are given when starting school and on leaving. After that, a booster should be given every 10 years—or more often if you are at special risk, for example, if you work on the land. In people who have not been immunized it is necessary to give an antitoxin after any serious wound (see Immunization).

It is possible to cut down the risks of contracting tetanus by careful cleansing of all wounds, no matter how minor, and the use of large doses of penicillin. However, adequate immunization can abolish the risk completely. This disease is often fatal and it is up to all of us to make sure that we are immunized.

People who work on the land—such as gardeners and farmers—are most likely to catch tetanus. The bacterium is commonly found in animal dung, a normal component of fertilized and cultivated soil.

Biophoto Associates

Brian Harris/Colorific!

Tetracycline

Q I am allergic to penicillin. Does this mean that I am also allergic to tetracycline?

A No. In fact, the tetracycline group of antibiotics could be very valuable to you simply because you are allergic to the penicillins. It is effective and safe against a wide range of common infections.

Q My doctor often gives me tetracycline for bronchitis. When I was pregnant, however, she no longer prescribed it. Why was this?

A Tetracycline shouldn't be used in pregnancy since it forms a deposit in the baby's teeth and stains them. The same thing happens to a lesser extent in the baby's bones. Tetracycline can also be deposited in the teeth at any age up to about eight or nine, so it is not generally given to children whose teeth are still growing.

Q My daughter is a nurse, and she tells me that many bacteria are now resistant to tetracycline. Does this mean that it is no longer useful as an antibiotic?

A Your daughter probably works in a hospital where tetracycline is not used frequently. Resistance can develop to tetracycline, and in a hospital the resistant bacteria can be passed from patient to patient very easily. However, there are some very important types of infection that will only respond to tetracycline, like typhus, psittacosis, and brucellosis.

Q My doctor gave me tetracycline and I got severe diarrhea. Am I allergic to this particular drug?

A No, it is not uncommon for people to get diarrhea as a result of treatment with any of the antibiotics. This is because the antibiotic not only kills off the bacteria that are causing trouble, but also kills bacteria that normally live in the colon (large intestine). This leads to a disturbance in its function, and diarrhea results.

Tetracycline is an important weapon in the doctor's armory of antibiotic drugs. It is used against many diseases, but judiciously, since resistance can develop.

Tetracycline is one of the most useful antibiotics (see Antibiotics). It not only provides effective treatment for a wide range of common diseases caused by bacteria, but also provides one of the only effective forms of treatment for a number of less common infections.

Tetracycline works by blocking the action of the ribosomes (the ribosomes are the cell's protein factory) within the bacteria. Although treatment with tetracycline will stop a bacterium growing, this does not mean that the drug will succeed in killing it off. For this reason, tetracycline is called a bacteriostatic drug (that is, one that stops bacteria) as opposed to the bactericidal drugs such as penicillin (see Penicillin), which actually kill off individual bacteria.

Effectiveness

Tetracycline is a very useful antibiotic because it is effective against a wide range of organisms, including those responsible for acne, bronchitis, gonorrhea, and types of pneumonia.

However, one of the problems that has occurred since its introduction in the 1950s is that a number of the common organisms causing infection have become resistant to the effects of tetracycline. This is a problem that occurs with many antibiotics, but it seems to be particularly so with tetracycline. Because there is a certain amount of resistance to the drug, it is used less in hospitals, where resistant strains of bacteria would have the opportunity to spread from patient to patient. There is much less chance that a patient attending his or her doctor's office would have caught a resistant bacterium, so the drug remains safe and effective for those people who are normally fit and who are removed from the risk of catching hospital infections.

Dangers

Side effects may include vomiting, diarrhea, nausea, and, rarely, rash and itching (see Side effects). However, the main danger of the drug is that it tends to get bound into growing bones and teeth. While there is little adverse effect on the bones, the teeth may become stained with defective enamel. It should therefore be avoided in pregnant mothers and in children whose teeth are still growing.

Both dishes contain a culture of a common bacterium called E. coli. However, in the dish where there is a pellet of tetracycline, there is no growth of the bacterium.

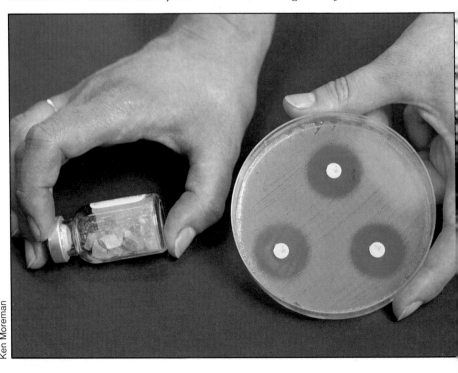

Ken Moreman

Thalassemia

Q If you have thalassemia, are there any special precautions that should be taken when you are pregnant?

A If you have been diagnosed as having one of the minor forms of thalassemia, the most important thing is to get genetic advice before deciding to have a family. It is particularly important to check that your husband does not have any signs of abnormal hemoglobin production, either in the form of thalassemia, or one of the related diseases like sickle-cell anemia. If he does, then it is important to seek expert advice. If your husband is clear, then you should have no problems with the pregnancy.

Q Is thalassemia common all over the world, or is it found only in certain places?

A Thalassemia tends to occur in the places where malaria is or has been common, but it is prevalent on the Mediterranean coast and in the Middle East and Far East. However, since the population of the world is now so mobile thalassemia can be found almost anywhere in the world, particularly in large cities.

Q I read somewhere that if you have had thalassemia you would have a natural protection against malaria. Is this true?

A It is thought that possessing one of the abnormal genes that gives rise to thalassemia gives some protection against the effects of malaria. Some doctors believe that this is because the red cells in the body of a thalassemic person are somewhat fragile, so that when the malarial parasite gets inside a red cell the cell breaks down and the parasite stops growing. In normal people, the parasite would continue to multiply. So those people with minor forms of thalassemia appear to have some protection against malaria. In addition, there is much more information available about thalassemia and its effects on the body. This means that medicine can offer more effective treatment than it could in the past.

Thalassemia is a blood disease and is one of the most common inherited diseases—especially in Mediterranean regions. Although it can be fatal in its most severe form, it more usually restricts a child's development.

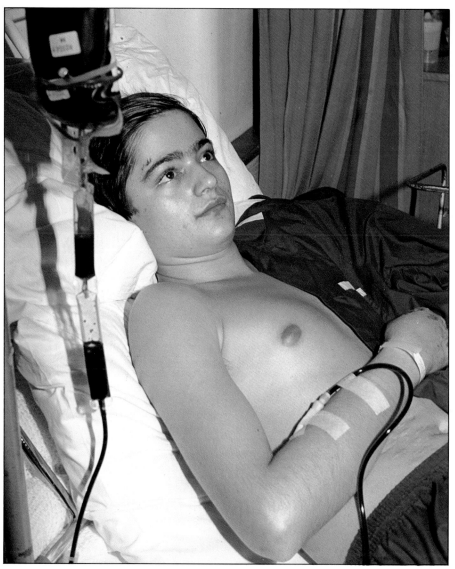

M. Adelman

Blood transfusions for some thalassemia victims are a way of life. The fragile red blood cells need constant replacement.

Thalassemia is a form of anemia, and it results from abnormalities in the structure of hemoglobin, the oxygen-carrying component of blood.

There are two basic forms of the disease: thalassemia major and thalassemia minor. In the minor form, there are usually no serious ill effects, but the major form can be fatal (see Anemia).

Causes

Hemoglobin is responsible for carrying oxygen from the lungs to the body tissues. It is made up from two substances that are chemically bound together: heme, the iron-containing central core of a hemoglobin molecule; and globin, the protein constituent that exists as a chain.

The body produces a number of different globin chains, but it is the alpha and beta chains that determine the thalassemic condition. Each molecule of hemoglobin has four globin chains attached to its central portion. Normal hemoglobin in an adult, called hemoglobin A, is made from two alpha and two

Thalassemia and malaria: are they connected?

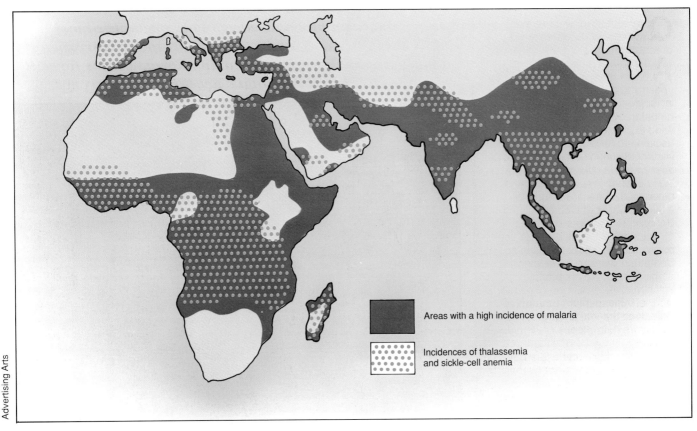

Areas with a high incidence of malaria

Incidences of thalassemia and sickle-cell anemia

beta chains The type of chain is determined by the genes inherited from our parents (see Genetics).

If the normal construction of the globin chain fails, then the makeup of the hemoglobin is affected and thalassemia is produced. The failure can be caused by both the presence of an abnormal gene, and an abnormality in what is called the transcription process: converting the genetic instructions into the production of new protein molecules.

Beta thalassemia

We inherit two genes from our parents that control the production of beta chains. If one of the genes is faulty, the outcome is beta thalassemia minor, a form of thalassemia that gives no serious trouble. However, when both genes are defective, then the very serious beta thalassemia major is produced.

In this disease the faulty hemoglobin, called hemoglobin F and normally only found in the fetus, is very slow to give up the oxygen to the tissues, and this leads to overstimulation of the bone marrow. The marrow expands and may deform the bones that contain it (see Marrow and transplants).

This longstanding and serious anemic condition is particularly dangerous for children because it restricts their growth.

Alpha thalassemia

Alpha thalassemia is slightly more complex, but not as serious, due to the fact that we inherit four genes that are responsible for the production of alpha globin chains. If one or two of these genes are defective in any way, then the result is alpha thalassemia minor, which is not serious; the sufferer has only slight anemia but will need treatment.

When there are three defective alpha genes, this produces a type of hemoglobin called hemoglobin H, which turns into hemoglobin H disease. The red blood cells break down easily and this leads to anemia and jaundice. Although this condition cannot be cured, it can be successfully controlled through blood transfusions, and the sufferer can lead a near normal life (see Blood, and Blood transfusion).

However, when all four alpha chain genes are missing, a type of blood is produced that is not compatible with life and the fetus either aborts or is stillborn.

Treatment

The treatment for the different types of thalassemia is similar; patients are provided with regular blood transfusions to keep the level of hemoglobin high, and so maintain the supply of oxygen to the tissues. The regularity of blood transfusions depends on the type and severity of

Thalassemia and sickle cell anemia are particularly common in certain areas of the world and, significantly, these are areas where malaria thrives. It is possible that genetic mutations that cause these blood diseases have an important side effect, and that they may offer some form of protection against malaria.

the anemia. Since frequent blood transfusions can result in a dangerous buildup of iron, some patients may need daily treatment with a special drug that allows excess iron to be excreted safely in the urine. Treatment may also include antibiotics to counter infection, and in some cases the spleen is removed.

Prevention

Genetic counseling is the only preventive measure that can be taken. Using simple tests it is possible to determine whether two people have the genes for beta thalassemia. Where this is found, one in four of the children are expected to have beta thalassemia major.

It is possible to analyze the blood of the fetus at about 20 weeks into the pregnancy to see if there are any beta chains being produced. If not, then a baby considered at risk is likely to have the disease, and it may be thought wise to terminate the pregnancy (see Screening).

Thalidomide

Q What is thalidomide and where did it come from?

A Thalidomide is the generic name for a drug marketed under a total of 51 trade names, including Distaval, Contergan, Kevadon, Asmaval, Tensival, and Valgraine. It is an hypnotic (sleep-inducer). Chemically, it is composed of carbon, nitrogen, oxygen, and hydrogen.

Thalidomide was invented and developed in West Germany by a company called Chemie Grünenthal, and was sold in 46 countries. In the UK it was distributed by the Distillers' Company (Biochemicals).

The inventor of the drug, Wilhelm Kunz, was trying to find a more efficient peptide (one of the molecules that make up protein) for use in antibiotics. Thalidomide was not a great improvement on existing peptides, and might have been abandoned had not Herbert Keller, one of Kunz's colleagues, noticed that its molecular structure was similar to some sedatives.

Grünenthal's tests showed that it was an effective sedative, with no side effects and, incredibly, no toxic effect at any concentration. It was thought to be the first totally safe sleeping pill ever discovered, and its early success in Germany contributed to its acceptance elsewhere in the world.

Q Could a tragedy like thalidomide happen again?

A In the wake of the thalidomide tragedy, many new controls were introduced to prevent any recurrence, and the drug companies now have much more sophisticated testing procedures than were available in the 1950s.

Nevertheless, it is both economically and practically impossible for any drug to be declared totally safe. No amount of laboratory and animal tests can reliably predict the long-term effects of a drug on humans. Even human tests are inadequate, since people are very different from one another. It is less likely now that a drug as dangerous as thalidomide could be marketed, but it will never be completely out of the question.

Once considered a wonder drug, the very name of thalidomide strikes a chill to the heart: thousands of babies suffered horrific deformities because their mothers took it in early pregnancy. What went wrong?

John Beckett

Thalidomide is a synthetic hypnotic drug composed of carbon, hydrogen, nitrogen, and oxygen. Its molecular structure is similar to that of some widely used and very effective sedatives such as glutethimide, although the similarity is slight. In the late 1950s and early 1960s, sleeping pills formed an enormous part of the drug market in the United States and abroad. Thalidomide was the first apparently safe sleeping pill, and it sold by the million.

This 20-year-old woman was born without proper limbs, yet has triumphantly overcome her handicaps. She works at an aid center for the disabled, and has recently passed her advanced driving test.

The "wonder drug"

Wilhelm Kunz, a chemist with Chemie Grünenthal in West Germany, invented thalidomide. His colleague Herbert Keller recognized the drug's sedative potential, and Grünenthal tested it for its efficacy

The molecular structure of thalidomide

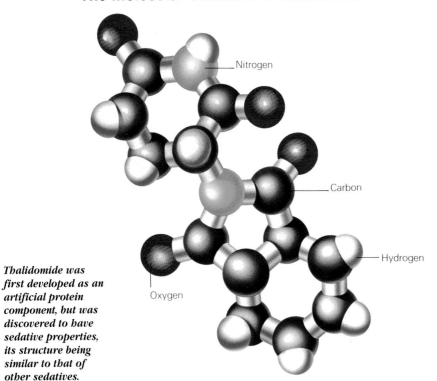

Nitrogen

Carbon

Hydrogen

Oxygen

Aziz Khan

Thalidomide was first developed as an artificial protein component, but was discovered to have sedative properties, its structure being similar to that of other sedatives.

and safety. There appeared to be no side effects and no maximum dose. The tests would later be questioned, but the company believed it had a wonder drug.

However, soon after the drug's introduction, side effects in adults were dizziness, nausea, wakefulness, numbness, shivering, and hangover. By the end of the first year, sales rose and Grünenthal dismissed the reports and made even stronger claims for thalidomide. A leaflet produced by the British distributors stated that "Distaval (thalidomide) can be given with complete safety to pregnant women and nursing mothers, without adverse effect on mother or child," even though no reproductive tests had been done.

Side effects

Adverse reports increased in number and confirmed that the drug caused peripheral neuritis: numbness in the extremities, cramps, pins and needles, weakness, and loss of motor control. Grünenthal continued to market the drug, and in May 1961 a thalidomide baby was born in Australia. It was badly malformed and died one week later, after unsuccessful emergency surgery. Within three weeks, two more such babies were born in the same hospital and obstetrician Dr. William McBride set out to find the cause. He discovered the common factor. All three mothers had taken only one drug: thalidomide.

It was not until similar reports were made in Germany, and after pressure from

the German press, that the company finally agreed to withdraw the drug in November 1961. Even so, governments were slow to respond and several hundred children were born malformed even after thalidomide's devastating effects were known.

A year after it was withdrawn in Europe, it was still available in Japan without prescription; the Swedish distributor continued to sell it in Argentina after it was banned in Sweden; in Italy it was still on sale, under 10 different trade names, 10 months after it had been withdrawn in Germany. Fortunately the Food and Drug Association banned the drug in the United States, and so spared much suffering.

The effect of the drug on the unborn child was horrific and widespread. It is thought that almost 100 percent of women who took the drug during the first trimester of pregnancy had deformed babies. Several babies were affected by a single dose. The first trimester of pregnancy is the crucial stage of fetal development when the limb buds form. Thalidomide arrested this growth and that of the internal organs.

Many of the children were born with such extensive deformities that they did not survive. Those that lived, about 7,500 worldwide, were sometimes so badly deformed that doctors and nurses were too upset to help the parents effectively, and divorce was not uncommon. This strain was made worse by the fact that at

the time no one but a few doctors, and Grünenthal, suspected the cause, and parents blamed themselves and each other for their children's deformities.

Often nurses were unable to tell parents what the baby looked like, and kept them apart until they left the hospital. As a result one mother discovered her child had no arms only after she got home. The failure to give parents adequate help, support, and guidance in accepting their handicapped children led to problems of rejection in some cases. Society recoiled from the children, emotionally and financially, and it was 10 years before financial settlements were made.

Could it have been foreseen?

Grünenthal claimed that it was not usual to test for reproductive effects, and that even if they had performed such tests they would have been carried out on

The crucial stage of fetal development

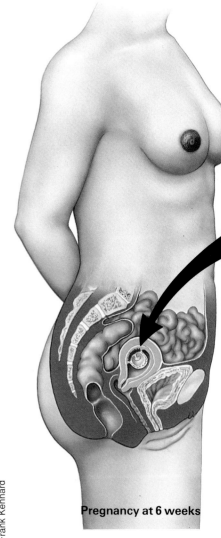

Frank Kennard

Pregnancy at 6 weeks

rats, which do not show the effect. In many larger companies, however, it was already routine to test on pregnant animals, and several laboratories, including Distillers', used rabbits, which do show the drug's teratogenic (deformity-causing) effects. It was known that drugs can cross the placental barrier and affect the unborn child, just as essential substances such as oxygen and nutrients do.

All of this, however, might have been excusably overlooked. What cannot be justified is that the drug was still being sold as safe for pregnant women long after it was known to cause serious neural side effects in adults, and that, even after the birth defects were discovered in Japan, over a year elapsed before it was withdrawn from sale in that country.

Partly as a result of this tragedy, in 1970 new controls were effected, such as the formation of the Committee on the Safety of Medicines in the UK, and aids to the disabled were made available. Even the regulations and sophisticated techniques that now exist cannot guarantee that this tragedy will not recur. The balance is in our favor because successes hugely outnumber tragedies. However, just one mistake like thalidomide can have calamitous effects.

The thalidomide story continues

As a result of the thalidomide disaster most doctors and pharmacologists wanted to have nothing more to do with the drug. However, there remained a few researchers who realized that such a powerful drug was likely to have some useful applications.

In 1964, careful observations of leprosy patients who were taking thalidomide suggested that the drug might help certain phases of the disease. Many trials have since proved that this is, indeed, the case. Thalidomide has no direct effect on the leprosy bacillus, but it has a powerful effect on one of the types of acute flare-up reactions of the disease that can cause serious tissue destruction (see Leprosy). The drug is effective in over 90 percent of cases and may bring about improvement within 24 hours. As a result it has now been used by leprologists for years.

Graft versus host disease is a complication of bone marrow transplantation. It is a reaction of the transplanted cells against the tissues of the recipient, and it occurs in about 40 percent of patients who survive transplantation. Unfortunately it has a high mortality rate. Trials have shown that thalidomide is a safe and effective drug for this serious condition. The drug is not a complete cure, but has proved the most effective therapy to date. It has been shown to be effective in 20 percent of cases that resist treatment with antirejection drugs such as corticosteroids and cyclosporin.

A research paper in the prestigious *New England Journal of Medicine* for May 22, 1997, reported that thalidomide had proved to be an effective treatment for the painful, debilitating, and persistent mouth ulcers that are a common feature of AIDS. In this trial, 55 percent of patients who received thalidomide had complete healing of their ulcers within four weeks. Only 7 percent of those who did not have thalidomide showed healing. Other trials have shown a cure rate as high as 81 percent. Thalidomide does not act against HIV, but may have a role in improving the general condition of people with AIDS (see AIDS).

Many other conditions have been shown to respond to, or to be helped by, thalidomide. These include various skin disorders caused by immune system malfunction; ulcerative colitis; rheumatoid arthritis; the genital and esophageal ulcers of Behçet's disease; and the severe and prolonged pain that often follows shingles (postherpetic neuralgia).

The continuing thalidomide story is not all positive, however. The known effects on the early fetus make it imperative that the drug should not be used on women if there is any possibility of pregnancy. If there is no alternative, contraception must be 100 percent effective.

In addition, other side effects of thalidomide, especially on the nerves, appear to be potentially more serious than had at first been thought. Because of these dangers, thalidomide is a strictly controlled drug, and supplies are available only under prescribed conditions. As a result, exhaustive clinical guidelines for the use of thalidomide worldwide have been produced for doctors.

During the second month of pregnancy, the fetal limb buds rapidly develop into fully formed limbs (below). Thalidomide arrested this development. Like most drugs, it was able to pass across the placenta by a simple process of diffusion.

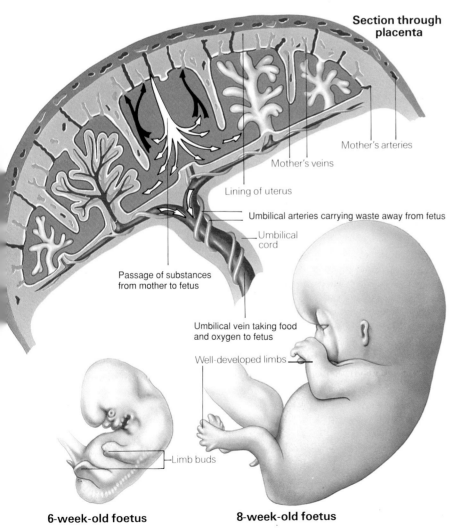

Section through placenta

Mother's arteries
Mother's veins
Lining of uterus
Umbilical arteries carrying waste away from fetus
Umbilical cord
Passage of substances from mother to fetus
Umbilical vein taking food and oxygen to fetus
Well-developed limbs
Limb buds

6-week-old foetus   **8-week-old foetus**

Therapy

The term therapy *covers a range of methods of treatment for physical and psychiatric disorders. Some have been scientifically proven to be effective in managing disease; others use methods that are not accepted as being scientific.*

Q What exactly does the word *therapy* mean?

A This is a very general term and, although it is often used to mean psychotherapy, it should not be limited to any one group. A therapy is a treatment of any kind for a medical or psychological disorder. A reasonably detailed medical dictionary will contain upward of 80 entries for various procedures or techniques that are described as therapies.

Q Does the word *therapy* imply that the method referred to actually works?

A Regrettably no. And this is where people are often misled. Strictly speaking one should not use the term unless there is good reason to suppose that the method is effective. No doubt people who develop new therapies believe that they do work but, unfortunately, the care with which some of these are tested often leaves much to be desired.

Q If a particular form of therapy makes someone feel better, isn't that a sufficient justification for its use?

A Up to a point. But scientific therapists make an important distinction between symptoms and the underlying disease process that causes them. Temporarily removing symptoms and making a person feel better can sometimes have serious consequences if it delays the start of conventional treatment that is rational and known to be completely effective.

Q Many people are convinced that homeopathy works. If this form of therapy is so illogical how is this possible?

A Feeling better has nothing to do with reason. If a particular treatment is followed by an apparent recovery, then this is more than likely to be attributed to the treatment, however illogical, and will be remembered. The many occasions when the same treatment has had no effect are ignored and forgotten.

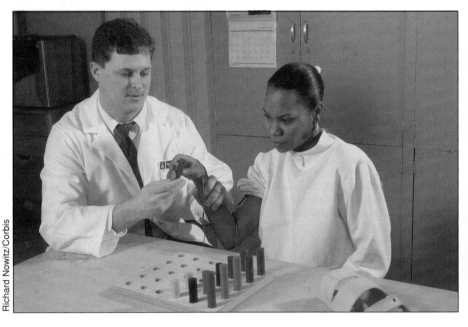

Richard Nowitz/Corbis

Therapy is any form of treatment intended to relieve a disorder or disease of the body or mind. The word is derived from the Greek *therapeia*, meaning "attendance," and is related to the Greek *therapeutikos*, meaning "to minister to." The word does not connote that the treatment is either correct or likely to be effective, but this is usually the implication. However, many therapies are based on ideas that do not stand up under close examination.

Since therapy covers all forms of medical treatment, it includes the use of drugs to treat disease, which is called pharmacological therapeutics, and all forms of surgery. These two major fields are covered in a number of other articles, including those on Antibiotics, Anesthetics, Barbiturates, Blood transfusion, Cosmetic surgery, Cough syrup, Donors, Emetics, Enema, Expectorants, Grafting, Hormone replacement therapy, Hysterectomy, Immunosuppressive drugs, Inhalants, Insulin, Joint replacement, Kidney transplants, Liniments, Manipulation, Medicines, Microsurgery, Morphine, Ointments, Open-heart surgery, Orthopedics, Pain management, Penicillin, Pharmacy, Postoperative care, Premedication, Prostaglandins, Quinine, Sedatives, Steroids, Surgery, Tetracycline, and Vitamins.

Orthodox medicine and surgery also incorporate a number of other therapies

Physical therapy is a scientifically proven therapy that aims to restore a patient's full range of movement and mobility after an injury or surgery.

that are covered in more detail in the articles on Flotation therapy, Occupational therapy, Osteopathy, Physical therapy, Radiotherapy, and Speech therapy. There are, in addition, many therapies that are not recognized by orthodox medicine as being supported by a rigorous scientific basis or as being sufficiently proven to be effective. These therapies are often described as being complementary to orthodox medicine, and few would object to this description or to their employment strictly in that role. Some people, however, take the view that these therapies are an adequate alternative to scientific medicine. This is not a view that can safely be maintained.

Alternative versus orthodox

Scientific therapies are based on demonstrable fact. For instance, there are certain virulent bacteria that, once established in the body, will kill unless the person concerned is given a selected antibiotic that will kill those bacteria. None of the complementary therapies will save that person. In that context, therefore, they are not acceptable alternatives. All bacterial infections and a great many viral infections can be completely cured by conventional medical or surgical treatment; none of them can be cured by complementary therapies. Many cancers will grow, spread, and kill the patient. Surgery and selected anticancer drugs can often destroy the cancer and save the patient. None of the complementary therapies can do this. None of the major diseases, such as diabetes, tuberculosis, rheumatoid arthritis, multiple sclerosis, cataract, chronic bronchitis, emphysema, cystic fibrosis, phenylketonuria, and leukemia, can be effectively treated by complementary therapies. If such therapies prevent or delay accurate diagnosis and rational scientific treatment of these diseases, the patient may suffer severely.

Many people turn to complementary therapies to find sympathy, understanding, compassion, and comfort because they are disenchanted with conventional medicine, perceiving it as cold, heartless, technology-based, and unconcerned with human values. There is substance in this view but, logically, it is a criticism of the way medicine is organized and of individual doctors rather than the discipline itself. The best doctors try to practice holistic medicine and are deeply aware of the importance of humanity and of the real aims of medicine—the promotion of human health and happiness. Unfortunately many doctors are driven by pressure of work and materialistic aspirations to turn what should be a humane and caring art into a commercial, money-centered enterprise. This is a reflection of society's current values.

Psychotherapies
These include Freudian psychoanalysis, a range of psychoanalytic methods based on schools that broke away from Freud, and numerous forms of psychotherapy involving single patients, families, or groups (see Behavior therapy, Counsel-

Richard Nowitz/Corbis

Water plays a role in more than one form of therapy. In hydrotherapy, patients lie in a warm bath or Jacuzzi, and physical therapy sessions (above) may take place in water.

ing, Gestalt therapy, Group therapy, and Psychotherapy). Psychoanalysis is now in sharp decline, as are many other therapies based on imaginary premises and the unsupported assertions of their founders, rather than on scientific principles. Currently, the field leader is cognitive behavior therapy, which is proving capable of correcting many psychological and behavioral disorders, especially phobias and many forms of anxiety disorder. It has even been successful in curing persistent unemployment.

Irrationally based therapies
Several therapies are explicitly based on premises that are known to be false or that cannot be sustained by reason. These include: acupuncture, acupressure, and shiatsu (the body contains meridians of energy, the blocking of which causes disease); aromatherapy (certain essential oils have healing properties if inhaled or massaged through the skin); chiropractic (many bodily disorders are caused by subtle displacement of the bones of the spine); colonic irrigation (toxins are absorbed from bacteria in the large intestine and these cause disease); color therapy (light of different colors can act therapeutically on body cells); crystal therapy (crystals such as quartz can be programmed by a therapist to increase the amount of healing in a room); herbalism (many plants contain therapeutically valuable substances that have been ignored by the drug companies); hydrotherapy (lying in a warm bath or Jacuzzi

John Greim/Science Photo Library

A psychotherapist interacts with his or her patients and encourages them to talk through their problems, rather than relying on drug treatment.

can positively affect your health); homeopathy (repeated massive dilution with vigorous shaking increases the potency of a remedy); iridology (zones on the irises of the eyes reflect various organs and parts of the body); mud therapy (covering the body with mud can effectively treat numerous disorders); naturopathy (diseases are caused by the accumulation of toxins in the body); reflexology (energy channels run from the toes to various parts of the body, each representing an organ); and rolfing (deep massage can significantly improve health).

Logically based premises
Although not scientifically accepted as having significant medical value, some complementary therapies encourage valuable physical and mental habits and attitudes that can help to promote health. These include the Alexander technique, art therapy, biofeedback, dance movement therapy, hatha yoga (see Yoga), meditation, mind-body therapy, relaxation, and tai chi.

The apparent success of complementary therapies and of activities such as faith healing depend on the effect they have on the patient's mind. This effect may be enhanced by impressive-looking equipment, impressive-sounding explanations, and by the amount of time devoted to questioning and examination, but it is unlikely to be sustained unless the patient is persuaded that the therapist is genuinely concerned.

An effective human interaction is the real basis of complementary medicine. The great pity for the vast majority of patients in need of help is that this can so seldom be a central feature of scientifically proven medicine.

Thermal imaging

Q When rescue workers use thermal imaging cameras to look for survivors after disasters, are they using the same technique as when my mother had thermography to diagnose her varicose veins?

A Yes. In rescue work, thermal imaging can locate survivors because their body temperature is higher than the temperature of their surroundings and this produces images of different intensity. In medicine, thermal imaging, or thermography, uses infrared rays emitted by the body to show areas of increased or decreased heat emission, which can indicate tumors, inflammation, or, as in your mother's case, abnormal blood supply.

Q My sister recently had a breast thermogram, and the doctor then arranged for her to have a mammogram. Why did she have to have two tests?

A A breast thermogram is a very safe, noninvasive technique that is used to detect abnormalities in the breast. It shows tumors as hot spots and cysts as cold spots. Unfortunately it cannot reliably distinguish between benign and malignant tumors, so if a hot spot is found the patient must have a mammogram to provide a more accurate diagnosis. Mammography carries a very slight risk of inducing cancer because it uses X rays, so some doctors prefer thermography if they think the problem is more likely to be a cyst than a tumor.

Q My father has rheumatoid arthritis and the doctor is monitoring his condition using thermography. Is it dangerous to have repeated thermograms?

A No. Thermography is a completely safe, noninvasive and nontraumatic technique. It relies on detecting the infrared radiation that is naturally emitted from your father's body. He will not be exposed to any external rays as he would be with an X ray or a computerized tomography (CT) scan, for example. Therefore it is an ideal technique when repeated testing is needed.

Thermal imaging is a diagnostic procedure that records any variations in the surface temperature of the body. It can be used for detecting a wide range of conditions, including tumors, inflammation, and abnormal blood supply.

A thermogram is a color-coded thermal map of skin surface temperature.

Thermal imaging, or thermography, is a diagnostic tool that provides clues to the presence of diseases and abnormalities that alter the temperature of the skin, such as circulatory problems, inflammation, and tumors (see Temperature).

Doctors have used the temperature of the body as an indicator of health for over a hundred years. The internal temperature of a resting healthy person is 98.6°F (37°C), and the body regulates this over a range of environmental temperatures—even though you may feel cold in winter and hot in summer, your internal temperature will stay around 98.6°F.

The skin plays a very important part in the regulation process, and its temperature can vary from about 86°F (30°C) to 95°F (35°C) depending on the environmental temperature. The skin temperature is also affected by the movement of air, since air carries heat away from the skin. Internal factors also have an effect on the skin temperature, because heat is conducted to the surface of the body from structures beneath the skin. It is these factors that form the basis of thermography.

How does thermography work?

Thermography is a noninvasive technique that can measure the temperature distribution over large areas of the surface of the body very quickly without bringing anything into contact with the skin. Every object emits infrared radiation and the intensity of this radiation is related to the temperature of the object—in this case the temperature of the skin surface.

Like visible rays, infrared rays travel in straight lines, and they can be reflected and refracted using mirrors and lenses in the same way as optical devices reflect and refract light. If the infrared rays can be detected and accurately measured, then the temperature of the object emitting them can be determined.

In thermal imaging machines the infrared radiation is detected by a photosensitive detector. The radiation emanating from a small area of the skin surface is focused into the detector. To allow the machine to view large areas of the skin it is placed up to 10 ft (3 m) away from the patient and oscillating mirrors or rotating prisms are used to scan the whole of the field of view.

Temperature distribution is obtained by amplifying the signal from the detector and displaying the result as a varying light level on an oscilloscope or a TV monitor. This picture can then be photographed using Polaroid film; the resulting photographs are called thermograms.

What is thermography used for?

The first medical application of thermography was in the 1950s, when it was used by a breast surgeon in the diagnosis of breast disorders. Since then its use has been expanded into several other areas.

Breast thermography: It is the influence on the skin temperature of the structures an inch or two below the surface that provides the information that is useful in the diagnosis of breast disorders. The vessels just below the skin affect the skin temperature and in normal breasts they show up as branching lines on the thermogram because of their higher temperature. The armpits (axillae) also show up as hot regions and in most patients the nipples are shown as cool. In breast cancer the affected area shows up as a hot spot because of an increase in the blood supply to the area and also because of the increased activity of the tumor tissue.

A hot spot is not used as a positive diagnosis on its own. If a hot spot is seen the patient will then have a mammogram (see Mammography). This is because in benign breast disease enlarged blood vessels may also produce hot regions. Cysts will usually show up as well-defined cold regions (see Cysts).

Circulatory problems: Thermography can be used to assess the efficiency of the blood supply in patients with peripheral vascular disease. Blocked arteries in the lower limbs produce an abnormal skin temperature distribution, which can be seen on the thermogram. Varicose veins can also be detected (see Varicose veins).

Cerebral (brain) circulation can be monitored by thermography because changes in the blood supply to the internal and external carotid arteries (that supply the brain) are reflected in changes in the temperature of the skin of the face and forehead. Narrowing (stenosis) of the internal carotid artery shows up as cool areas over the eye region and the middle forehead (see Arteries and artery disease).

Bone and joint disorders: Disorders such as inflammation and bone cancer can show up on thermograms. Thermography shows the rise in temperature in joints affected by rheumatoid arthritis and is useful for monitoring the progress of the disease. The inflammation produced by a slipped disk sometimes shows up, but the results are usually not accurate enough to be useful in diagnosis (see Cancer, Rheumatoid arthritis, and Slipped disk).

Thyroid disorders: Active thyroid tissue shows as a warm area on a thermogram.

Thermography is a very useful technique for distinguishing benign thyroid nodules (adenomas), which show as cold spots, from malignant nodules (thyroid cancer), which show as hot spots. A scan of the thyroid by radioisotopes detects nodules, but cannot distinguish between benign and malignant nodules (see Thyroid).

Results and outlook

Because so many factors affect skin temperature, in most cases the results of thermography are not sufficiently reliable to allow a conclusive diagnosis; further tests are usually needed to confirm the underlying condition. For example, in breast disease thermography is usually carried out with mammography, which is more accurate at detecting abnormality. But since mammography uses X rays it carries a low risk of inducing cancer, especially if the accumulated dose of X ray is increased by repeated examination. Thermography can be used regularly without risk to the patient, who need only be referred for mammography if the thermogram shows anything suspicious (see X rays).

As the apparatus becomes more accurate, it should be possible to obtain the information to make more positive diagnoses using thermography. Its great advantage is that it is totally noninvasive and nontraumatic for the patient, which is so beneficial when repeat testing is needed.

A thermogram of a woman's body, showing the breast. Areas of different temperature are color coded, the hottest are white, yellow to red, and the coolest blue, purple to black.

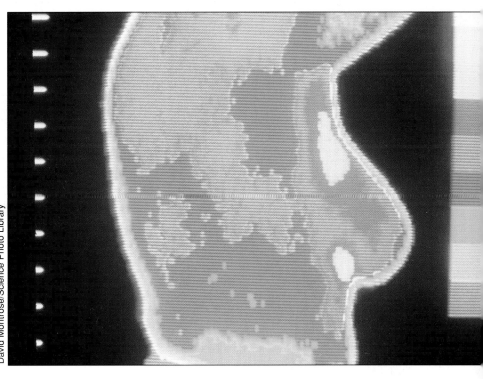

David Montrose/Science Photo Library

Thirst

Q When it is very hot and I am thirsty, I get much more relief from having a really cold drink than I do if I have a tepid one. Is there a physical reason for this, or is it just psychological?

A The amount of fluid your body receives is the same whatever the temperature of the drink you take. However, the relief of thirst depends to a large extent on the stimulation of your mouth and throat as you drink. It is possible that cold fluids stimulate the linings here more than tepid fluids. Similarly, hot tea is thirst-quenching even on hot days, again because hotter drinks stimulate the throat more than tepid ones.

Q My husband has very bad bronchitis and has to breathe through his mouth most of the time. He says that doing this seems to make him very thirsty. Why does this happen?

A One of the things that stimulates our brains to make us thirsty is when the lining of the throat and mouth get dry. People with bronchitis or asthmatic attacks who have to breathe through their mouths get very dry in the mouth through evaporation of the water on the lining. This stimulates the thirst centers, despite the fact that the actual water content of the blood is adequate.

Q Why do people who have diabetes get so thirsty before the disease is diagnosed and treatment begins?

A In people with diabetes, the main change that occurs in the blood is that there is too much sugar. This problem spills over into the urine, and its presence there prevents the tubules of the kidney from properly controlling the amount of water that is lost. The first symptom that most diabetics notice, therefore, is that they have to drink more than usual to alleviate their thirst. Eventually they can no longer satisfy this thirst and may, in fact, become dehydrated unless they begin to receive medical treatment for their condition.

Taking a drink to quench a thirst is not only immensely pleasurable, it is also absolutely vital for maintaining adequate amounts of water in the body's fluids.

Sally and Richard Greenhill

The delicate chemical processes that keep us alive demand that the amount of water in the body is kept very constant. Our sense of thirst is one of the most vital of our appetites because it insures that the chemical equilibrium is maintained. Sensitive centers within the brain monitor the amount of water in the body's fluids. These respond quickly to any significant change, producing the sensation of thirst that drives us to seek replenishment if we become short of water.

Remarkably, sensors in the throat seem to be able to assess accurately when we have drunk enough, even before the centers in the brain signal that the amount of water in the body is adequate. As a symptom, excessive thirst is an important indicator that fluids have been lost. It can point to abnormalities in the kidneys (see Kidneys and kidney diseases), to the presence of excess sugar in the blood (which causes excess water loss; see Diabetes), and to damage to those brain structures that participate in keeping the water balance in order.

The mechanics of thirst
The main control center for our sense of thirst is deep in the brain just below the thalamus, and this is known as the hypothalamus (see Hypothalamus). Small groups of nerve cells in this gland are sensitive to the amount of water in the blood. If the amount of water in the blood compared to the amount of salts and other substances diminishes, these cells are stimulated and, in addition to producing the hormones that make the kidneys conserve water, produce the sensation of thirst. These cells are also stimulated by sudden changes in the volume of blood in the circulation, such as occurs after a hemorrhage (see Hemorrhage).

The other change that makes us thirsty is when the lining of our mouth and throat becomes dry. This stimulates nerve endings in the lining, which are also connected indirectly with the thirst centers in the hypothalamus. Simply moistening the mouth has a powerful effect in reducing the signals to the brain that fluid is in short supply.

When we have been deprived of water and are then allowed to drink, we rapidly take enough water to replenish our stocks; we stop before the water has had time to be absorbed and change the blood enough to reduce the stimulus to the water-sensitive cells in the hypothalamus. This illustrates the fact that there is some sort of metering mechanism in the body that assesses accurately when we have drunk enough liquid.

Closer ... there ... oh! That first glorious gulp from a water fountain quenches even the mightiest thirst and makes us drink until we're fit to burst. While we can remain for long periods without food, regular intake of liquids is vital. Our thirst is a sign that a drink is absolutely essential.

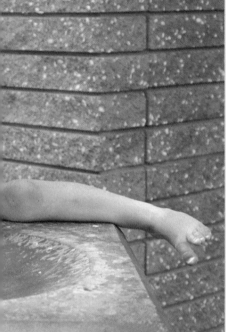

Roger Payling

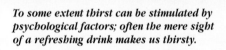

The sensors that control this metering are in the mouth and throat (see Mouth, and Throat). They coordinate with the thirst center in the brain through relays in the brain stem. In humans, this metering mechanism is not as accurate as it is in other animals, probably because we have superimposed on it certain psychological and habitual factors that are partly in control of our drinking behavior.

Thirst and illness

People are sometimes unable to compensate for dehydration by taking a drink, for example, when they are unconscious and cannot respond to messages from the thirst center in the brain. Thus, when people are very sick they may get dehydrated, especially if they lose fluid by vomiting and diarrhea (see Dehydration).

Very occasionally, the thirst area in the brain is damaged by a stroke or tumor, and does not respond normally to the changes in the water content of the blood. More often, psychiatric disease, such as certain psychoses, disrupts a person's behavior to such an extent that he or she ignores the signals from the hypothalamus and becomes dehydrated.

In hot climates, like those of the southern states, dehydration during strenuous exercise or work can be a real danger. Make sure you drink plenty of liquids.

To some extent thirst can be stimulated by psychological factors; often the mere sight of a refreshing drink makes us thirsty.

Thirst can be a symptom of many different types of disease, and its presence in someone who is sick is often a useful clue to the doctor.

The common factor in people who suffer from abnormal thirst is that they are dehydrated. This may be brought about because of kidney damage, which may affect the kidney's ability to respond to signals from the brain to retain water. When there is an excess of sugar in the blood, as in diabetes mellitus, the excess spills over into the urine and disrupts mechanisms in the kidneys controlling water retention (see Diabetes).

In an uncommon disease called diabetes insipidus the hormone normally produced by the hypothalamus to retain water may not be manufactured or, more rarely, the kidneys themselves may be unable to conserve water.

Finally, internal hemorrhage, while producing the more obvious changes in the circulation, also produces thirst. This is not so much an aid in diagnosis of the problem as a guide to the treatment (by blood transfusions, for example), since continuing thirst tells the doctors that the effects of the hemorrhage have not been reversed.

Throat

Q What should I do if I swallow a fish bone and it gets stuck in my throat?

A First try the old remedy of swallowing small amounts of bread. If you are lucky this will catch on the bone and dislodge it, carrying it down into your stomach. However, if this fails you should go immediately to a hospital emergency room, where they will be able to remove it.

Q Some time ago I had difficulty swallowing, which gradually became worse. My doctor sent me for an X ray and then prescribed iron tablets. I am much better now, but want to know why iron pills could have cured my throat trouble.

A From your description, it sounds as if you had a condition known as pharyngeal web, which occurs in people with iron deficiency anemia. In addition to difficulty in swallowing, patients complain of a sore tongue, cracks at the corner of the mouth, and brittle fingernails. In such cases an X ray of the pharynx will reveal a fine web that appears partially to obstruct the food passage. This complex symptom is known as the Patterson Brown-Kelly syndrome. It is very important to recognize it and treat it by reversing the iron deficiency; if it is not treated the difficulty in swallowing can become much more serious.

Q Why is laryngitis more serious in children than it is in adults?

A A child's airway is much smaller than that of an adult. When it becomes inflamed the lining swells and constricts the airway, and the smaller the airway the more potential there is for serious obstruction. In children, inflammation of the larynx makes it more sensitive to any agents that pass down the throat. Such agents can produce bouts of coughing and spasms of the vocal cords that make it impossible to breathe. In severe cases it is necessary to admit the child to the hospital to treat the inflammation intensively.

The air we breathe has to pass through the throat on its way to the lungs, as does our food before reaching the digestive tract. Any obstruction to this vital passage can represent a serious threat to life.

The term *throat* is used to describe the area that leads into the respiratory and digestive tracts. It extends from the oral and nasal cavities to the esophagus and the trachea, and is made up of two main parts: the pharynx and the larynx (see Larynx and laryngitis, and Pharynx).

Structures of the throat

The pharynx is a muscular tube lined with mucous membrane. For practical

Anatomy of the throat

The main component of the throat is the pharynx, a muscular tube about 5 in (13 cm) long stretching from the base of the skull into the esophagus. It is the passage

through which everything we eat, drink, and breathe has to pass, the junction point of all nasal and oral passages. It is also connected to the ears by drainage channels—the eustachian tubes—which help to equalize air pressure on each side of the eardrums.

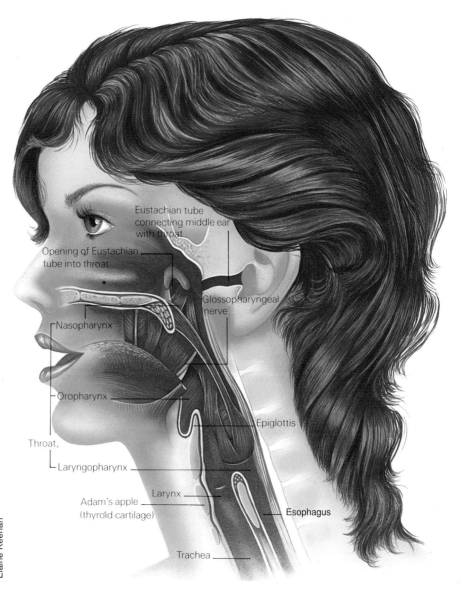

Eustachian tube connecting middle ear with throat

Opening of Eustachian tube into throat

Glossopharyngeal nerve

Nasopharynx

Oropharynx

Epiglottis

Throat,

Laryngopharynx

Larynx

Adam's apple (thyroid cartilage)

Esophagus

Trachea

Elaine Keenan

purposes it is divided into three areas. The part behind the nasal cavity is called the nasopharynx; the area behind the mouth the oropharynx; and behind the larynx the laryngopharynx. Clumps of lymphoid tissue lie in the lining of the pharynx; these are the adenoids in the nasopharynx and the tonsils in the oropharynx. They protect the entrance to the food and air passages.

The other major part of the throat—the larynx—is situated in front of the laryngopharynx and is made up of a framework of cartilage that is swathed in muscles both internally and externally, and is lined by a respiratory membrane.

The larynx is a specialized section of the windpipe. It has a flap valve—the epiglottis—hovering over the inlet to the airway, which acts as a type of umbrella against a shower of food and liquid when we eat or drink.

The vocal cords are located in the larynx, and held in place by special cartilages. They are suspended across the airway and produce sound when vibrated by air movement (see Vocal cords).

Functions of the throat

Because the throat is an assembly of different components, it has a variety of functions. The most obvious of these is to channel food and liquid into the digestive tract, and air into the lungs; this essential task is carried out by the pharynx.

The movements of the pharynx must be coordinated to insure that the respiratory gases end up in the lungs and food and liquid ends up in the esophagus. This is achieved by a plexus, or network, of nerves—the pharyngeal plexus. Its activity is controlled in the lower brain stem, which brings together information from both the respiratory and swallowing centers higher in the brain (see Brain).

When food is thrown into the oropharynx by the tongue, it is swiftly sent into the esophagus by a wave of muscular contractions that travel down the pharynx (see Esophagus). At the same time mechanisms are triggered to prevent the food from entering the larynx.

No less important are the functions of the larynx, which are to produce sound and to protect the airway. Like the pharynx, the larynx achieves these functions through a complex coordinated nerve supply to its muscles. The nerves that supply the larynx are under the same central influence in the brain as the nerves that supply the pharynx.

Throat disorders

The pharynx and larynx are prone to a number of infections caused by viruses or bacteria, and also to damage by physical agents, such as excessive smoking or

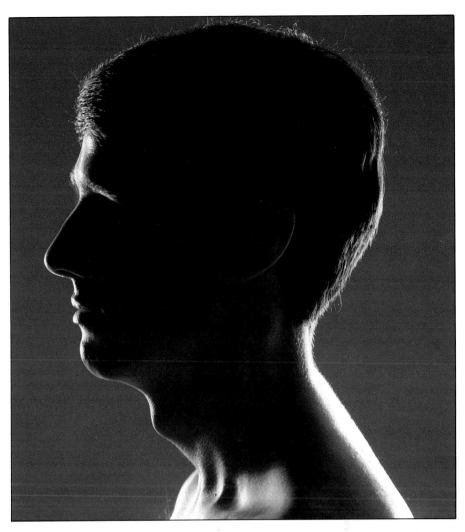

Roger Payling

drinking. Either of these factors can lead to, for example, chronic laryngitis or pharyngitis. Other throat infections include nasopharyngitis, a viral infection of the mucous membranes lining the nasopharynx. This begins with a burning feeling in the throat that builds up in intensity and is aggravated by speaking and swallowing. The discomfort is accompanied by a general feeling of malaise, which lasts from one to two days.

Nasopharyngitis is often confused with tonsillitis. Because the tonsils and the nasopharynx are adjacent to each other an infection in either area gives rise to similar symptoms. However, in tonsillitis the symptoms are much more severe.

The nasopharynx is also the site of the adenoids, and repeated infections in this area can cause the adenoids to enlarge. Patients with excessively large adenoids are unable to breathe through the nose and have persistently gaping mouths. An increase in adenoid tissue may block the natural drainage channel—the eustachian tube—from the middle ear and cause an accumulation of fluid in this cavity. In severe cases deafness may result, and the

The thyroid cartilage surrounding the larynx creates the projection called the Adam's apple. It is more prominent in men because they have larger vocal cords.

condition also predisposes to recurrent attacks of otitis media (infection of the middle ear; see Otitis). Children are most affected, and are frequently admitted to the hospital for drainage of the middle ear fluid and removal of the adenoids (see Adenoids).

Papillomatosis is caused by a virus that affects the larynx; it occurs in both children and adults. The virus is very similar to that which produces warts on the skin. As the papillomata increase in size they restrict the passage of air and may even choke the patient. Like warts on the skin, the growths will eventually disappear spontaneously, but in severe cases surgery is required to remove them.

Throat cancers

Cancer of the pharynx is an unusual condition that occurs in middle and old age. Patients complain of a progressively painful difficulty in swallowing. The pain

Q My husband has just been told that he has cancer of the larynx. What are his chances of being cured?

A Most forms of cancer of the larynx respond well to treatment. With modern radiotherapy techniques a cure rate of about 90 percent is common. However, the doctors will want to keep a close eye on your husband for the rest of his life, to treat any recurrent problems as they arise.

Q What is the correct action to take when someone is choking on something they have swallowed, such as a bone or a peanut?

A First take hold of the person firmly from behind and give a very strong and very sharp bear hug. If the patient is a child, turn him or her upside down to do this. In most patients this will dislodge the object explosively.

Q Why are disorders of the throat often accompanied by pain in the ear?

A Throat infections may cause pain in the ear because of the phenomenon of pain referral. This occurs when the same nerve supplies the two different, but close-lying structures. The patient is unable to discern from which site the pain arises.

Q My son is always getting ear infections and we have been told that he should have an adenoidectomy. Will this definitely cure him?

A It is never possible for a doctor to guarantee that any treatment will be totally successful. However, very enlarged adenoids are frequently implicated in recurrent otitis media (an infection in the middle ear) and it is only right to remove them in the hope that this is the cause of the problem. It is very important to try to minimize infectious attacks in the ear and prevent the deafness that can be associated with them, so if your ear surgeon recommends an adenoidectomy you should seriously consider it.

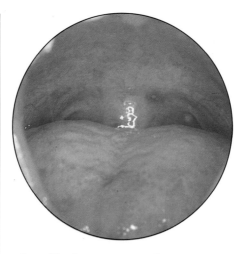

Caused by the streptococcus bacterium, strep throat is a common throat infection that can be very painful.

is experienced not only at the site of the disease but also radiating to the ear. In a large number of patients a lump appears on one side of the neck. Although cancer of the pharynx is an extremely serious condition, a high proportion of patients can be greatly helped by either radiotherapy or surgery (see Radiotherapy).

Cancer of the larynx is a more common throat cancer. It is a form of cancer that can be cured if the disease is diagnosed and treated early. It occurs most frequently in late middle age and is much more common in men than in women. Most patients are, or have been, heavy smokers for much of their life (see Cancer).

Progressive hoarseness is the most common symptom, and patients may also complain of an odd feeling in the throat, slight difficulty in breathing, pain in their ear, or pain radiating from the throat to the ear. Occasionally they may cough up a small amount of blood.

Most cases are cured by a course of radiotherapy. However, in a few cases the disease recurs or fails to respond to radiation treatment and surgery is necessary.

Foreign objects in the throat

A wide variety of foreign objects have been found in the pharynx, ranging from fish bones to coins and bottle tops. Any foreign object in the throat is potentially dangerous because it can perforate the pharyngeal wall and set up serious infection in the surrounding tissues.

Patients who have swallowed a foreign object that has become lodged in the throat are rarely in any doubt about its presence; every attempt to swallow even their own saliva is excruciatingly painful. If the object is lodged high in the pharynx it is usually possible to remove it in the emergency room of a hospital. However, if it is lodged lower down, for example, in

the laryngopharynx, it must be removed under general anesthesia.

Foreign bodies that are inhaled into the larynx can threaten a patient's life and little time should be lost in getting treatment. The younger the patient the more serious the condition, since the diameter of a child's airway is so narrow that even a small object is likely to obstruct it totally.

Removal of any object from the larynx is a matter of surgical urgency, and may require a temporary tracheostomy to protect the lower airway and maintain adequate breathing. Recovery from this surgery is swift (see Tracheostomy).

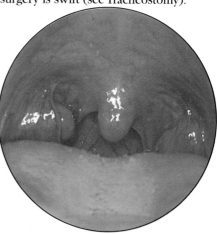

Infection can spread rapidly throughout the throat; in this case tonsillitis, usually caused by a streptococcus, has developed.

Home help for a sore throat

A sore throat that accompanies a common cold or other minor infection can be treated at home. Here are some proven remedies you might try.

Make up a gargling solution by dissolving two teaspoonfuls of household salt in a cupful of hot, but not boiling, water. Stir until the salt has dissolved, then use to gargle. Make sure you spit the solution out of your mouth when you have finished.

Alternatively, you can use an aspirin gargle by dissolving two soluble aspirin tablets in a cup of hot water. If you swallow this after gargling, the aspirin will relieve some of the pain and reduce any fever you might have.

Drink plenty of hot liquids and try to eat only soft or liquid foods, such as soups, so that you do not take anything into your throat that might cause further damage or inflammation.

Lozenges can be effective in soothing a sore throat and can prevent the throat from becoming dry. Keep the lozenge as far back on your tongue as you can for maximum benefit.

Thrombosis

Q Will giving up smoking really help to lessen my chances of suffering from a coronary thrombosis?

A There is no doubt that if you smoke cigarettes you stand a far greater chance of having a heart attack as well as developing chronic bronchitis or cancer. Doctors are now convinced that as soon as a person quits smoking, the chances of contracting these life-threatening conditions decrease. Five years after stopping smoking a reformed smoker is at no greater risk from a heart attack than someone who has never smoked.

Q Is it true that some doctors prescribe rat poison for thrombosis?

A It is true that the anticoagulant drug warfarin is also used to kill rats and mice. This group of anticoagulants was discovered when cattle feeding on sweet clover were found to be suffering from bruising and hemorrhages. A powerful anticoagulant was discovered in the plants on which the cattle were grazing. Warfarin is commonly used to prevent thrombosis and is prescribed only in very small doses. Blood clotting is carefully controlled by the doctor, who usually orders a blood test every few weeks.

Q Can the contraceptive pill cause thrombosis? I read that this could happen and it has made me very wary since I am thinking of going on the Pill.

A There tends to be a higher incidence of thrombosis in women who take a high dosage oral contraceptive, particularly if they are over 35, overweight, and smoke. However, the modern low dosage estrogen Pill has only a very small risk of causing thrombosis—indeed a smaller chance than in pregnancy itself. Of those women who do develop thrombotic side effects, the majority suffer from thrombophlebitis of the legs, and should immediately see a doctor and arrange to start some alternative form of birth control.

Heart attacks, strokes, and even varicose veins all have a single cause—a thrombosis, which is a blood clot in an artery or a vein that blocks circulation. Can anything be done to minimize the risk of this occurring?

People who smoke, the obese, and the diabetic are more prone to thrombotic diseases, but they can occur among the healthy. However, risks can be reduced and some preventative measures taken.

Thrombus formation

The blood forms a clot (or thrombus) as a normal, healthy protective process by which bleeding from a damaged blood vessel is stopped and the repair process begins. There are three stages in the process of stopping bleeding from a small blood vessel—constriction, formation of a platelet plug, and clotting.

As soon as bleeding begins, the damaged vessel constricts, slowing blood flow, and attracting platelets to the site of the damage. Platelets are tiny blood cells that suddenly become sticky and adhere to each other and to the lining of the vessel, temporarily plugging the hole. Finally

a clot will form. Thromboplastin, an extract from the blood vessel wall, oozes from the torn edges of the vessel. This starts a chain reaction in which fibrinogen, a soluble blood protein, is changed into long strands of fibrin, forming a meshwork to trap passing red blood cells and platelets. In the last stage of clot formation, the fibrin mesh tightens, fluid is squeezed out of the clot, and the torn vessel walls pull together (see Blood).

How a thrombosis occurs

When blood circulation through the heart, limbs, or the brain is sluggish, or the blood contains an excess of clotting factors, or the blood vessels are affected by atheroma, a clot may block a major

Doctors encourage patients to become mobile as soon as possible after surgery to reduce the likelihood of thrombosis.

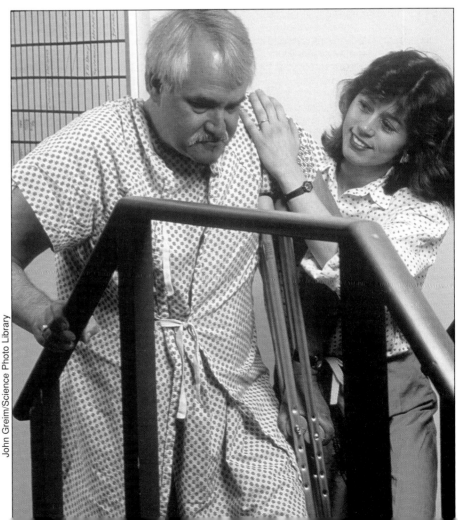

John Greim/Science Photo Library

Q A friend told me that you can get gangrene from a blood clot. Is she correct?

A Indirectly, yes. Gangrene occurs when living muscle and skin are deprived of blood supply and begin to die. Gas gangrene is a complication of massive penetrating wounds contaminated by *Clostridium welchii*, a bacterium normally growing in the intestine. Gas gangrene of the arm or leg was commonly seen following bullet or shrapnel wounds, which were left unattended until only amputation of part of the limb could prevent infection from affecting the whole body. Dry gangrene is less dramatic but more common. It often occurs when a blood clot blocks the blood flow in an artery supplying blood to an arm or a leg. Fingers or toes are usually affected first by discoloration, cold, and sometimes pain. Eventually the digits may turn black and the gangrene spreads up the limb to a level that is determined by the site of the blockage.

Q I had rheumatic fever as a child and have been told by my doctor that I have a damaged heart valve. He has prescribed an anticoagulant drug for me. Why is this necessary?

A Rheumatic fever was once a very common childhood disease. It is less common now, but many sufferers have been left with narrowed or stiffened heart valves. These produce murmurs, or abnormal sounds, which are detected during a medical examination. Damaged valves often interfere with the pumping action of the heart and can lead to irregularities of heart rhythm. Both these complications can result in blood clotting in the chambers of the heart. To make the blood clot more slowly, and prevent clots from forming, anticoagulant drugs such as warfarin are prescribed. But often the only way to improve the performance of the heart and prevent further damage is to replace the damaged valve with a metal or plastic valve. Replacement valves still need anticoagulant protection, and most doctors advise patients to remain on warfarin or similar drugs.

artery or vein. The thrombosis may occur in different parts of the body.

When thrombosis occurs in one of the coronary arteries of the heart, a patient will have a heart attack or myocardial infarction. Thrombosis in the brain results in a stroke. If thrombosis develops in a leg vein it causes phlebitis, and if it occurs in the artery supplying a limb it may result in gangrene (see Gangrene).

An embolism occurs when a thrombus forming in a major blood vessel, or on the lining of the heart, breaks loose. It is swept away by the bloodstream and becomes lodged in a narrow vessel, completely cutting off the blood supply to part of the lung or brain, or to an arm or leg. Because of the anatomy of the circulatory system, thrombosis in a leg vein may break loose to form a pulmonary embolism in the lung. If the clot originates from a neck artery, it may be carried into the brain to produce a cerebral embolism (see Circulatory system).

Why does a thrombosis occur?
Thrombosis nearly always results from one or a combination of the following: cardiovascular disease, prolonged immobilization, the aftermath of major surgery, pregnancy, or the Pill.

Some individuals are more susceptible to thrombosis than others. In these cases there is usually both an abnormality of blood vessels, and a hypercoagulable state in which the blood has a tendency to clot more easily than normal. Any attempt to reduce the risk of thrombosis must either entail preventing or correcting the disease in the heart or blood vessels, or reducing the ease with which clotting occurs in the blood.

Disorders of the blood vessels
As we grow older signs of degenerative disease become more marked in the major arteries. Pathologists describe this degenerative process as atheroma, and the effect on the blood vessels as arteriosclerosis, or hardening of the arteries. Arteriosclerosis is most likely to occur first in the heart and the major arteries, where the arteries are subjected to the most stress. Not surprisingly, when the blood pressure is abnormally high, then arteriosclerosis develops early in the blood vessels supplying the heart, brain, and limbs. The arteries become narrower and more rigid, which has the effect of significantly reducing the flow of blood.

Atheroma in its earliest form can be detected in childhood. Tiny yellowish flecks develop in the linings of the major arteries, particularly where they branch or split into smaller tributaries. By middle age the flecks have become distinct streaks, rich in cholesterol. The lining of

the vessel may then become roughened and cracked. Platelets are attracted to the cracked surface and a small clot may grow into the cavity of the artery. This may create a turbulence in blood flow, which may finally tear the clot loose, resulting in a dangerous embolism of the brain or the limbs.

The chambers of the heart are a common place for clots to form, particularly in the heart valves. This is especially likely to happen if the valves are already damaged or narrowed. Rheumatic fever in childhood is still the most common cause of valvular disease, although it is rare in today's children. Some people in the middle or older age group are seeing their doctors with illness brought on by an attack of rheumatic fever in childhood (see Rheumatic fever).

A thrombus may form in the heart's atria if they are beating irregularly or fibrillating. Occasionally after a severe coronary thrombosis a whole area of the left ventricle, the main pumping chamber of the heart, becomes thin, wasted, and fails to contract effectively. This is a likely site for a thrombus which all too often leads to a serious embolism (see Heart).

Coronary thrombosis
Coronary thrombosis is the common cause of what is generally called a heart attack, and what doctors usually refer to as myocardial infarction. One person in three will be affected by coronary artery disease, and it is still the most common single cause of death in the developed world. Until the age of 70, about four times as many men as women suffer a coronary thrombosis. Women over 70 are just as likely to be affected as men (see Heart attack, and Heart disease).

To prevent thrombotic diseases

- quit smoking
- if you are overweight, start to rid yourself of those extra pounds
- diabetics should stick religiously to their diet and take their medication
- attend prenatal clinic regularly for checkups if you are pregnant
- after an operation, follow your doctor's orders and get mobile as soon as possible
- don't cut down on your medication if you feel well but suffer from high blood pressure
- embark on a program of regular exercise; a thrombosis is much less common in individuals who are fit and active, regardless of age

One of the most common places for a clot to form is in the heart. This cross section of a coronary artery clearly shows a small clot that has grown within it.

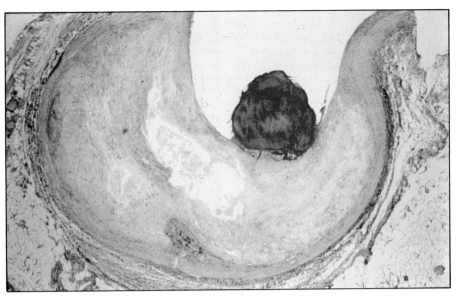

CNRI/Vision International

Those most at risk of a heart attack are male, overweight, have a diet rich in fats, and lead a stressful life with minimal exercise. In addition, diabetics, and people whose families have a history of heart attacks, are also prone to it. However, the biggest group of risk takers is smokers; a cigarette smoker is five times more likely to suffer a heart attack than a nonsmoker.

Causes, symptoms, and treatment

The two coronary arteries embedded in the muscular walls of the heart divert oxygen-rich blood, fresh from the lungs, to small vessels that feed all parts of the heart muscle. It is vital that these arteries remain open; even a slight narrowing may cause symptoms during times of exertion.

Persons at risk from coronary disease have a tendency to form fatty deposits that roughen the lining of the arteries

No matter what age you are, quitting smoking, keeping to a healthy, balanced diet, and getting regular exercise will help to reduce the risks of thrombosis.

and narrow the central channel. If the blockage occurs gradually, the person may experience pain only on exertion. This is typical of the pain of angina, and usually is severe enough to make the sufferer stop what he or she is doing. The angina pain then subsides. Although it is often frightening, it serves as a warning, making the sufferer rest long enough for

blood flow to be restored to the oxygen-starved muscle before serious damage can be done, and allowing time for new circulatory channels to open up over the following weeks.

When a coronary thrombosis develops at a site of narrowing, it completely blocks blood supply to part of the heart muscle. That part will be so severely damaged it

Elyse Lewin/Image Bank

Q Six months ago I had deep vein thrombosis which was a complication of my hysterectomy, but my leg still swells from time to time. Is this usual?

A The veins in the legs contain valves which allow blood to flow against gravity toward the heart, but prevent backflow stagnation of blood in the lower legs and feet. When a blood clot forms in these veins, the valves are often damaged. The clot is eventually digested and removed by enzymes in the blood, and blood flow is restored. For many weeks after the thrombosis, increased pressure may force fluid into the tissues causing the legs to swell, notably after a person stands for a long time. If you've had deep vein thrombosis, you should avoid long periods standing, try to do some exercise such as walking, and wear support hose. This will usually help to relieve the symptoms.

Q Can varicose veins be dangerous or are they just unsightly?

A Varicose veins are rarely more than an unsightly nuisance. Some people can develop painful, and hard, red swollen areas known as superficial thrombophlebitis. Varicose veins increase the danger of a deep vein thrombosis after an operation or pregnancy. It is not uncommon for a cut or fall to cause serious bleeding from a prominent varicose vein. If you suffer from varicose veins avoid prolonged standing, and wear special support hose. In serious cases an operation on the veins may be required to deal with the condition.

Q A girl at work suffers from something called phlebitis. What is it?

A Phlebitis is an inflammation of a vein, usually in the leg, caused by a blood clot forming in the vein. It is fairly painful, and the area may be red, swollen, and tender to the touch. Fortunately phlebitis usually disappears in a week or two without any serious consequences, but there may be recurrent attacks throughout a person's life.

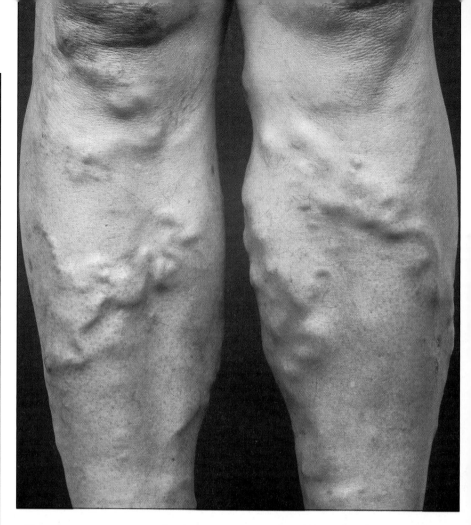

One of the most common causes of thrombosis is varicose veins, a problem for some pregnant women. The veins can often cause itching, sometimes pain and, although rarely, skin ulceration. The symptoms can be alleviated by taking frequent rests and by wearing support hose.

will cease to contract normally; the symptoms, then, will be sudden and severe. Patients experience crushing chest pain, which is sometimes also felt in the arm and jaw; they may feel breathless and sweat profusely. These symptoms do not always begin when the person is being particularly energetic, and do not usually improve even when he or she is resting.

Coronary thrombosis almost always requires treatment in the hospital, though patients will be allowed out of bed for short periods within the first two weeks and will embark on a program of graduated exercise. It is believed that once a firm scar has replaced the damaged heart muscle, exercise will encourage the formation of new channels to replace the thrombosed artery (see Exercise).

Cerebral thrombosis

Strokes are one of the most common causes of death and disablement. Those most at risk are people who suffer from high blood pressure, or who are diabetics, have a high serum cholesterol, and who smoke. Strokes may run in families. Some people with heart disease are predisposed to strokes (see Stroke).

Causes, symptoms, and treatment

A stroke can be caused by bleeding from a weakened artery into the brain (cerebral hemorrhage), a sudden blockage of an artery by a flake of material that has come adrift from a diseased artery or from the heart (embolism), or a more gradual blockage of an artery by clot formation within a diseased artery of the brain (cerebral thrombosis). The arterial disease that predisposes to all three types of stroke is arteriosclerosis (see Arteries and artery disease).

The effects of a stroke depend entirely on the size and situation of the affected area of the brain. If the right side of the brain is damaged, there is usually weakness, paralysis of the facial muscles, with loss of sensation in the left arm and leg. If the left side of the brain is affected, the patient may lose total or partial control of speech and be paralyzed on the right side of the body (see Brain damage and disease).

Cerebral thrombosis produces sudden paralysis or weakness that begins to improve within hours of the stroke occurring. Recovery is helped by early encouragement of the patient, and physical therapy and/or speech therapy. A high proportion of stroke victims make a full recovery, but in the rest the degree of recuperation will depend on the severity of the initial damage to the brain.

Thrombophlebitis

Phlebitis is an inflammation of a vein; it is usually associated with a blockage of the vein by a blood clot. The clot forms in a limb—frequently in the leg and, rarely, in the arm (see Phlebitis).

Causes, symptoms, and treatment

Thrombophlebitis can either be a superficial or deep vein. The most common cause of superficial thrombophlebitis is varicose veins. The veins lie directly under the skin and at points connect with the deeper veins. If the blood flow is sluggish, with the blood's component parts settling out, clotting may occur and the veins will become inflamed. In most cases, varicose veins, which are more common in women, are no more than an unsightly nuisance. They are made worse by standing and pregnancy, and frequently cause itching, sometimes pain, and rarely ulceration of the skin.

At times they can cause more serious problems, especially during pregnancy or when a patient is confined to bed by some immobilizing illness or after surgery. The veins may then become painful and hard. The inflammation usually disappears on its own, but a hot water bottle will give relief.

Deep vein thrombophlebitis is more serious and is likely to occur in varicose vein sufferers. When varicose veins are so large that most of the blood being pumped back from the legs to the heart is carried in dilated veins beneath the skin, the blood flow through the main leg veins can be so slow as to encourage formation of an extensive clot. The thrombus, in addition to causing a painful, hot swollen limb, can permanently damage the valves that insure the blood flows toward the heart and against the force of gravity. In the majority of patients the thrombosis resolves completely and normal blood circulation is restored, but in a few the aching and swelling of the limb may recur on prolonged standing.

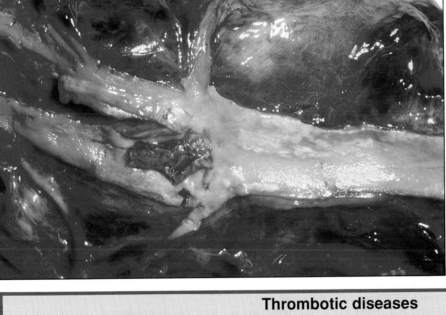

Biophoto Associates

A thrombosis can sometimes be fatal: here a clot has completely enveloped the internal carotid artery in the neck.

Thrombotic diseases

Disease	Causes	Symptoms	Dangers	Treatment	Prevention
Coronary thrombosis	Stress. High blood pressure. Diabetes. Arteriosclerosis (hardening of the arteries)	Faintness. Breathlessness. Increasing, crushing chest pain	Irregular heartbeat. Low blood pressure. Congestion of the lungs. Other thromboses	Bed rest. Pain relief. Oxygen. Drugs to stabilize heart rhythm and blood pressure	Quit smoking. Lose weight. Get regular exercise. Avoid stress
Cerebral thrombosis and embolism	Heart disease. High blood pressure. Also arteriosclerosis	One-sided weakness of the face, arm, and/or leg. Loss of feeling. Drowsiness. Difficulty with speech. Unsteadiness	Chest infection. Pressure sores. Stiffening of joints. Depression	Retraining exercises. Speech therapy. Anticoagulant drugs	Quit smoking. Have your blood pressure checked frequently
Venous thrombosis (phlebitis)	Immobilization. Major surgery. Varicose veins. Pregnancy and occasionally the contraceptive pill	Pain and swelling. Also tenderness. Discoloration of the lower leg	Pleurisy. Massive embolism of the lung. Postphlebitic limb	Rest and elevation of the limb. Support hose. Exercise. Anticoagulant drugs	Patients with varicose veins: wear support hose. Phlebitis sufferers: seek specialist advice during pregnancy, or before starting the Pill, or undergoing surgery
Arterial thrombosis and embolism	Heart disease. Diabetes. Smoking. Also arteriosclerosis	Limb pain. Numbness and cold. Blackening of fingers or toes	Gangrene	Bed rest. Surgery. Anticoagulant drugs	Quit smoking. Diabetes sufferers: stick closely to diet

Thrush

This common infection of the skin and the body's internal lining membranes affects people of all ages, but is particularly likely to affect certain groups. It may be a trivial disorder or a life-threatening disease.

Q Isn't thrush just an infection of babies' mouths?

A Thrush is common in babies but it is by no means confined to them. Nor is it restricted to their mouths. The infection can involve both the exterior and the interior of the body. It is as common in the diaper area as in the mouth.

Q What is a mucous membrane, and what is its connection with thrush?

A All the surfaces of the body are covered with a special nonstick layer. On the outside this is called epidermis and is the outer part of the skin. On the inside it is called mucous membrane. The most accessible parts of the mucous membrane are in the mouth and nose, and the genital area. Thrush fungus grows well on mucous membranes, so is commonly found in these two areas.

Q Why is thrush so common in people with diabetes?

A Diabetic people have sugar in their urine, and the thrush fungus thrives on carbohydrates. In females with diabetes, especially, there is a risk of thrush in the area around the urinary outlet and the adjoining vaginal area. Once established, such a thrush infection can spread widely.

Q Why are people with AIDS especially prone to thrush?

A The thrush fungus is found everywhere and minor infections are common, but are easily dealt with by our immune systems. If the immune system is not working properly, as in AIDS, all kinds of infections can easily become established. This is especially true of thrush.

Q Is thrush caused by a single kind of fungus?

A No. There are many different species. However, they are all similar in appearance and effect. Most cases of thrush in otherwise healthy people are caused by two *Candida* species of fungi.

National Medical Slide Bank

Thrush is the common term for what is medically known as candidiasis—an infection with a fungus of the genus *Candida*. It is one of the most common human infections and is usually of minor importance. Inapparent thrush infections are far more common than is generally supposed. The fungus is present in the mouths, throats, and intestines of 50 percent of people in the United States. It is present in the vaginas of 30 percent of pregnant women and 20 percent of nonpregnant women, and is present on the skin of 5 percent of all people. These figures indicate that thrush is predominantly an infection of the internal membranes of the body rather than of the skin.

The nature of thrush

The *Candida* genus contains many different species, most of which can affect human beings. The majority of human thrush infections are caused by either *C. albicans* or *C. tropicalis*.

Candida gets its name from the typical white curdy appearance of the fungus when it is present on mucous membranes. The Latin term *candida* is the feminine form of the word *candidus*, meaning "white." Some of the other *Candida* species, such as *C. parapsilosis*, *C. guilliermondii*, and *C. krusei*, mainly affect

Thrush is a fungal infection that is particularly common in babies. It is most likely to occur in a baby's mouth (above) or diaper area.

people with immune deficiency problems (see AIDS, and Immune system).

Candida fungus can exist in a yeastlike form that reproduces by budding, or in the form of a mass of branching filaments, or hyphae, that spread throughout any area that provides suitable nutrients. This form is called a mycelium. The yeastlike pattern is most common in immunocompromised people and in those receiving treatment with antifungal drugs in whom the underlying factors encouraging thrush have not been dealt with. It is also common in people who have acquired their infection from tubes passed into the body for surgical purposes and which have then been left in place for long periods of time. The most persistent and hard to treat thrush infections are those that form a mycelium. In this form the fungus adheres tenaciously both to human tissues and to surgical equipment.

The risk of serious thrush infections in people who are in none of these categories is very small. Unfortunately thrush infections are common in the hospital. This is because hospital patients often have surgical incisions, transfusion, drainage, and other tubes that breach the surface of the body. They are also commonly being given broad spectrum antibiotics (see Antibiotics). An additional concern arises from the fact that, although there are antifungal drugs effective against the common species of *Candida*, some of those strains that occur in hospital-acquired infections are able to resist these drugs.

Severity

The severity of a thrush infection depends on the amount of nutrient available to the fungus. *Candida* fungus lives on glucose or glycogen, the storage form of glucose (see Glucose). If these nutrients are present in the body's secretions the fungus will grow and spread.

Glucose and glycogen are present in increased quantities on the mucous membranes of pregnant women, women taking oral contraceptives (see Oral contraceptives), people with diabetes (see Diabetes), and those taking steroid drugs (see Steroids). People whose diabetes is well controlled and who keep their urine largely free from glucose are much less likely to develop thrush than those whose diabetes is poorly controlled; and if they do contract it, it will be less severe. Similarly, people on low dosage steroids are less likely to develop severe thrush than those on long-term, high dosage steroids.

Broad spectrum antibiotics can kill most bacteria but they do not have any effect on fungi. Their effect on the bodily secretions is to prevent the usage of glucose by other organisms and to leave more available for the *Candida* species present. They may also destroy helpful bacteria, such as the lactobacilli of the

vagina, which produce an acid (lactic acid) that is harmful to the thrush fungi and other organisms.

Effects of thrush

On mucous membranes such as the inside of the mouth or in the genital area, thrush appears as separate, raised, white patches on an inflamed base. These may cause pain but are often symptomless. If the fungus spreads down into the esophagus there may be severe pain behind the breastbone, with pain and difficulty in swallowing.

Women with vaginal thrush will usually have a creamy or cheesy vaginal discharge, severe itching, pain on sexual intercourse, and pain on urination. Sexual partners are readily infected. Vaginal thrush is most common during pregnancy, and in women who are taking oral contraceptives. A high proportion of cases of mucosal and vaginal thrush occur after taking a course of antibiotics.

Thrush of the skin most commonly affects the groin, armpits, and the skin between the buttocks and under pendulous breasts. The affected areas are moist and red and have irregular margins. Many small satellite areas, like little blisters, commonly surround the main patches of infection. The skin around the nails may also become infected, especially if it is allowed to remain constantly wet. Thrush of the nails results in reddened, swollen, and painful nail folds, sometimes with exuding pus. If neglected, the nails themselves may become involved and will become thickened, hard, yellow, and discolored, and may separate from the nail bed (see Nails).

There is a form of thrush that affects the skin, the nails, the hair, and the mucous membranes. This is called chronic mucocutaneous thrush and it is particularly persistent. About half the people with this form have an underactive thyroid gland (see Thyroid). This is a strange form of immune deficiency that is limited to defense against *Candida* species and some of the other fungus skin infections. There is no problem with other infections and the condition, although distressing, is limited to the skin, the skin appendages, and the mucous membrane surfaces adjoining the skin.

It is only in people with severe immune deficiency that thrush may become a life-threatening condition. In such cases the fungus can affect any organ or part of the body. For example, it is quite common for the *Candida* fungus to settle inside one or both eyes where it can severely damage vision. Fungus infection of the inside of the heart is also common in immune deficiency. These widespread infections are

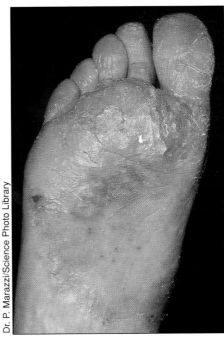

A thrush infection may occur on the soles of the feet, particularly in people with moist, sweaty feet. It can be successfully treated with an antifungal cream.

most likely to occur in immunocompromised people who have to be artificially tube fed or who require long-term fluid infusions into the bloodstream.

Treatment

The first step in successful treatment of thrush is to remove, if possible, the underlying factor or factors that are encouraging the infection. There is little point, for instance, in repeatedly applying antifungal creams in a case of genital thrush in an uncontrolled diabetic. For the great majority of cases of minor thrush, however, local treatment with such creams will be highly effective.

Mucous membrane or skin thrush will respond readily to creams or lotions containing antifungal drugs such as clotrimazole, nystatin, or miconazole. For more serious internal infections and for very severe external infections, treatment by mouth is often necessary. A single dose of the drug fluconazole is capable of curing most cases of vaginal thrush. However, it is sometimes necessary for the woman's sexual partner to be treated also. Persistent infections of the mouth may require the use of lozenges of clotrimazole. Gargling with suspensions of antifungal drugs is also useful. Suitable pediatric medication is available for babies and children.

In all cases the treatment of thrush is a matter for a doctor and should only be undertaken under medical supervision.

The risk of thrush

The people most likely to acquire thrush are:

- people with diabetes
- pregnant women
- women using oral contraceptives
- intravenous drug abusers
- people with AIDS
- those with other forms of immune system disorders
- those on immunosuppressive drugs for organ transplants
- people on long-term, large dosage steroid drugs
- those taking long-term antibiotics
- people with leukemia
- people with cancer

Thymus

Q Is it possible to live without a thymus?

A As we grow older it seems that all of us live without a thymus since, unlike almost all the other organs, it grows smaller after the age of puberty. It can be difficult to find at all in elderly people. This ties in with its function in making the immune system work properly. Normally we will have come into contact with, and gained immunity to, most of the important infections that the immune system is designed to repel in the first few years of life. If a baby is born with an absent or inadequate thymus it has problems repelling infection. So although the thymus is essential early in life, it can be removed in later years.

Q My brother-in-law said that he had to have X-ray treatment for his thymus when he was a baby because it was too big. Is this common?

A It is no longer the practice to irradiate excessively large thymus glands in children. However, before the importance of the thymus gland to the developing immune system was realized, this was a common treatment.

Q My brother has myasthenia, and now the doctors say that they are going to remove his thymus. I thought that myasthenia was a nervous disease, and I don't see what a gland in the chest has got to do with it. Can you explain?

A Myasthenia is a nervous system disorder and symptoms include weakness and tiredness of the muscles, which gets worse during the course of the day. The disease is caused by the formation of antibodies to the junctions between the nerves and muscles by the body's own immune system. These antibodies attack the junction, and the nerves cannot instruct the muscles to move. Since the thymus is very much involved with the control of the immune system, it has been found that removing the thymus is effective in helping some sufferers.

Until comparatively recently the role of the thymus in the body was a mystery. But research has shown that it plays a vital role in the body's defenses against disease.

Over the last two decades it has become clear that the thymus sits at the center of the remarkable web of interconnected organs and tissues that make up the immune system, which defends the body from attack by infection.

There is still a certain amount of ignorance about exactly how the thymus does its job, but it is now known that it is essential for the proper running of the immune system, and that it has really carried out its major function during the first few years of life.

Where is it?
The thymus is found in the upper part of the chest, where it lies just behind the breastbone (sternum). It consists of two lobes that join in front of the windpipe (trachea). In a young adult it measures a

The thymus is at its most vigorous in the first years of youth, setting up immunity to disease; its function fulfilled, it shrinks into insignificance in old age.

few centimeters in length and weighs about 0.5 oz (15 g). However, unlike any other organ in the body, it is at its largest at around the time of puberty, when it may weigh as much as 1.5 oz (43 g).

In a baby the thymus is very large compared to the rest of the body, and it may extend quite a long way down the chest behind the breastbone. It grows quickly until about the age of seven, after which it grows more slowly until the child reaches puberty (see Puberty).

After the age of puberty the thymus starts to shrink in size—a process called involution—until in an elderly person the

Size and location of the thymus

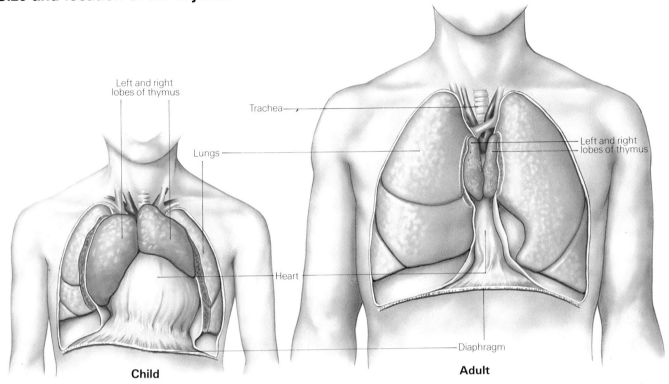

Child

Adult

Left and right lobes of thymus

Lungs

Heart

Trachea

Left and right lobes of thymus

Diaphragm

Frank Kennard

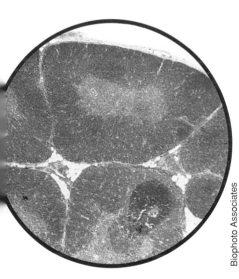

Biophoto Associates

The relative sizes of the thymus in an adult and a child (above) graphically demonstrate its importance in establishing the body's immune system early in life. In adulthood it actually shrinks. Low-power magnification of a section through a normal thymus shows up some of its structure. The large purple masses are the lobes of this vital organ (left).

only thymus tissue present may be a bit of fat and connective tissue

Structure and function

The thymus is made up of lymphoid tissue, epithelium, and fat. The lymphoid tissue consists of many small round cells called lymphocytes, which are the basic unit of the immune system. These cells are also found in the blood, the bone marrow, the lymph glands, and the spleen, and they can be seen traveling into the tissues as part of the inflammatory reaction.

The outer layer of the thymus, which is called the cortex, has many lymphocytes. Inside this is an area called the medulla,

which contains lymphocytes and other sorts of thymus cells as well.

There seems to be little doubt that in the early years of life the thymus is concerned with programming the way in which the immune system works, and, in particular, it seems that the thymus is responsible for making sure that the system does not turn its activities against the body's own tissues.

It is now thought that the thymus is responsible for many of the most important aspects of the immune system. There are two main sorts of immune cells in the body and they are both different sorts of lymphocytes. The T or thymus cell lymphocytes are under the control of the thymus and are responsible for the recognition of foreign substances and for many of the ways in which the body attacks them. The other sort—the B lymphocytes—are responsible for making antibodies to foreign substances.

The exact ways in which the thymus goes about controlling its T lymphocytes

is not known, but one important mechanism has come to light. It seems that about 95 percent of the new sorts of lymphocyte that are made in the thymus are in fact destroyed there, before they ever have an opportunity to get out into the rest of the body. The probable reason for this is that they would have the potential for turning against the body itself, and the only cells that the thymus allows to develop are those that will attack outside or foreign substances.

What can go wrong?

If the thymus is regarded as an isolated organ then it must be said that it is rare for it to give rise to any trouble. However, it is important to remember that the T lymphocytes it controls are the most central part of the body's immune system, and the activity of this system is extremely important in almost all serious diseases (see Immune system).

In the thymus itself, as opposed to the wider aspects of its function, two main problems may occur. First, the thymus may fail to develop properly in babies and, as might be expected, this leads to a failure of the immune system and a failure to resist infection, which may prove fatal. Fortunately this is not a common problem. Second, tumors can occur in the thymus. These are called thymomas, and they are treated by surgery followed by X-ray treatment (see Tumors).

Thyroid

Q I am very nervous and anxious all the time and I seem to be very irritable with my children. Is it possible that I have an overactive thyroid?

A Yes, although there may be some initial difficulty in differentiating between symptoms of the disease and those of pure anxiety. This thyroid disorder is often associated with weight loss, and there may be the characteristic protruding eyes of Graves' disease, which is the main form of thyrotoxicosis or overactive thyroid. If you find that you are shaky and have a lot of difficulty tolerating heat, then these symptoms might suggest that your thyroid is at fault. The tests for thyrotoxicosis are straightforward and if your doctor suspects that this might be the trouble, he or she will arrange for you to have a blood test to confirm the diagnosis.

Q I have an overactive thyroid and my doctor is sending me to the hospital to see a specialist. I am terrified that I will need surgery; do you think this will be necessary, and are there any other forms of treatment I can try?

A It is possible that you will be advised to have surgery, although your worries about having it might lead the doctor to suggest alternative treatment. First, you could be given pills to take for about 18 months to suppress the activity of the gland. This has the disadvantage that the condition might recur in the future. Second, you could be given treatment with radioiodine (radioactive iodine that is taken up by the thyroid), which reduces the level of thyroid activity. This has the advantage of being simple, and the condition is unlikely to recur. However, this type of treatment is not given to very young people or to women who might become pregnant, since there is a theoretical risk of it causing cancer in the patient or in any children that may subsequently be born. There is also a definite risk of underactivity of the thyroid occurring after treatment, but this, in turn, is very easy to control.

Problems associated with the thyroid and the hormone it produces are fairly common. However, many of the disorders respond extremely well to treatment and can be completely cured once they have been identified.

The thyroid gland

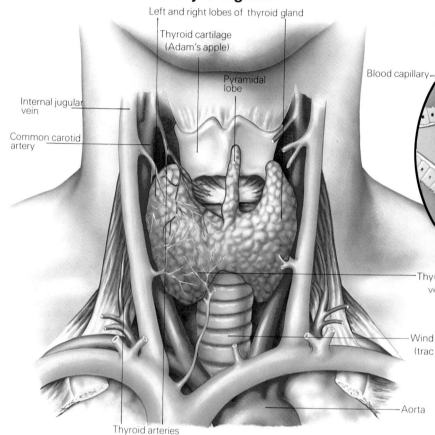

Left and right lobes of thyroid gland
Thyroid cartilage (Adam's apple)
Pyramidal lobe
Blood capillary
Internal jugular vein
Common carotid artery
Thy v
Wind (trac
Aorta
Thyroid arteries

Frank Kennard

Problems associated with the thyroid gland cause the most common types of hormonal disorders, and affect large numbers of people. Many of these problems can be completely cured by administering the hormone that is produced by the gland. This can be easily prepared and is given by mouth.

Of the wide range of thyroid disorders, by far the most important are those of overactivity (thyrotoxicosis or hyperthyroidism) and underactivity (myxedema or hypothyroidism). Both of these problems are a lot more common in women than in men, and up to 2 percent of the adult female population may have difficulty from an overactive thyroid at some time in their life, with underactivity being only slightly less common. One other disorder is worth noting here—thyroiditis, which is an inflammation of the thyroid as a result of a viral infection.

Where is the thyroid gland?
The thyroid gland is located in the neck just below the level of the larynx, which can be seen or felt as the Adam's apple. There are two lobes to the gland, and these lie just in front and at either side of the windpipe, or trachea, as it passes down the front of the neck. The two lobes are connected by a small bridge of tissue, and there may be a smaller central lobe called the pyramidal lobe. In an adult the thyroid gland weighs about 0.7 oz (20 g).

What does it do?
The function of the gland is to make the thyroid hormone thyroxine. When the gland is examined under a microscope many small follicles can be seen; these are islands of tissue containing collections of colloid, a protein substance to which the thyroid hormone is bound and from

The anatomic drawing (below left) shows the position of the thyroid gland in relation to the surrounding structures in the throat, which include the Adam's apple and the trachea. The insert is a section of the thyroid, which clearly shows the cells that produce and store the essential hormone thyroxine.

...tion through thyroid

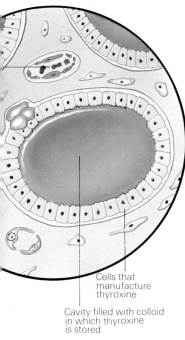

Cells that manufacture thyroxine

Cavity filled with colloid in which thyroxine is stored

which it can be released under the influence of enzymes.

Once thyroxine has been released from the gland into the bloodstream it is probably taken up into all the cells of the body. There appears to be a receptor on the surface of the cell nucleus that responds to the hormone. The overall effect of the hormone is to increase the amount of energy that the cell uses; it also increases the amount of protein that the cell manufactures. Although the exact role of the hormone in the cell is not known, it is essential for life.

The thyroid gland contains iodine (see Iodine), which is vital for its activity. This is the only part of the body that requires iodine and it is very efficient at trapping all the available iodine from the blood. An absence of iodine in the diet results in malfunction of the thyroid and growth of the gland, a condition called endemic goiter.

Control of thyroid activity

The thyroid is one of the endocrine glands (see Glands), and like so many of them it is under the control of the pituitary gland. The pituitary produces a hormone called thyroid stimulating hormone (TSH), which increases the amount of thyroid hormone that is released. The amount of TSH produced by the pituitary increases if the amount of thyroxine circulating in the system falls, and decreases if it rises. This system, called negative feedback, results in a relatively constant level of thyroid hormone in the blood.

The pituitary gland is itself under the influence of the hypothalamus, and the amount of TSH it produces is increased if a substance called TRH (TSH-releasing hormone) is released from the hypothalamus.

This situation is further complicated by the fact that thyroid hormone comes in two versions, according to the number of

In some areas of the world, such as the Matto Grosso in Brazil, the normal diet lacks iodine. This deficiency causes the thyroid to malfunction and swell, leading to endemic goiter, the disfiguring condition this woman is suffering from.

iodine atoms that it contains. Most of the hormone released from the thyroid gland is in the form of tetraiodothyronine, which contains four iodine atoms and is known as T_4. However, the active hormone at the cell level is triiodothyronine, which contains three iodine atoms and is known as T_3. Although the thyroid releases some T_3 into the blood, most of its output is T_4, and this is converted into T_3 in the tissues. Sometimes the tissues switch the way that they convert T_4 to produce an ineffective compound called reverse T_3. This means that there will be less thyroid hormone activity in the

Q I know a lot of people who have had thyroid problems, and most of them are women. Is it really so much more common in women than in men?

A Yes. Underactivity of the gland happens in about 14 in every thousand women and only about one in every thousand men. Overactivity occurs in at least 20 in every thousand women, but again in only about one or two in every thousand men.

Generally thyroid disorders are quite common, with over 3 percent of women likely to have some type of thyroid difficulty. Most disorders can be treated effectively.

Q I had an overactive thyroid and was treated with pills. Although I have been better for the past two years, the clinic still insists on seeing me. Why is this necessary?

A Thyrotoxicosis responds well to treatment with pills. However, the disease has a great tendency to recur and there may be several years between attacks. It is important to diagnose the disease in the early stages, since it is not only easier to treat, but irreversible changes in processes such as the heart rhythm may occur if the disease is allowed to progress too far. For these reasons the doctors will want to keep an eye on you.

Q Is it true that your hair falls out if you have myxedema?

A Myxedema is underactivity of the thyroid gland, and it leads to dry, coarse hair that is very difficult to manage. The disease is also associated with alopecia, where the hair roots die and the hair falls out. However, this is not a direct result of the low thyroid levels.

Q Do thyroid disorders tend to run in families?

A Yes they do, and this is quite common. It is also interesting to note that although one family member might have an overactive thyroid, another might have an underactive thyroid.

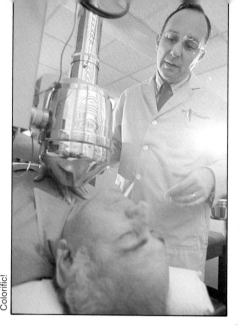

Colorific!

One of the tools that is used for diagnosing a malfunctioning thyroid and for detecting and identifying nodules in the tissue of the gland is an isotope scan (above).
This bulbous red mass (above right) is a grossly enlarged thyroid gland that was removed. It measures over 10 in (25 cm). A thyroidectomy—surgery to remove overactive tissue—may be necessary to combat hyperthyroidism. The scar left by the surgery is insignificant (right).

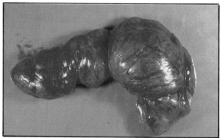

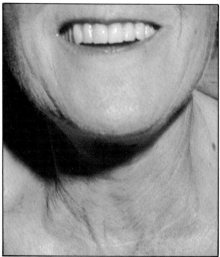

tissues even though the actual amount of hormone in the bloodstream remains at an adequate level.

Goiter

Any enlargement of the thyroid gland is called goiter. Small but visible goiters are found in about 15 percent of the population, and are about four times more common in women than in men. Usually these are of no significance (see Goiter).

In the past, iodine deficiency was the main cause of goiter, but now most are caused by overactivity of the thyroid or are simple goiters that are not related to any abnormality of thyroid function. In a few cases goiters are isolated lumps (nodules) in the substance of the thyroid, and these should be investigated using an isotope scan to see whether the lump is composed of functioning tissue. If it is not, and if an ultrasound scan shows that it is solid, then it could be malignant and may need a surgical exploration.

Overactive thyroid glands

Most cases of thyroid overactivity are caused by Graves' disease. A goiter is usually present and the eyes become protruding and staring—a sign that many people associate with thyroid problems. It is the basic disease process that causes the symptoms, and not the overactivity.

Graves' disease is caused by the presence of antibodies in the blood. Although these antibodies do not destroy thyroid tissue, they stimulate the gland to produce thyroid hormone. It is not known why some people are more prone to making these antibodies than others, although there is certainly genetic susceptibility. This can be demonstrated by the fact that many sufferers have a specific type of tissue group.

The effects of an overactive thyroid are: weight loss, increased appetite, anxiety and nervousness (sometimes with a tremor), palpitations of the heart, sweating, intolerance of heat, and irritability. In addition to eye problems there may be weakness of the muscles, particularly at the shoulders and hips.

Once Graves' disease is suspected then the majority of cases can be diagnosed very simply by measuring the level of thyroid hormone in the blood. Often the T_3 level is measured as well as, or instead of, the T_4 level, since T_3 is always raised in Graves' disease but it is possible to have the disease with a normal T_4 level.

Treatment is to suppress thyroid activity. This can be done with pills, which must be taken for a year or more. If the gland is very large then it may be appropriate to surgically remove some of it. The alternative is to give a dose of radioactive iodine. This is taken up by the thyroid so it presents no danger to other tissues. It will reduce the level of thyroid activity over the course of approximately six weeks.

While the hormone levels are being brought under control the symptoms can

Thyroid problems

Problem	Cause	Effects	Treatment
Simple goiter	Unknown	Swelling of the thyroid, producing a swelling of the neck	Often unnecessary, but in many cases the problem responds to low doses of thyroid hormone pills
Endemic goiter	Lack of iodine in the diet	May lead to deficiency of thyroid hormone	Replacement of iodine in the diet
Myxedema or hypothyroidism	Inadequate levels of thyroid hormone in the blood. May be caused by Hashimoto's disease or autoimmune thyroid failure	Problem develops slowly, leading to dry, rough skin, tiredness, intolerance of cold, increase in weight, constipation, hoarse voice, and deafness	Replacement of thyroid hormone in pill form
Thyrotoxicosis or hyperthyroidism	Most commonly Graves' disease; others include nodules in the thyroid, either single or multiple	Increase in appetite (often with weight loss), sensitivity to heat, disorders of heart rhythm, nervousness, tiredness, and sweating. In some cases there is muscular weakness	Various treatments, including use of pills, surgery to remove overactive thyroid tissue, and use of radioactive iodine administered by mouth
Graves' disease	Presence of antibodies in the blood, which stimulate the thyroid	Causes thyrotoxicosis; also affects the eyes, causing the pop eyes associated with overactive thyroid	Troublesome eye problems can necessitate surgery, either to tack down the lids to protect the eyes, or to try to reduce the amount of eye protrusion
Thyroiditis	Inflammation of the thyroid gland resulting from a viral infection	Painful swollen gland that may come on suddenly. Mild thyrotoxicosis may result	Usually unnecessary; painkillers may be given. In severe cases steroid drugs are sometimes used to reduce the inflammation
Dyshormonogenesis	Inherited abnormality in the way the gland makes hormones. Of six different types the most common is Pendred's syndrome, which is associated with deafness	A low level of hormone in the blood may cause the same effects as myxedema. There is often a large goiter	Thyroid hormone
Congenital hypothyroidism (cretinism)	Failure of the fetal thyroid to develop	Mental and physical retardation is the major effect; it occurs in about one in every 4000 births	Early diagnosis is vital, since with prompt thyroid treatment there will be normal development; retardism will otherwise occur

Problem	Incidence	Treatment
Cancer: (1) Papillary	The most common type; occurs in young people, including children	By surgery, followed by radioactive iodine treatment if necessary. Outlook is good
(2) Follicular	Slightly less common; also occurs in young people	As for papillary carcinoma. Outlook is good
(3) Anaplastic	Uncommon; occurs in the elderly	Surgery is often impossible. X-ray treatment may be used
(4) Medullary	Very uncommon. Familial	Surgery. Outlook is good in most cases

be decreased by drugs that block the effects of epinephrine, since high levels of thyroid seem to produce an increased response to epinephrine.

Underactive thyroid glands

Underactivity of the thyroid gland (myxedema) is also caused by antibodies in the gland, which seem to destroy it. Hashimoto's disease is very similar, except that the antibodies set up a long-term inflammation of the gland, causing goiter but leading to thyroid failure.

In many cases weight gain results, together with a lack of energy, dry thick skin, intolerance of cold, a slow heart-beat, hoarseness, deafness, and a typical puffy face. The presence of hypothyroidism makes elderly people much more susceptible to hypothermia.

Underactivity of the thyroid is readily diagnosed by blood tests. The level of T_4 is reduced, but this is not conclusive since a reduced T_4 level can also occur when the thyroid is functioning normally—in severe illness, for example. Much more important is the high level of TSH that is found in the blood in myxedema, because the pituitary gland tries to stimulate the thyroid to produce enough hormones.

Once a diagnosis is made, the thyroid hormone T_4 can be given by mouth. The dose is built up fairly gradually since there is a risk of making patients with heart disease worse; myxedema predisposes to coronary artery disease since it causes a very high level of cholesterol.

Patients with myxedema must continue to take medication for the rest of their lives. Although Graves' disease is not quite as easy to treat as myxedema, the results of treatment in both cases is usually satisfactory, and the outlook is very good in both conditions once the early difficulties have passed.

Tinnitus

Commonly described as ringing in the ears, tinnitus is a disturbing symptom of some problems with the ears and hearing. Although often annoying, it is not dangerous.

Q My son is always going to heavy metal rock concerts where I have heard that the music is extremely loud. Will he get tinnitus?

A There is every chance that he will get temporary tinnitus—a ringing or high-pitched tone audible only to himself—after going to a very loud rock concert. However, it is unlikely that he will do himself any permanent damage, or get long-term tinnitus, unless he goes every night or joins the band! If he does something crazy like putting his head close to the speakers then he might do himself some permanent harm; but he, and for that matter anybody, is more likely to get tinnitus on being exposed to loud noise every day at places of work. Ear protectors should be worn whenever you come into contact with prolonged noise. People who shoot for sport must also wear ear protectors since repeated loud bangs are likely to cause ear damage and tinnitus.

Q I have tinnitus in one ear only, and although it doesn't worry me too much, my doctor says I should have a checkup once a year. Is this really necessary?

A Tinnitus in only one ear, called unilateral tinnitus, is likely to be caused by some disease that might eventually need treatment. The cause of your tinnitus may not be obvious at the moment, but your doctor is being very prudent in making sure that you are seen every year for a checkup.

Q I have very loud and unbearable tinnitus and have begged my doctor to remove the hearing apparatus from my ears but he refuses. Why will he not do this for me?

A Although tinnitus can be aggravating, there is every chance that you will come to learn to live with it. Also, in refusing to destroy your ability to hear, by removal of the cochlea, your doctor is correct as, even after this, you may still have the tinnitus. In fact, it could be worse than before.

John Watney

Tinnitus, the sensation of noise in the ears or head, is a symptom that affects more people than is generally realized. The sound is perceived by the sufferer even though it has no origin outside the body. Although it is rarely the symptom of any serious disease, it can be extremely disturbing to the person who has it. The sound perceived can vary between a ringing, a hissing, a buzzing, and a roaring noise; but the nature and quality of the sound has actually very little to do with the causes.

The effects of tinnitus vary greatly. In some the noise is soft and barely noticeable, while in others the noise is crashingly loud and can prevent the person from sleeping. The cause of this often distressing symptom can arise in any section of a person's hearing apparatus, from the outside of the ear to the intricate neural pathways in the brain (see Hearing).

Outer ear causes
In the outer ear there are two common causes. The first, and most common, is impacted wax, often caused by people trying to clean their ears out with cotton swabs, or the corner of a handkerchief. The quick and simple way to remove it is by syringing (see Syringing), in which a doctor washes the wax away with water.

The other cause in the external ear is infection by a bacteria or a fungus. In this

The constant attack on the ears by noisy industrial machinery—in this case the high-pitched yowl of a woodcutter—can cause the unpleasant ringing in the ears characteristic of tinnitus. Wearing ear protectors is a necessary precaution, but it can make conversation difficult.

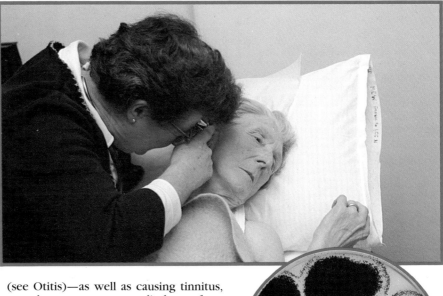

John Watney

Ken Moreman

Old age may bring on increasing deafness, a common degenerative process that is almost always accompanied by tinnitus. It should be checked by a doctor (top). The fungus Aspergillus niger *(above) is responsible for a painful infection of the outer ear, whose symptoms include tinnitus.*

(see Otitis)—as well as causing tinnitus, can also cause a mucus discharge from the ear, a raised temperature, and deafness. Again, treatment for this is with antibiotics and also with decongestant nasal drops.

Chronic infection of the middle ear is usually rather more difficult to detect. The symptoms, although broadly similar to those of acute otitis media, are extremely variable and can be intermittent. Rarely the patient suffers vertigo. If this happens, the patient must seek medical help rapidly to avoid severe and permanent hearing damage (see Vertigo).

Tinnitus is an early symptom of the other type of problem in the middle ear. In this condition, otosclerosis, new bone is deposited around the stirrup bone (stapes) and it prevents it from moving freely and transmitting sound properly from the eardrum to the inner ear. The patient becomes progressively more deaf, but fortunately there is an operation in which the stapes is removed and a plastic replacement fitted. This restores the hearing and any remaining tinnitus is usually masked by the increased volume of external sound heard by the patient.

Inner ear causes

In the inner ear there are the very delicate receptor cells in the cochlea. Damage to these cells is probably the most common cause of tinnitus. The damage can have several causes, the most usual of which is the simple degenerative aging process that produces deafness. Although the degree of deafness and the age of onset vary greatly there is almost always some tinnitus (see Deafness). Often, patients complain bitterly about it at night because then there is no other noise to mask the tinnitus. Another increasingly common cause of tinnitus is cochlear damage caused by sudden loud noises or

prolonged exposure to noises of lesser intensity. Where there is loud, constant noise, especially in the workplace, ear protectors should be worn.

Some drugs, when given in high doses, also cause cochlear damage, and thus tinnitus, and care should always be taken if a drug is likely to give this side effect. There is a disease called Ménière's disease (see Ménière's disease) that involves tinnitus, and a rare benign tumor called an acoustic neuroma that gives tinnitus, usually only in one ear.

In general, tinnitus caused by damage to the cochlea can be difficult to treat. Often, a hearing aid that boosts sounds from outside the head will make the tinnitus sufferer less aware of their tinnitus (see Hearing aids). Also, devices that appear to mask the sound give some relief, as do relaxant pills. However, the vast majority of people suffering from tinnitus learn to live with their condition.

case the patient complains of both tinnitus and some kind of irritation, often accompanied by localized pain that is made worse by moving the outer ear. There is also some deafness and a scant, watery discharge. Fortunately treatment is simple, with antibiotics and steroid drops that quickly clear up the infection. After such treatment, the tinnitus abates.

Middle ear causes

Tinnitus also crops up in association with problems in the middle ear. The two main causes are infection and otosclerosis.

As with most types of infection, there are acute and chronic types. Acute infection of the middle ear—acute otitis media

Tiredness

Q Do ordinary tonics, bought without prescription, have any value?

A Tonics are very much out of fashion at the moment. Nevertheless, there is no harm in taking them providing that they do not lull you into a false sense of security and become an inadequate substitute for getting proper advice. In effect, none has the near-miraculous properties that are sometimes claimed for them. If symptoms persist, you must go to your doctor to find out what is really the matter.

Q What is the difference between laziness and tiredness due to illness?

A This is not nearly as easy to determine as you might think, which is why people often mistake one for the other. In general, the lazy person bucks up and finds an almost overwhelming amount of energy when something that he or she very much wants to do turns up, whereas the truly exhausted person cannot summon up enthusiasm for anything. If in doubt, it is wise to suspect a physical cause until a succession of negative medical tests make it increasingly unlikely.

Q My mother, who is now 81, is becoming increasingly feeble and lethargic lately. She feels sure that it is all due to her age and refuses to go to her doctor about it. Is there anything I can do about it?

A Although there is often some loss of energy in old age it should only be slight and gradual. Anything more than that should not be accepted as either normal or inevitable and ought to be looked into, since it can very often be corrected. Anemia and inadequate nutrition in general (often the consequence of a reluctance to shop for and prepare proper meals) are both common in old people. Try to persuade your mother to see her doctor about her tiredness, if necessary making the arrangements and taking her yourself.

It is perfectly natural to feel really worn out at the end of a hard day at work, after strenuous exercise, or after a couple of nights' poor sleep. However, tiredness can be one of the first signs of a serious underlying illness.

Tiredness of one sort or another is one of the most common of complaints. Usually it is short-lived and quite normal. However, because it can be the first and sometimes the only indication of something more serious, continuing or persistent tiredness should always be looked into.

Tiredness is often thought to be normal in old age, and certainly there may be a decline in normal vigor (see Aging). In many old people, however, what they may accept as the normal tiredness of aging can sometimes be due to a slowly developing anemia or even a poor diet. So tiredness should never be regarded as normal or inevitable until other causes have been ruled out, since many conditions can easily be corrected.

One of the most important features of tiredness due to illness is that it occurs in circumstances when normal tiredness would not be expected. Thus, although tiredness is normal at the end of the day, after a sleepless night, following severe exertion, in the weeks after an illness or surgery, during pregnancy, or after confinement, tiredness occurring at other times is abnormal, and is likely to be due to disease of some sort. Persistent tiredness should therefore always be investigated, particularly when it is accompanied by symptoms of weakness.

Causes due to illness

Tiredness due to illness may result from either physical or mental disorder, or a combination of the two. Probably the most common physical cause is infection in some part of the body (see Infection and infectious diseases), and this is one thing that doctors look for in cases of persistent tiredness. Established or well-developed infectious diseases such as measles, chicken pox, and influenza (especially if they are accompanied by fever) are expected to make us feel tired

The pain on the faces of the crew shows clearly how these oarsmen are totally exhausted after forcing themselves through the extreme physical trial of a boat race.

A tired baby can sleep anywhere, especially closely cuddled up to its mother (left). The baby's blissful oblivion blots out all the racket of this vibrant African street market.

You don't need to wield a pickax all day to feel tired after work. Sitting in an office, or dealing with difficult problems and people, can be just as tiring (below).

A quiet nap in the sun after lunch is one of the pleasures open to the retired person (below right). It is natural for the patterns of sleep to change in old age.

and run down (see Chicken pox, Influenza, and Measles). Tiredness by itself may also be an indication that an infection is on the way, as in the day or two leading up to flu.

Tiredness that develops or persists for no apparent reason is often due to a localized pocket or focus of infection in some part of the body. A chronic dental, throat, or sinus infection, or a hidden abscess somewhere in the body, can be common causes. Up until midcentury, one of the most likely and most feared causes was a developing tuberculosis infection, in which tiredness was often the only symptom. Unfortunately tuberculosis is once again resurgent (see Tuberculosis).

Another common cause of persistent tiredness occurring on its own is anemia (see Anemia). Even a slight fall below normal in the level of hemoglobin (the oxygen-carrying chemical in the blood) will cause some degree of tiredness and lack of energy. Some hormone disorders may also show themselves primarily in terms of tiredness (see Hormones). The most common of these are lack of thyroid hormone, as in myxedema, and lack of insulin, as in diabetes (see Diabetes).

Another type of metabolic tiredness, though not usually caused by hormone disorder, is obesity (see Obesity). Those who are overweight do, however they may try to disguise it, generally get much more easily tired than other people. This is partly a direct metabolic effect and partly due to the extra energy used up in carrying the additional fat around all the time.

TIREDNESS

The underlying disease that doctors are most concerned to rule out in cases of unexplained tiredness is cancer (see Cancer). Again, tiredness may be the only indication that all is not well with the patient in the early stages of cancer, no matter in what part of the body it is developing. Cancer, however, is sometimes accompanied by a falling off in appetite and a loss of weight as well.

Sometimes the origin of tiredness is due to mental or emotional causes rather than to some physical disease. Boredom makes for feelings of tiredness; prolonged anxiety is exhausting; and depression is certain to make one feel dispirited and sluggish. The sleeplessness that often goes with these conditions will aggravate the tiredness.

It is thus clear that although tiredness can be due to minor and only temporary conditions, it may also be the symptom of something much more serious, the first indication of an underlying disorder that ought to be investigated and corrected. If you have tiredness that does not correct itself within three or four weeks, you should go to your doctor.

Assessing tiredness

In order to assess tiredness and unravel its cause, the doctor has to do several things. He or she will first of all need to have a full account of what has been noticed as wrong, so that he or she has a clear idea of its duration, extent, and the full range of its effects. Because tiredness can be such a vague and variable condi-

Without an occasional break, anyone doing a repetitive job will become fatigued from the combined effects of boredom, noise, and unrelieved concentration.

tion, this is one of the medical situations in which the patient's account of the circumstances, and description of what has been noticed, is particularly important. The doctor's questioning and the examination that will probably be necessary will have to cover all the possible causes and this may involve virtually any part of the body.

Treatment

It is unlikely that the doctor will prescribe any medicine until he or she knows the cause of the tiredness, since effective treatment is likely to depend on it. In particular, he or she is very unlikely to give any kind of stimulant drug to relieve tiredness. This can only provide a very short-term and completely artificial boost, cannot get to the heart of the matter, and can easily lead to addiction.

The doctor may suggest adjustments in lifestyle or diet, and will want to make sure that the patient is getting enough rest and relaxation. He or she may prescribe a tonic, but the effect of this, apart from possibly stimulating the appetite, is largely psychological.

If a tonic is bought from the drugstore, you must make sure that it does not become a dangerous substitute for getting the tiredness properly investigated and treated by a doctor.

Tongue

Q Is it really possible to be tongue-tied, or is this just a figure of speech?

A It was once thought that babies were tongue-tied if they could not put their tongues out, but it has now been found that as a child grows in the first year or two of life, so the strand of tissue beneath the tongue, linking its underside to the floor of the mouth, elongates and makes the tongue properly mobile. Only in very exceptional circumstances is it necessary for that strand of tissue, the frenulum, to be cut to give the tongue greater mobility and improve a child's speech. In modern parlance, of course, to be tongue-tied means simply to be incapable of speech for a short time, especially through shyness or surprise.

Q What should you do if someone accidentally swallows his or her tongue?

A Unless you are trained in first aid it is important not to try to pull the tongue back to its normal position—you may well end up doing more harm than good and choking the patient. Lie the person down in the recovery position with the chin forward so that the airway is as clear as possible and call for help immediately.

Q Why is it that smoking makes my tongue furred and yellow?

A Smoking furs the tongue because it tends to dry the mouth and thereby prevents the body's natural washing process from taking place. The cells of the tongue and mouth wear out and are replaced extremely rapidly, and the remains of dead cells, plus dried mucus and the remains of food, form a furry deposit on the tongue if not washed off. The effect of smoking is to inhibit the action of the salivary glands, thereby slowing this cleaning mechanism. The yellow color of the fur is produced by the staining action of the tars in tobacco. There is one very simple answer to this problem—quit smoking.

The tongue is one of the body's muscles, but a muscle of a remarkable kind. Not only are its movements vital for speaking and eating, but it also contains thousands of taste buds that give us our sense of taste.

The tongue is shaped like a triangle—wide at the base and tapering almost to a point at its tip. It is attached at its base or root to the lower jaw, or mandible, and to the hyoid bone of the skull. At its sides the root is joined to the walls of the pharynx, the cavity that forms the back of the mouth (see Mouth).

The middle part of the tongue has a curved upper surface, while its lower surface is connected to the floor of the mouth by a thin strip of tissue called the frenulum. The tongue's tip is free to move, but when a person is not eating or speaking it normally lies neatly in the mouth with its tip resting against the front teeth.

The sense of taste

The structures that give the tongue its characteristic rough texture are the ridged folds, or papillae, that cover the upper surface of the front two-thirds of the tongue. Largest of these are the eight to 12 V-shaped, or vallate, papillae that form the border between the ridged and unridged areas. Because the papillae are so numerous, they provide a huge surface area to accommodate the 9000 or more taste

Licking a Popsicle is a study in contrasting sensations: flavor explodes onto the tongue, while the frostiness lends a biting effervescence to the taste.

Steve Bielschowsky

The tongue: its position and structure

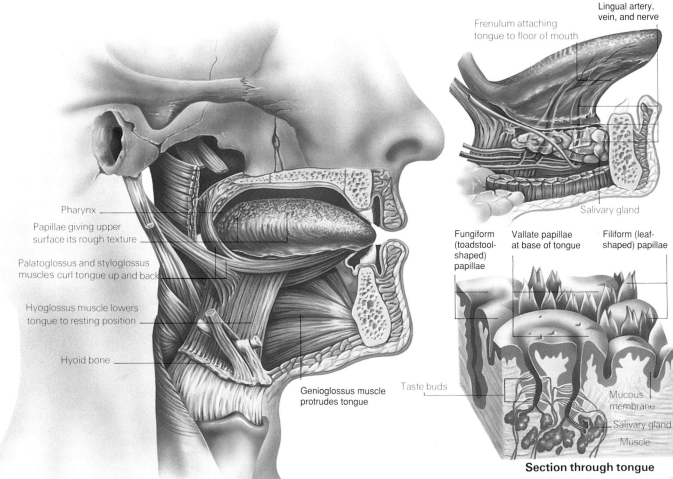

Frenulum attaching
tongue to floor of mouth

Lingual artery,
vein, and nerve

Salivary gland

Fungiform
(toadstool-
shaped)
papillae

Vallate papillae
at base of tongue

Filiform (leaf-
shaped) papillae

Pharynx

Papillae giving upper
surface its rough texture

Palatoglossus and styloglossus
muscles curl tongue up and back

Hyoglossus muscle lowers
tongue to resting position

Hyoid bone

Genioglossus muscle
protrudes tongue

Taste buds

Mucous
membrane

Salivary gland

Muscle

Section through tongue

buds with which the human tongue is equipped (see Taste). This large surface also creates a vast platform on which substances can be dissolved, tested, and tasted. Dissolving is a vital part of the tasting process because the taste buds will not work unless they are presented with molecules in solution.

The taste buds nestle in the valleys of the papillae and consist of bundles of hairlike cells, which project into the valley. Nerve fibers connected to the hair cells run to the brain and to the salivary glands that are situated around the borders of the mouth.

When food is taken into the mouth, nerve cells in the tongue first feel it and test it for texture and temperature. As the taste buds become stimulated by chemical messages arriving from dissolved foodstuff molecules, they send messages to the salivary glands, which pour their secretions into the mouth, not just to help soften the food but also to assist the dissolving process (see Saliva).

These illustrations show the position of the tongue and surrounding musculature (above); the underside, with its blood and nerve supply (top right); and the upper surface with papillae (above right).

As a result of the combined action of the nerve cells in the tongue, messages are passed to the brain about the taste of food and about its texture and temperature, to give a total impression of each mouthful (see Nervous system). Because of the tongue's millions of minute undulations, chemicals may be trapped in the valleys for some time, allowing a taste to linger in the mouth long after a mouthful of food or drink has been swallowed.

Movements of the tongue

The actions of the tongue are determined by the muscles it is made up of and to which it is joined, and by the way it is fixed into position in the mouth.

The tongue itself contains muscle fibers running both longitudinally and from side

Sally and Richard Greenhill

to side, and these are capable of producing some movement. However, the actions of the tongue are given huge versatility by the contractions of a variety of muscles situated in the neck and at the sides of the jaws. The styloglossus muscle in the neck, for example, is responsible for bringing the tongue upward and backward, while the hyoglossus, also in the neck, brings it back down again into the normal resting position.

In eating, one of the tongue's main jobs is to present the food to the teeth for chewing and to mold softened food into a ball, or bolus, ready for swallowing. These actions are performed by a range of curling and up and down movements. When the task has been completed (or sooner in someone who gulps his or her food) the tongue pushes the bolus into the pharynx at the back of the mouth from where it enters the esophagus and is swallowed into the stomach.

The actions of the tongue are important to human communication through the enunciation of speech (see Speech). The difference between a crisp, clearly spoken "s" sound and the fuzzy tone of a lisped one is, for example, all to do with tongue action. To discover the range of positions your tongue must adopt during speech, try saying the sounds of the alphabet out loud, then intone common characteristics such as "sh" and "th." You will find that there is a precise tongue position for each sound, and that it is vital for enunciating consonants in particular.

Ian Turner/Rex Features

Injuries and disease

It is easy for the tongue to be accidentally injured, and this often happens when a person bites his or her own tongue.

Because it is so richly supplied with blood vessels, the tongue bleeds profusely when injured. If bleeding is severe, the best sort of first aid is to sit the person upright and, with a clean wad of tissue or a folded handkerchief, try to grip the bleeding area between your thumb and forefinger. If the injured person is an adult, and has not sustained severe injuries elsewhere on the body, he or she may be able to grip his or her own tongue, but in any case you should try to keep up a steady pressure for about 10 minutes. If an injury

As well as having a role in taste, eating, and speech, the tongue can be used to help express a person's feelings.

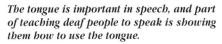

The tongue is important in speech, and part of teaching deaf people to speak is showing them how to use the tongue.

is only minor, give the person an ice cube to suck. Following accidents, the tongue can block the airway. If someone is unconscious after an accident, lie him or her down in the recovery position, chin forward, to leave the airway clear.

The tongue is not often prone to disease, mainly because of the antiseptic action of the saliva that bathes it. The most common problems are ulcers (see Ulcers) and the yeast infection *Candida* (see Thrush). Unless ulcers are very large and/or painful, the best treatment is to use a proprietary mouthwash or gel, or to suck lozenges formulated to treat the problem. Also pay attention to your teeth—they may be the cause of the trouble.

There is a possibility of carrying the genital herpes virus on the tongue and of tongue cancer (see Cancer). Both these diseases are extremely serious, so it is vital that you see your doctor if you notice any abnormal swelling or pain in your tongue, or if you have persistent ulcers.

The tongue as an indicator

The color, texture, and general state of the tongue can arouse a doctor's suspicions about disease, but rarely tells the whole story on its own. Normally, the ridged papillae are cleared of accumulating debris by the washing process, which is affected jointly by the saliva and the movements of the tongue. If fur accumulates on the tongue it is usually because the flow of saliva is impaired. This may be because you are thirsty or because your appetite is reduced or impaired for some reason, such as a digestive upset, but it could also stem from a psychological problem.

If you have persistent discoloration or pain, you should always bring this to the attention of your doctor. As is the case with so many disorders, the sooner treatment can begin, the better the chances of a total recovery.

Tonsils

Q How soon after having an attack of tonsillitis is it safe to have surgery to remove the tonsils?

A Two to three weeks is the accepted period, after which time the risk of abnormal postoperative bleeding returns to normal. If a child is having attacks of tonsillitis every 10 days and is due for a tonsillectomy, the doctor will put him or her on a course of antibiotics for three weeks before the planned surgery. This eliminates the possibility of the child being sent home when he or she is taken to the hospital for surgery.

Q Should I suck aspirin rather than swallow them when I have a sore throat?

A No, this is not advisable. In fact, sucking aspirin can be dangerous, because it can cause a chemical burn on the mucous membranes lining the mouth and the throat.

Q Will I be more prone to infections after I have had my tonsils out?

A No. Your tonsils probably only have a significant function during the first few years of life, which is one of the reasons why doctors prefer not to remove the tonsils from a child who is still very young.

Q My three-year-old son has very frequent attacks of tonsillitis, but the surgeon is reluctant to remove his tonsils. Why is this?

A At three years of age your son will probably weigh between 26 and 40 lb (12 to 18 kg) and therefore his total blood volume will be between 2 and 3 pt (950 and 1400 ml). A loss of 0.3 pt (120 ml), which is the average loss for the operation, would deprive him of between 8 and 12 percent of his blood and cause a dangerous condition. Should he bleed heavily after the operation his condition would become very serious indeed.

The tonsils have a role to perform in the body and should be allowed to carry it out. Throughout life, however, they are subject to a variety of diseases for which removal is sometimes the only appropriate remedy.

Position of tonsils

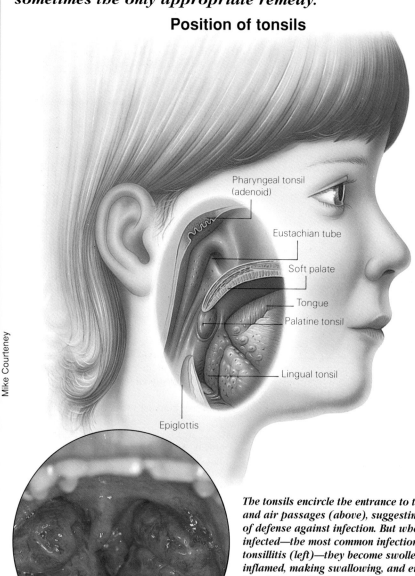

Mike Courteney

- Pharyngeal tonsil (adenoid)
- Eustachian tube
- Soft palate
- Tongue
- Palatine tonsil
- Lingual tonsil
- Epiglottis

The tonsils encircle the entrance to the food and air passages (above), suggesting a role of defense against infection. But when infected—the most common infection being tonsillitis (left)—they become swollen and inflamed, making swallowing, and even breathing, difficult and painful.

The tonsils are part of a ring of lymphoid tissue (Waldeyer's ring) that encircles the entrance to the food and air passages in the throat (see Lymphatic system). Although the tonsils are present at birth they are relatively small. They grow rapidly during the first few years of life, only to regress after puberty. However, they do not disappear completely.

Function

The exact function of the tonsils is not known, but it has been suggested that they may play a significant role in the body's defense mechanisms (see Immune system). They are ideally situated to monitor ingested material and to react to those materials that could pose a threat to the well-being of the body.

The tonsils provide immunity against upper respiratory tract infections by producing lymphocytes (see Lymphocytes). In addition the tonsils produce antibodies that deal with infections locally.

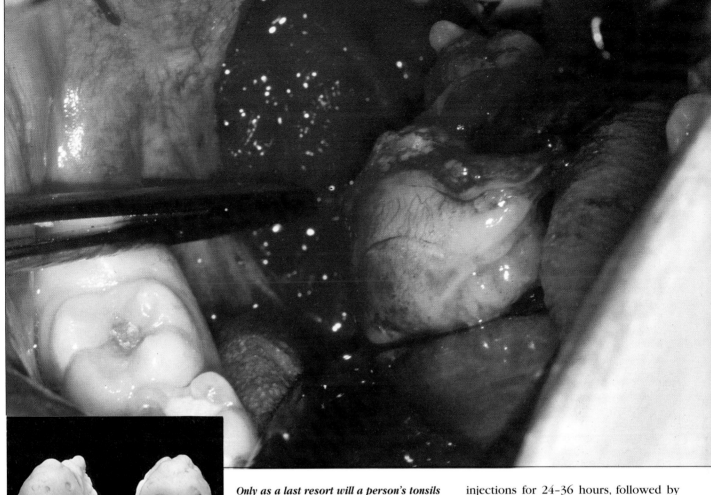

Only as a last resort will a person's tonsils be removed. They are dissected from the pharyngeal wall while the patient is under general anesthesia (above). These removed tonsils (left) show patches of scar tissue from repeated bouts of tonsillitis.

Tonsillitis

Almost everyone suffers an attack of tonsillitis at some time in life. The organism causing the infection is usually a bacterium called streptococcus (see Bacteria).

It is often easy to tell tonsillitis from a simple sore throat since it lasts considerably longer—approximately a week. Symptoms vary with the severity of the infection, but they always include marked discomfort in the pharynx (see Pharynx), making swallowing painful. Pain from the throat may also be felt in the ears. Some patients also experience discomfort on turning their head because of swelling of the glands in this region.

A fever almost always accompanies the infection, but it varies in degree. Children, for example, tend to develop higher temperatures and consequently more symptoms (such as malaise and vomiting) than adults. Some children may have no symptoms in the throat, but will complain of abdominal pain instead.

When the tonsils are infected they become enlarged and inflamed. Specks of

pus (see Pus) exude from their surfaces. The infection responds well to antibiotics, and improvement can be expected within 36–48 hours. Symptoms can be alleviated by eating soft foods and drinking plenty of liquids. Painkillers such as aspirin both relieve the pain and reduce the temperature.

Tonsillitis tends to occur most frequently between the ages of four and six years, and then again around puberty. The more often the tonsils are infected the more prone they are to persistent and recurrent infection. A stage is reached when removal of the tonsils is the only sensible way of controlling the illness.

In some cases an infection is so severe that an abscess forms in the tissue around the tonsils (see Abscess). This is called peritonsillar abscess, or quinsy. Quinsy usually affects one side of the tonsils and is very rare in children. The affected tonsil swells to a considerable extent, and may prevent swallowing altogether. Local inflammation contributes to this by limiting the opening of the jaw. Oral antibiotics are not only difficult to swallow but also rarely effective. Higher doses of antibiotics are given by intramuscular

injections for 24–36 hours, followed by oral antibiotics. If the quinsy is ripe, that is, the abscess is pointing, recovery may be accelerated by lancing the abscess and allowing the pus to drain.

In exceptional cases an infection is not limited to the tonsils, but spreads both down the neck to the chest and up toward the base of the skull—a parapharyngeal abscess. This is a life-threatening condition and requires urgent admission to the hospital, where the abscess can be drained and massive doses of powerful antibiotics given. Patients who have had quinsy are thought to be more susceptible to this complication and are therefore advised to have their tonsils out even if they have not been troubled previously by recurrent tonsillitis.

Viral infections of the tonsils

Tonsillar tissue can be affected by viral infections, which commonly lead to a sore throat. Symptoms are similar to those of tonsillitis, but are milder and last for only 24–48 hours.

The tonsils are also affected in infectious mononucleosis (see Infectious mononucleosis), when a sore throat is accompanied by severe lassitude, joint pains, and generalized swelling of all the lymph glands. In this condition the tonsils are covered by a white membrane, and the adjacent palate is dotted with splinterlike hemorrhages. Neither of these conditions is an indication that a tonsillectomy is nec-

Q My husband will shortly be going into the hospital for a tonsillectomy. How long will he have to stay off work and how should I look after him at home?

A Most adult patients take about two weeks to recover completely. This includes one week in the hospital and at least one week resting at home. It is very important that you encourage your husband to eat as abrasive a diet as he can tolerate so that the site of the operation is kept clean. If it was your child who was having surgery, the recommendation would be the same, with the additional precaution that he or she should not come into contact with other children for at least a week.

Q If a person's tonsils are larger than normal, should they be removed?

A The size of the tonsils alone rarely necessitates their removal. However, in a few cases the tonsils are so enlarged that they obstruct the passage of air and a tonsillectomy must be performed. The obstruction occurs mainly at night. While the person is asleep he or she stops breathing intermittently, causing him or her to wake up. There can be far-reaching consequences of this condition, called sleep apnea. Subjects may become lethargic, undergo personality changes, and may even become incontinent. Very rarely the chronic deprivation of oxygen can lead to heart failure and irregularities of the heart rate.

Q Is it true that some children have to have their tonsils removed to stop them from going deaf?

A Yes. In children, attacks of tonsillitis may precipitate attacks of otitis media (an infection of the middle ear) or it may prevent a complete recovery from secretory otitis media, a condition known more commonly as glue ear. In these cases the surgeon may advise tonsillectomy to prevent possible damage to the middle ear and avoid the deafness which, although temporary, is associated with these conditions.

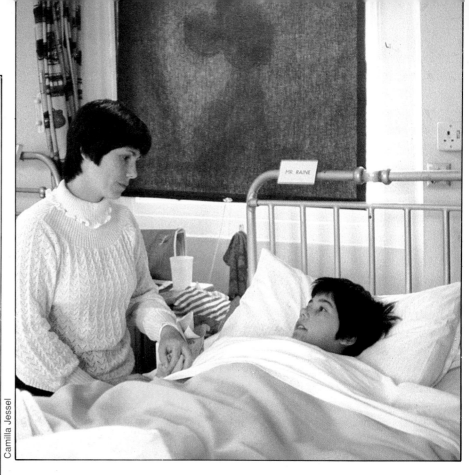

Camilla Jessel

essary, since both occur just as frequently in people who have had surgery to remove their tonsils for a variety of other reasons.

Tonsillectomy

A tonsillectomy is performed under general anesthesia. The tonsils are dissected away from the pharyngeal wall and the resulting bleeding is controlled by ligatures. On average about 0.3 pt (120 ml) of blood is lost during surgery, irrespective of the patient's age. Surgeons are therefore very reluctant to operate on children who are very small or below the age of four, since this amount of blood loss is a significant proportion of their total blood volume. If surgery is necessary, however, the child will be given an intravenous infusion for about 12 hours after the tonsillectomy.

The only serious complication that may occur after a tonsillectomy is further hemorrhage. When this occurs it is usually within the first hours after surgery and requires a return to the operating room for further ligation (see Hemorrhage).

Bleeding may also occur six to ten days after surgery if the tonsil bed becomes infected. Patients most commonly affected are those who eat poorly postoperatively or who have had an attack of tonsillitis immediately before admission to the hospital. This late bleeding is treated with antibiotics, but if the patient has lost a lot of blood a transfusion or a course of iron tablets may be necessary to stimulate rapid replacement of the lost blood.

Although children recover very quickly from a tonsillectomy, being in the hospital can be a lonely experience. The reassuring presence of a parent, especially just before and after surgery, helps speed recovery.

Children tend to recover from surgery more quickly than adults and only require one or two days in the hospital. Adults, however, may need four to five days' hospitalization before they are fit enough to be discharged.

Tumors of the tonsils

Tumors of the tonsils are uncommon but may occur at any age (see Tumors). Lymphomas may cause a sudden tonsillar enlargement and are usually associated with swollen glands in other parts of the body—for example, under the arms and in the groin. In general they respond well to treatment, and a large proportion of patients are cured.

Another type of tumor is known as squamous cell carcinoma. It occurs in the older age group and men are more frequently affected than women. The condition results in a unilaterally enlarged and painful tonsil, which may be ulcerated. Variable degrees of difficulty and pain on swallowing are experienced, and in advanced cases it may even be impossible for the patient to swallow his or her saliva. Similarly, as the disease progresses the tumor spreads to the glands in the neck. With early treatment a recovery rate of at least 50 percent can be expected.

Total allergy syndrome

Q Is total allergy syndrome a condition that appears suddenly, or does it develop over a period of time?

A People with extensive allergies usually displayed some allergic tendencies in childhood, suffering from such conditions as eczema, asthma, or hay fever. The number of foods and other environmental substances that they are allergic to may increase as they grow older. This, of course, produces a tremendous strain on even the most robust personality. It is hardly surprising that in some people other symptoms and patterns of behavior that are not due to immune problems start to occur.

Q How common is total allergy syndrome?

A On the whole, doctors do not regard total allergy syndrome as a separate disease in itself, although there certainly are extreme forms of allergic susceptibility. The term *total allergy* is a misnomer, since even the most severely affected patients can tolerate certain foods. Nevertheless, however the disease is classified, it is clear that only a very few people with allergic tendencies ever develop a sensitivity to more than one or two substances.

Q Is total allergy syndrome a purely modern-day disease as people have said?

A People who have multiple allergies are sometimes said to be allergic to modern society. That does not necessarily mean that severe allergy never existed before. Its apparent novelty owes much to the fact that a term has only recently been coined by the media to describe it. In spite of this, however, it is possible to expect the increased numbers of additives in the food we eat, or the wide range of cosmetics available, to cause an increase in the incidence of allergic disease, if only because there are now many more substances for people to be allergic to.

We all know of people who are allergic to something, but the term total allergy syndrome *has recently been coined to describe an allergic response to everything. Does this condition really exist, or is it a misnomer?*

Sufferers with what is called total allergy syndrome seem to become severely ill when exposed to any of a wide range of substances in their environment.

All types of allergic disease are a result of a defect in the body's immune system. When a substance recognized as foreign enters the body, it provokes the production of substances called antibodies. When the foreign substance enters the body again, the antibodies bind to the intruder, rendering the body immune. Unfortunately some people form antibodies to quite harmless substances, and the binding of antibody to intruder may inappropriately trigger off the release of a number of other chemicals concerned with the body's defense. These produce unpleasant effects such as asthma, runny nose, skin rashes, and vomiting.

Most people with an allergic predisposition become sensitized to just one or two substances, and their symptoms on reexposure are generally mild. In the more severe cases of allergy, however, not only are the symptoms more alarming, with such things as joint pains and bleeding from the large intestine, but people may become sensitive to a variety of substances, particularly foods.

However, some symptoms in the so-called total allergy syndrome are not likely to happen as a result of immune disorders. In particular, allergy does not make people lose consciousness, although it may certainly cause headaches and a disabling sense of ill health.

There is also an alarming range of substances that can produce allergies, and in the case of food allergy it is the rule rather than the exception to be allergic to more than one food. It seems very likely that multiple food allergy is at the basis of total allergy. Some sections of the medical profession are skeptical. It is not surprising that some people may suffer from the stress of the situation, with the result that anxiety symptoms occur that are not directly related to any action of the immune system (see Anxiety).

Treatment

It is very difficult to help people whose disease has made such an impact on their lives that they are thought to suffer from the total allergy syndrome. Drugs have only a limited place in the treatment of allergy, and the basis of treating the food allergies is to identify the foods responsible and exclude them from the diet.

Sufferers from total allergy syndrome sometimes feel that the only safe environment is their own home.

Zefa

Touch

Q Why do babies touch as well as look at everything around them?

A When we are babies we train our brains to match the sight of an object with its feel. When we are older, these earlier experiences enable us to predict what the texture of an object or surface is without touching it.

Q When someone has had a stroke and is paralyzed down one side, does this mean that he or she will have lost the sense of touch on that side?

A Not necessarily. Some people who have been paralyzed by a stroke will have retained their sense of touch on that side, providing the damage has been confined to the movement control parts of the brain. If the area of damage is sufficiently large to have involved the touch analyzers in the brain or their connections, then the sense of touch will be damaged.

Q I have noticed that on very cold days my sense of touch is poor. Why is this?

A In very cold weather two things are working against the touch receptors just below the skin in the fingers. The cold itself will be reducing their efficiency, and blood will have been diverted away from the skin in order to minimize heat loss; this relatively poor blood supply will further impair the ability of these nerve endings to send concise messages to your brain.

Q Is it true that blind people have a better sense of touch than the sighted?

A A blind person will have the same equipment in his or her nervous system for touch perception. What makes blind people able to use it more effectively than those with full sight is the practice that this sense has had in the absence of sight. The brain has come to rely on touch to a much greater extent, and so the analysis of touch has become more efficient, enabling, for example, the rapid reading of Braille.

Touch is so fundamental to life that most of us never think of how the many sensations we feel are produced: how, for instance, we can tell silk from sandpaper, or recognize an object simply by the way it feels on the skin.

Sandra Lousada/Susan Griggs Agency

Touch is one of the first ways in which young babies explore their world, and it remains our most intimate way of relating to our environment. We have a wide range of receptors in our skin that are sensitive to different types of pressure. Through these we are constantly able to monitor our immediate surroundings and keep our brains in touch with the surfaces on which we sit, the objects we grasp, and so on. However, our sensation of touch is complex and is therefore sensitive to disturbances in many parts of the nervous system (see Nervous system).

The sensory receptors

Just below the surface of the skin there are many nerve endings with varying degrees of sensitivity. These allow the nervous system to be supplied with different types of touch sensations (see Skin and skin diseases).

Wrapped around the base of the fine hairs of the skin are the free nerve endings, which respond to any stimulation of the hair. These touch receptors are the least sophisticated in structure and rapidly stop firing if the hair continues to be stimulated. Receptors found in greater numbers in the hairless part of the skin, for example, on the fingertips and lips, are formed into tiny disks. Because the nerve fibers are embedded within these disks they respond more slowly to pressure and continue to fire when the pressure is maintained. Other more structurally complicated receptors are formed by many membranes being wrapped around a nerve ending like an onion skin, and give responses to more constant pressure. In addition, the information that all receptors send into the nervous system tends to be influenced by the temperature at which they are operating. This explains why our sense of touch can be impaired in cold weather.

The distribution of the different types of touch receptors reflects their particular job. The receptors around the base of body hair send messages from large areas

The touch receptors in our skin are so sensitive that they respond to the gentlest stroking of a blade of grass.

From a very early age we begin to use our sense of touch to help us get to know the shape and feel of everything around us (left)—even Mom!

of the skin about the pressure stimulating them. They rapidly stop their flow of information once we have been warned of the presence of objects, for example, an insect on the skin. On the hairless skin more sophisticated receptors give continuous information, allowing objects to be felt as the brain gathers this information into a coherent picture (see Brain).

Analysis in the spinal cord

Some of the fibers conveying touch information pass into the spinal cord and, without stopping, go straight up to the brain stem. These fibers deal mainly with sensations of pressure, particularly a specific point of pressure. Therefore they need to send their messages directly to the higher centers of the brain so that this well localized sensation can be assessed without confusion from any analysis in the spinal cord.

Other nerve fibers bringing information of more diffuse touch enter the gray matter of the spinal cord and there meet a network of cells that perform an initial analysis of their information. This is the same area that receives messages from the pain receptors in the skin and elsewhere. The meeting in the spinal cord of messages dealing with both touch and pain allows for the mixture of these two sensations, and explains such responses as the relief of painful stimuli by rubbing (see Spinal cord).

Touch pathways

Touch receptors in the skin relay their messages to the cerebral cortex via two specific pathways in the spinal cord: one for well-localized touch sensations, the other for more diffuse touch.

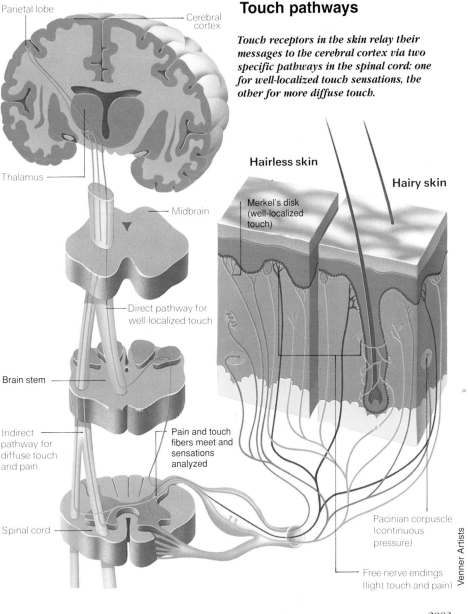

Parietal lobe

Cerebral cortex

Thalamus

Midbrain

Direct pathway for well-localized touch

Brain stem

Indirect pathway for diffuse touch and pain

Spinal cord

Hairless skin

Hairy skin

Merkel's disk (well-localized touch)

Pain and touch fibers meet and sensations analyzed

Pacinian corpuscle (continuous pressure)

Free nerve endings (light touch and pain)

Venner Artists

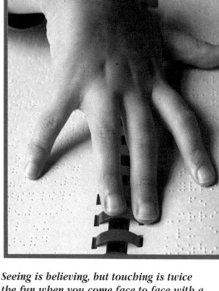

Owen Franken/Corbis

John Walmsley

John Walmsley

Seeing is believing, but touching is twice the fun when you come face to face with a real live woolly sheep for the very first time (top left).

The various touch receptors in our skin are very discerning. If a shape is drawn on the hand, for instance, we can often tell what it is without looking (top). This is obviously important to someone who is blind, since the ability to define shapes is fundamental to reading Braille (above).

We can all get enjoyment from the way things feel—from the delicious sensation of kneading soft, pliable modeling clay (left) to the decidedly more delicate sensuousness of soft, tactile material such as silk when it is worn next to the skin (far left).

Steve Bielschowsky

Rex Features

This spinal cord analysis filters the sensations, which are then sent upward to the brain. The gray matter of the spinal cord here acts as an electronic gate so that pain information can be suppressed by the advent into the cord of certain types of touch impulse, limiting the amount of trivial information that needs to be transmitted to the higher centers.

This division of the touch pathways to the brain into two streams—one of which goes fairly directly up to the brain stem, and the other that is first analyzed by the cells of the spinal cord— enables the fine discriminating aspects of touch to be preserved. This means we can estimate accurately the amount of

pressure in a touch and its position, but if the pressure is too great, or too sharp, the pain analyzers become involved through the connections in the spinal cord and tell us that the touch is painful as well (see Pain, and Pain management).

The sensory sorting house
Whether touch sensations from the skin have come by the more direct route or after analysis in the spinal cord, they eventually end in the compact knot of gray matter deep in the center of the brain, called the thalamus.

The direct touch fibers will have already relayed once in the brain stem and then will have crossed over to the other side, streaming to the thalamus in a compact bundle. The other fibers will have crossed over to the opposite side of the spinal cord after their relay in the gray matter there; so all our touch sensations from one side of the body are analyzed by opposite sides of the brain.

In the thalamus these pieces of information from various different types of receptor in the skin are assembled and coordinated. This enables the brain's highest centers in the cerebral cortex to put together a picture of the sensations of touch of which we become conscious.

The final analysis
The area of the brain that enables the complex array of touch sensations entering the nervous system to be consciously perceived is the middle section of the cerebral cortex. As with all other sensory information, touch is analyzed by the cortex in a series of steps, each increasing the complexity of the sensory perception. From the thalamus, the raw data is projected to a narrow strip in the front of the parietal lobes.

This primary sensory area of the cortex processes the information before relaying it to the secondary and tertiary sensory areas. In these latter areas the full picture of the site, type, and significance of the touch sensations we feel is produced and correlated, along with memories of previous sensations and sensory stimuli coming via the ears and eyes. The latter coordination is achieved easily because the areas for vision and hearing back onto the areas for touch.

Touch sensations are also coordinated here with the sensations of what position our limbs, joints, and digits are in. This is vitally important as it enables us to determine an object's size and shape, and helps us distinguish one object from another.

Problems
Damage to the nervous system at many different levels can alter our ability to feel and notice things that touch our skin.

How this affects us depends largely on the exact place in the nervous system that the damage occurs.

Damage to the peripheral nerves, which may happen in alcoholism or in diabetes, for example, can affect the sense of touch (see Alcoholism, and Diabetes). However, it takes extensive damage for the sense of touch to be lost completely or severely diminished.

Often people with such disorders feel pins and needles in their hands and feet for some time before any alteration in their sense of touch. The ability of the fingers to make fine touch discrimination may be involved, and sufferers may report that it feels as if they have gloves on all the time. Instead of being lost or diminished, the sense of touch can also become distorted as a result of damage to the peripheral nerves, so that a sufferer may say that smooth surfaces feel like sandpaper or warm surfaces feel hot.

Much greater distortion of the sense of touch, however, arises from disease in the spinal cord, for example in multiple sclerosis (see Multiple sclerosis). The cross connections that arise in the spinal cord if it is diseased, or even pressed upon from the outside, produce distortions of touch that can be disabling and unpleasant. Apart from noticing a feeling of numbness, the hands may have lost their ability to make properly coordinated touch perception, for example, in picking the correct coin from a pocket, or the feet may feel as if they are walking on cotton balls instead of firm ground.

Similar types of symptoms can arise from damage to the same touch pathways through the brain stem all the way to the thalamus. Thalamic damage, which happens after strokes, for example, can produce bizarre alterations of touch so that a simple pinprick produces unpleasant, spreading, electric shocklike sensations, or the gentle stroking of a finger may be felt as an unpleasant burning spreading over the skin (see Stroke).

Damage to the parietal lobes of the cerebral cortex, common in strokes and tumors of the brain, may disrupt touch sensations in other ways. If the thalamus is still intact (it is often involved in the disease as well), then the touch will be felt, but the localization of the touch will be inaccurate—it may, for example, be felt on the other side of the body. If the parietal lobe is not functioning, the correlation of different types of sensation will not occur (see Brain damage and disease).

For instance, usually, when the hand or skin is drawn upon, a person will be able to distinguish letters and numbers, but someone with parietal lobe damage will not recognize shapes, although he or she will be aware that a touch has occurred.

Tourniquet

Q How long is it safe to leave a tourniquet on a limb?

A The time varies depending on the nature of the tourniquet. Damage can result from pressure on the nerves, and from the limb being deprived of blood for too long. Therefore every effort should be made to release a tourniquet every 20 minutes, and it should not be left on for more than an hour. When it is first applied, a label should be made out with the time written on it. This label should be affixed to the patient prominently so that it is clear when the tourniquet must be loosened.

Q My son cut his hand with a knife the other day and by the time I had brought him to the hospital he had lost a lot of blood. Should I have used a tourniquet?

A No. You probably could have stopped the bleeding by holding his hand above his head and pressing on the bleeding point with a pad. A tourniquet applied by an inexperienced person is likely to cause unnecessary injury.

Q When I had a blood test at the hospital, the doctor put a tourniquet on my arm. Is this the same sort of tourniquet that is used in emergencies?

A No. The sort that you had was a venous tourniquet. This means it only exerted enough pressure to obstruct the flow of blood in the veins, so that the arteries could carry on pumping blood into your arm, but the blood could not get out of your arm. This enlarged the veins, making it easy for the doctor to insert a needle into one of them to obtain blood.

Q What is the best thing to use for an emergency tourniquet?

A Any piece of material that can be tied around the limb may be used. The main thing is that it must not be stretchable, and must be reasonably wide so that it does not cause injury to the limb. A piece of cutlery, such as a spoon, may then be used to tighten it.

If used at the wrong time and by inexperienced hands, a tourniquet can do more harm than good. But it can halt severe blood loss from a limb in an emergency.

Co Rentmeester/Life Magazine/1967/Time Inc./Colorific!

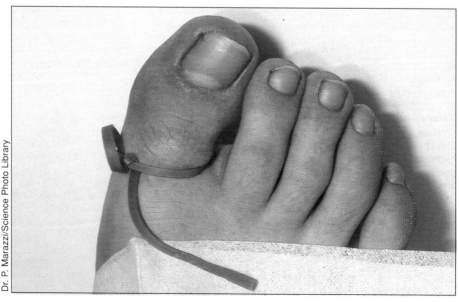

Dr. P. Marazzi/Science Photo Library

There is no place where immediate medical attention is more urgently needed than on a battlefield. In such a situation, someone's life can be saved by a skillfully applied tourniquet. This will prevent excessive blood loss from a wound until the patient can receive adequate hospital treatment.

What to do if a limb is bleeding

- Get the patient to lie down
- Elevate the limb high in the air
- Exert direct pressure over the wound, using a handkerchief or towel as a pad if dressings are not available. Wait for at least five minutes before releasing pressure on the pad and looking underneath
- Apply a tourniquet only if the above measures fail
- Release the tourniquet every 20 minutes
- Seek medical help immediately in cases of severe bleeding

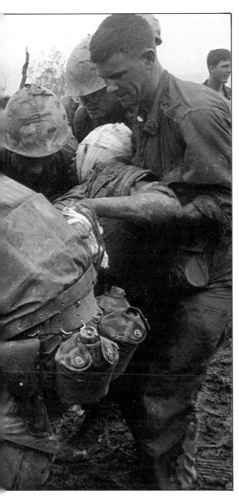

A tourniquet is essentially a bandage that, when placed around a limb and tightened, cuts off the blood supply to the part of the limb beyond it. It does this by squeezing closed the arteries (see Arteries and artery disease, and Blood). Its use in medicine goes back thousands of years, but generally it is not employed as much today as it was even 50 years ago.

It has two main purposes. First, in an emergency it can be used to stop major bleeding from a limb. Second, it can be used during surgery, providing a bloodfree area for the surgeon to work on.

The correct application of a tourniquet can, in some circumstances, be life saving, but it should be stressed that incor-

A tourniquet in the form of an elastic band has been applied to provide a blood-free area for the surgeon to work on during surgery to remove an ingrown toenail.

rect use can lead to a worsening of the situation, and even to permanent damage to the limb. Normally it is best to stop bleeding from a limb with firm pressure over the bleeding area.

Dangers

A tourniquet has the potential to be dangerous in several ways. For instance, if it is applied too tightly, or around part of the limb insufficiently covered with muscle, this could lead to nerves being damaged (see Nervous system). Also leaving the tourniquet on too long may cause serious damage and ultimately tissues can die because they are deprived of blood.

Paradoxically, if the tourniquet is not tight enough, there may be an increase in the amount of bleeding. In this situation if the tourniquet is tight enough to block the veins, where blood is at a very low pressure, but not tight enough to block the arteries, where blood is at high pressure, the blood is still able to get into the limb along the arteries but cannot return via the veins. If there is a cut in a large vein, the bleeding will increase due to the increase in pressure in the veins from blood that cannot return (see Circulatory system).

Finally, during the period a tourniquet is in place the blood vessels can increase in diameter in response to the lack of oxygenated blood in the limb. On release of the tourniquet these vessels can bleed freely, actually giving worse bleeding than before. Because of all these dangers a tourniquet should not be used to control bleeding unless it is absolutely essential.

Use of tourniquets

Before taking the drastic measure of applying a tourniquet, there are certain things that can be tried to stop the bleeding. The first thing to do is to elevate the limb. This causes the blood to be pumped against the force of gravity, and if the

bleeding is at the end of the limb it may stop at once. Firm pressure on the bleeding area may stop the bleeding. In an emergency, a clean handkerchief or a towel will be suitable to use as a pad.

If you are faced with bleeding you must keep up the pressure for at least five minutes. Only if this and elevation of the limb fail to stop or keep the bleeding to a reasonable level should the use of a tourniquet be considered. Tourniquets can be made and used in the following way. A bandage, or a handkerchief or scarf, is tied loosely around the limb, over a muscular part, and then tightened by inserting a rod under it, between the limb and the bandage, and twisting the rod so that the bandage tightens. The tourniquet should feel really tight, and there should be an obvious lessening in the amount of bleeding within about half a minute.

If the patient cannot be taken to the hospital immediately, the tourniquet should be released completely every 20 minutes or so to prevent any damage to the limb caused by blood starvation.

Tourniquets in surgery

Tourniquets are also used in planned surgery to enable the surgeon to operate without blood interfering with what he or she is doing. Typically tourniquets are used during surgery on joints, such as cartilage and tendon operations.

The limb is emptied of blood by winding a special rubber bandage tightly around the limb from the end of the limb, toward the body, gradually squeezing out the blood but without losing any. A special tourniquet is then placed around the upper part of the limb. The tourniquet consists of a hollow rubber tube that can be inflated to the desired pressure using a pump. Finally, the rubber bandage is removed and the surgery is then performed.

Toxic shock syndrome

Q Does toxic shock syndrome only affect women?

A No. However, the problem seems to be largely confined to women, and in the vast majority of cases it has occurred during the course of a period. The syndrome was first recognized in children and teenagers, and only four of these original cases had started their periods, although three of them actually got the disease during the course of a period.

Toxic shock syndrome has been reported in a number of men, all of whom had a skin infection with a staphylococcus. One of these was a plumber who had cleared a lavatory blocked with tampons.

Q Is toxic shock syndrome really a new disease, or did doctors not realize it existed?

A This really does seem to be a new disease. It may have occurred from time to time in the past, but it seemed to start in earnest in the late 1970s. The first report was in 1978, and over 300 cases in 1980 were recognized in America. The disease appears to be caused by toxins (poisons) produced by the staphylococcus— a common bacterium that infects the skin—and it may be that there has been some change in this organism to make it responsible for this new disease.

Q Can you get the syndrome more than once?

A Yes. Some women have even had up to five attacks. One of the things that seems to prevent repeated attacks is treatment with an antibiotic that will kill the staphylococcus so that it is no longer in the vagina during periods.

Q Will using tampons increase the risk of getting toxic shock syndrome?

A The chances are slim. The disease seems to be much more common during the course of a menstrual period, and sufferers almost invariably were tampon users, but millions of women use tampons with no ill effects at all.

First described in America in 1978, toxic shock syndrome now appears to be a worldwide phenomenon. It nearly always affects young women who are almost invariably tampon users and develop the condition during periods.

Toxic shock syndrome is a potentially fatal illness that almost exclusively affects women during the course of their periods. There is very good evidence to suggest that its occurrence is related to the use of tampons during periods, particularly the new superabsorbent varieties that are based on a rayon and cellulose compound. However, this evidence is not conclusive, and it is very important to remember that millions of women use tampons without any ill effects. As a recent American study has shown, the syndrome only occurs in about 6 out of every 100,000 women.

Causes

The important ingredients in causing the syndrome seem to be the occurrence of a period, probably the use of a tampon, and the presence of staphylococci in the vagina. Although staphylococci are not invariably found in the vagina, they are present in many more cases with the

How toxic shock syndrome occurs

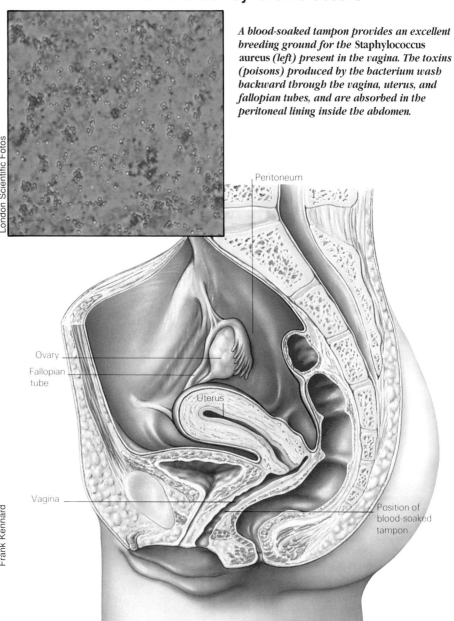

A blood-soaked tampon provides an excellent breeding ground for the Staphylococcus aureus *(left) present in the vagina. The toxins (poisons) produced by the bacterium wash backward through the vagina, uterus, and fallopian tubes, and are absorbed in the peritoneal lining inside the abdomen.*

London Scientific Fotos

Frank Kennard

Peritoneum

Ovary

Fallopian tube

Uterus

Vagina

Position of blood-soaked tampon

syndrome than not. It has been suggested that when the staphylococcus is present in the vagina and a period starts, then the presence of a blood-soaked tampon will provide an excellent culture medium on which the organisms can grow. It is thought that the symptoms result from the production of a toxin (poison) by the staphylococcus, which may then wash backward up through the vagina, uterus, and fallopian tubes to be absorbed from the peritoneal lining inside the abdomen.

About 95 percent of reported cases have happened in women who are having periods. The syndrome tends to occur in very young women, with the average age of 23, and 30 percent of cases involve girls aged between 15 and 21. No particular type of tampon has been associated with the disease, although it is possible that the new superabsorbent types, which have become widely used since the 1970s, may have some part to play. This led, in America, to the withdrawal from the market of a tampon made by a certain manufacturer.

Curiously the disease seems to be less common in women who are using a contraceptive pill. This could perhaps be explained by the fact that the amount of menstrual flow is reduced, but this can't be the only explanation.

Symptoms and dangers
Toxic shock syndrome is characterized by a high fever of over 102.2°F (39°C), low blood pressure (shock), a flattish skin rash that leads to loss of skin from the hands and feet after a week or two, and often a very marked eye infection.

Additionally there will be involvement of at least four of the body's main systems. Failure of the kidneys is very common, as is diarrhea. There is nearly always myalgia: aching pains in the muscles of the sort people get with flu. Headaches and disorientation occur, and there may be evidence of disturbance of the function of the liver.

Typically the illness develops suddenly on the fourth day of a menstrual period. The fever occurs first, and there may be abdominal pain. Watery diarrhea develops during the first 24 hours in most cases. Then myalgia occurs: it is extremely painful in the muscles and the skin. The rash appears during the first 24 hours, but it may not be noticed and may be mistaken for the first flush of fever. Later it becomes more marked, usually affecting the fingers, and sometimes the palms of the hands and the soles of the feet.

As the disease progresses, other problems such as pain in the joints and discomfort on looking toward a light (photophobia) may occur. The kidneys often fail, and stop passing enough urine to

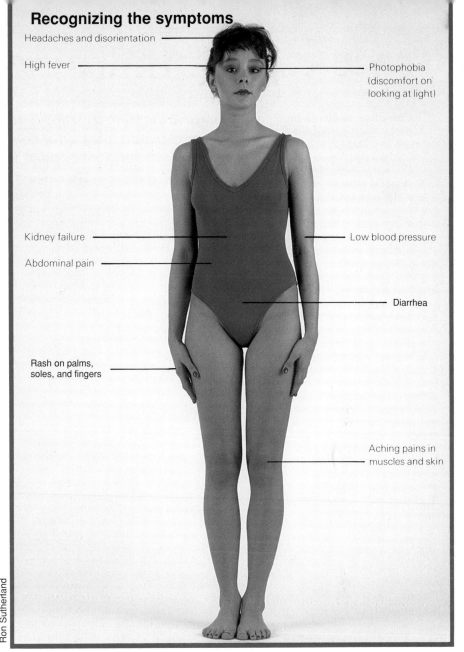

Recognizing the symptoms

- Headaches and disorientation
- High fever
- Photophobia (discomfort on looking at light)
- Kidney failure
- Low blood pressure
- Abdominal pain
- Diarrhea
- Rash on palms, soles, and fingers
- Aching pains in muscles and skin

Ron Sutherland

eliminate waste products, hence the level of waste products in the blood starts to rise. The kidney failure is probably related to the drop in blood pressure, since the kidneys are sensitive to any changes in the amount of blood flowing to them.

Most patients recover after 10 days, but at a rather late stage the skin is lost from the palms and soles, and often from the face and even the tongue. The death rate from the disease is not easy to assess, but it is probably around 2 or 3 percent.

Treatment and outlook
The most important aspect of the treatment is quickly to replace fluid intravenously in order to correct the working of the circulation. The other problems that can happen have to be faced as they occur, and a patient who has difficulty breathing might have to be put on a respirator. There is no evidence that the infection with staphylococci involves the

blood, but it is worthwhile treating the patient with antibiotics to eradicate the organisms from the vagina.

Not only may this hasten recovery from the illness, but it may also prevent the possibility of repeated attacks.

Prevention
The best way to avoid the syndrome is to ensure that tampons are changed regularly and frequently during a period. Although there is no direct evidence that this helps, it seems reasonable on the basis of what we know of the disease. If possible, use external protection in the form of sanitary pads during the later stages of the period, rather than using tampons (see Menstruation).

Although there seems little doubt that the disease is directly related to the use of tampons, few women would be prepared to forego their use completely to avoid such an uncommon condition.

Trace elements

Q Can trace elements be poisonous if they are present to excess?

A Certainly. An example is Wilson's disease, which affects the liver and the brain and results from an excess of copper. Cobalt can also be toxic in very high doses (20–30 mg a day), and can lead to heart failure. Smaller doses can also be poisonous if combined with a low protein diet and high alcohol intake.

Q Do you need extra trace elements to remain healthy?

A No, any normally balanced diet should contain more than enough of all the trace elements, and it is possible that taking supplements could prove dangerous because many of the trace elements can cause illness if they are present in the body in excessive amounts.

Q Are trace elements different from the essential minerals in our diet?

A No, trace elements are also minerals. They differ from the more important minerals, such as sodium and potassium, only because minute amounts (traces) are required in our diet.

Q Why are trace elements thought to be so important?

A The bodily functions rely on a vast number of chemical reactions continually taking place in a controlled way. All of these reactions involve the major organic chemical elements carbon, oxygen, and hydrogen. They may also involve other elements that are widespread in the body, such as sodium or calcium. However, a few of the enzymes that control these interrelated reactions need another substance in order to work properly. Often this substance is a metal, and most of the essential trace elements are, in fact, metals. An example is zinc, which is one of the chemical building blocks for vital enzymes, including the enzyme that breaks down alcohol in the liver.

In the human body, that wonder of complex chemistry, trace elements play vital roles. But too much of them, as well as too little, can cause illness.

Steve Bielschowsky

Zinc is a good healing element, and is particularly beneficial to the skin. Adhesive bandages impregnated with zinc are easy to use and are ideal for the minor cuts and abrasions common to children.

A balanced diet includes protein, starch, fat, and also the vitamins and minerals that we need to keep us healthy. Some minerals are required in such tiny amounts that they are called the trace elements, since a tiny trace of them is all that is required by the body.

In terms of quantity most of our needs are catered to by the three elements carbon, oxygen, and hydrogen, and to a lesser extent nitrogen; we take in kilograms of these substances every day. Relatively large amounts of other elements such as sodium, potassium, and calcium are also required, and we normally take in a few grams of these in our normal diet every day. However, trace elements such as copper, fluorine, and iodine, which are just as essential for normal life, are needed only in minute quantities. For example, we only need a few thousandths of a gram of copper and even less of such elements as iodine and chromium. The body relies on remarkably few elements to set up the complex and intricate web of chemical reactions that keeps us alive and healthy.

What they do

Trace elements have a very important role in bringing about the activity of the body's various enzymes (see Enzymes). Their function is to assist in chemical reactions in the body and, although they initiate a process, they remain unchanged at the end of the reaction. This means they act as catalysts.

All the enzymes are proteins, and what each one does depends on the shape into which the long, stringlike protein molecule winds itself. Trace elements play a role because it seems that a few of the body's enzymes require strong chemical forces produced by atoms of certain metallic elements to attain the correct shape for action. Therefore most of the trace elements we need are metallic and they either form part of the structure of an enzyme, or they take part in chemical reactions in the body. Also a few trace elements seem to be part of the structure of other important substances in the body. Fluorine is associated with the structure of bones and teeth, and iodine is an essential constituent of the thyroid hormones.

Harmful trace elements

Traces of some substances often present in food or air are not only of no value but can be positively dangerous. Metals such as lead, mercury, and arsenic are all poisonous in sufficient quantities and have absolutely no use within the body.

Apart from the purely poisonous metals, it is possible to accumulate high levels of normally beneficial, essential trace elements that can then cause illness. In hemochromatosis, an abnormality of the transport of iron in the blood leads to an accumulation of iron in the liver and pancreas. This can cause cirrhosis and diabetes. A genetic-linked disease called Wilson's disease can also occur where the copper metabolism becomes disorganized, leading to accumulations of copper in the heart and liver.

In other circumstances accidental intake leads to poisoning by metals that are essential only in very small amounts. The most notorious example of accidental excess was in Quebec, Canada, where cobalt was added to beer to improve the froth, and therefore put a better head on a glass of beer. This led to an outbreak of heart failure in beer drinkers, as the cobalt slowly poisoned the heart.

Zinc

Zinc is an important trace metal and is found in comparatively high concentrations in the skin, the eyes, the liver, the pancreas, and in bone.

Trace elements: sources and functions

Element	Source	Role
Iron *10 mg	Meat and some green vegetables	Essential for formation of oxygen-carrying pigments such as hemoglobin (in blood) and myoglobin (in muscle). Deficiency leads to anemia
Iodine *100 micrograms	Seafood. Added to salt in US and UK	Forms part of thyroid hormone. Deficiency results in endemic goiter
Copper *1.5 mg	Seafood, nuts, vegetable oils	Handles oxygen in cells; helps in formation of blood and melanin. Deficiency may lead to anemia, weakened or impaired respiration and growth, poor utilization of iron, especially in babies
Zinc *10–20 mg	Eggs, meat, fish, oats, nuts	Keeps skin healthy. Essential for action of many enzymes. Deficiency leads to retarded growth, late sexual maturation, hair loss, dermatitis, anorexia, vomiting
Manganese *2–4 mg	Mainly vegetables; also legumes and pasta	Part of several enzymes; essential for activating others. Involved in handling fat and excretion of products of protein breakdown. Deficiency leads to subnormal growth, deficient tissue respiration, menstrual irregularities, trouble in nervous system
Fluorine *500 micrograms	Water	Builds healthy teeth and bones. Deficiency contributes to tooth decay and weak bones
Chromium *10 micrograms	Water, oils, meat	Deficiency predisposes to diabetes
Selenium *100 micrograms	Cereals (depends on soil content)	Essential for working of red blood cells. A deficiency has no known effect in humans
Silicone *minute quantity	Vegetables	Forms part of connective tissue structure. A deficiency has no known effect in humans

* Daily requirement (mg = one-thousandth of a gram; microgram = one-millionth of a gram)

Structure of thyroxine

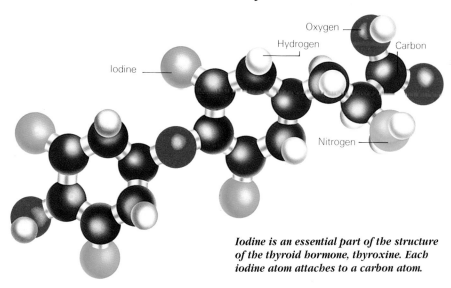

Iodine — Hydrogen — Oxygen — Carbon — Nitrogen

Iodine is an essential part of the structure of the thyroid hormone, thyroxine. Each iodine atom attaches to a carbon atom.

One of the first discoveries about the importance of zinc was the realization that deficiency leads to disease. In some parts of both Egypt and Iran there is a deficiency of zinc in the diet. In these areas there is a tendency for boys not to mature properly, and not to go through puberty. This leads to people over 20 having the appearance of 10-year-olds. Adding zinc to the diet of these boys brings about rapid maturation.

More relevant is the role that zinc plays in the healing of the skin. Zinc given in tablet form can help to speed up healing of various types of wounds. Also, in recent years, a disease called acrodermatitis enteropathica has been recognized. Here, the skin produces eczemalike symptoms; this happens particularly in the skin of infants being weaned. The condition results from poor absorption of zinc and it responds well to zinc treatment.

Tracheostomy

The windpipe can become obstructed as a result of blockage, disease, or injury, making breathing extremely difficult. In such cases, a tracheotomy—surgically creating a hole in the trachea—can be a lifesaver.

Q Is it possible to speak with a tracheostomy, and does a tracheostomy have long-term effects on the voice?

A Usually it is not possible to speak with a tracheostomy in the first few weeks. However, a special tube can be inserted after a while, and by covering the outside end of the tube with a finger the air can go straight up into the larynx. Sometimes the voice may be weaker after a tracheotomy, but should eventually regain its normal strength, depending, of course, on the original reason for performing the surgery.

Q Is it easy to do an emergency tracheotomy if you come across someone who is choking to death?

A No. A tracheotomy may seem simple, but it is not. However, if you are sure that the obstruction is at the back of the throat and if all else has failed—that is, the obstruction cannot be removed through the mouth or by performing the Heimlich maneuver, and there is no chance of a medical person being found—a cricothyroidotomy is an easier procedure. Here, a small cut is made about 1 in (2.5 cm) below the Adam's apple until the windpipe is entered.

Q If someone has a temporary tracheostomy, is it always necessary to have another operation to close the hole?

A No, not always. Usually as soon as the tracheostomy tube is taken out the hole starts getting smaller. Eventually it should heal up on its own, but if there is a persistent leak, minor surgery may be needed.

Q How long can someone have a tracheostomy for?

A There is no limit to the length of time that someone can have a tracheostomy. Of course if it is a temporary one, then every effort will be made to remove the need for it, but there are many people who have had a tracheostomy for years.

The actor Christopher Reeve, celebrated for his role as Superman, has had a tracheostomy since becoming paralyzed after breaking his neck in a riding accident.

The word *tracheotomy* is derived from two Greek words, *trachea*, the windpipe, and *tomy*, to cut. It should not be confused with the word *tracheostomy*, which means the actual opening in the trachea. Tracheotomy means the act of making that opening.

When is it necessary?

There are various reasons for performing a tracheotomy. Sometimes it is performed because of an obstruction in the upper part of the windpipe. Making an opening below the obstruction will allow the patient to breathe until the obstruction can be removed. The obstruction can be the result of injury to the mouth or the back of the throat; inflammation (see Inflammation), causing swelling of the upper airway; or a tumor in the larynx (see Larynx and laryngitis, and Tumor). It may be sudden or gradual in onset, and consequently the tracheotomy may have to be performed as an emergency or as planned surgery.

Sometimes the tracheotomy forms part of another surgical procedure. For instance, a tumor of the larynx (voicebox) may sometimes necessitate the removal of the larynx. After this procedure the patient will have a permanent tracheostomy.

A tracheotomy may be performed when a patient has to be attached to a respirator for a long period of time. This will usually be performed as a planned procedure and is most commonly done because the person has lost the ability to breathe naturally, for example, as a result of paralysis caused by disease or following an accident. A patient who has lost the ability to keep saliva and other secretions out of the trachea because of coma or a specific swallowing problem may also require a tracheotomy.

For short periods, a tube can be passed through the mouth or nose into the trachea, but if these tubes are left in place for more than about 7–10 days, the lining of the trachea may be damaged. This could lead later on to narrowing of the trachea. Another advantage of performing a tracheotomy in this situation is that the dead space—the space that is taken up by the air in the mouth and the air passages—is greatly diminished, making breathing more efficient. Also sucking out unwanted secretions from the chest in a patient who cannot cough is much easier when the suction tube can be passed through the tracheostomy and straight down into the lungs.

How it is done

A tracheotomy may be performed under local or general anesthesia. The surgeon first makes an incision in the patient's skin overlying the trachea, in the midline halfway between the Adam's apple and the top end of the sternum (breastbone). The tissues under the skin are divided, and the trachea is exposed. Quite often there is a band of tissue across the front of the trachea. This is part of the thyroid gland (see Thyroid), and it has to be divided between ligatures or it will bleed profusely. A small vertical incision is then made in the trachea itself and a metal or plastic tube is inserted. If the patient cannot breathe unaided, the tube is connected to a respirator.

After surgery, the hole between the trachea and the skin of the neck, which is called the tracheostomy, has to be kept open using one of these special tubes. If the tube were not left in the trachea, the hole would gradually close; in fact, if a tracheostomy is only to be temporary then it will eventually be allowed to close when it is no longer needed by simply taking out the tube and waiting for the hole to close on its own.

A week or so after the tracheotomy has been performed the tube will be taken out for a few minutes, and then it will be reinserted. Later, when the tissues have formed a definite track, the patient can change his or her own tube.

Problems with tracheostomies

There are a number of complications associated with tracheostomies, such as blockage of the tube, hemorrhage from veins around the trachea, and narrowing of the trachea. However, the main problem from the patient's point of view is that he or she cannot speak. The air is diverted away from the larynx, and so cannot make the vocal cords sound (see Speech, and Vocal cords). This can sometimes be overcome later on by the insertion of a special tracheostomy tube that has a valve in it to allow air to pass out of the lungs up into the larynx, provided that the patient covers up the outlet with his or her finger.

A tracheotomy is rarely used in emergency situations where, for example, a person is choking. Apart from the obvious disadvantages of doing anything that would take time, in the heat of the moment it would be very difficult to assess the whereabouts of the obstruction. Obviously if the trachea were obstructed anywhere below the point where a tracheotomy is usually performed, then there would be no point in doing one. The obstruction has to be sited either at the back of the mouth or throat, or in the larynx, for a tracheotomy to be effective.

If someone is choking on, say, a piece of meat during a meal, immediately try to remove the foreign body that is causing the obstruction. This might be possible by passing a finger into the mouth and trying to hook the object out, or by performing the Heimlich maneuver.

Cricothyroidotomy

In an emergency, an operation called a cricothyroidotomy may be performed. This consists of cutting a hole in the lower part of the larynx, just where it joins the trachea between the thyroid and cricoid cartilages. The advantage of a cricothyroidotomy over a tracheotomy is that this part of the windpipe is nearer to the surface of the skin, and so the surgery can be performed much more quickly. The disadvantage is that it may cause permanent weakness of the voice, and possibly also permanent narrowing of the air passages.

Creating a tracheostomy

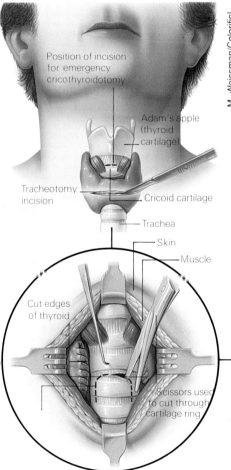

M. Weissman/Colorific!

Position of incision for emergency cricothyroidotomy

Adam's apple (thyroid cartilage)

Tracheotomy incision

Cricoid cartilage

Trachea

Skin

Muscle

Cut edges of thyroid

Scissors used to cut through cartilage ring

After the incision has been made in the trachea, just below the Adam's apple, a special tube may be inserted into the tracheostomy to facilitate breathing.

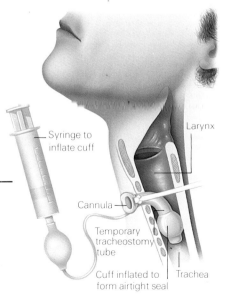

Syringe to inflate cuff

Larynx

Cannula

Temporary tracheostomy tube

Cuff inflated to form airtight seal

Trachea

Traction

Q How long is traction likely to last before taking effect?

A This, of course, depends on the condition it is being used to treat. In the case of a fractured thighbone (femur), it would have to be maintained until the bone was strong enough for normal movement and weight bearing. This could be anything up to three to four months. If the traction were removed too soon, the bone might refracture or slowly bend through the healing fracture to cause a deformity. The amount of time could, however, be reduced by combining traction with other forms of treatment. Where traction is used to treat a dislocated hip, the joint would need to be rested for several weeks to prevent further damage. And where it is being used to relieve back and neck pain, the traction can be applied either for short periods once or twice a day, or for continuous periods of one to two weeks.

Q Is traction more effective in children since their bones are still growing?

A Traction itself does not cause a bone to grow faster. For example, you couldn't make a short leg longer in a child simply by applying traction to it for a long time. But traction is often used in children, for fractures of the thighbone or femur, as a safe and effective way of getting the fracture to heal in a good position.

Q Can you have a course of traction as an outpatient as you can with other kinds of treatment?

A Yes. This is called intermittent traction. It is used for many types of back pain, such as a slipped disk. This is usually done in the physical therapy department and is combined with other forms of treatment such as heat and exercise. Traction relieves painful muscle spasm by pulling gently in the opposite direction. Sometimes it also pulls the vertebrae slightly, enabling the slipped disk to move away from the crushed nerve, again lessening the pain.

Widely used for fractures, dislocations, and painful conditions of the skeleton, traction has long been, and will continue to be, a valuable form of treatment.

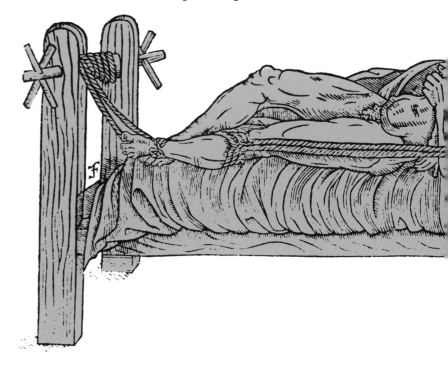

Ann Ronan Picture Library

Although traction may appear to be a crude and rather old-fashioned form of treatment, it is as yet unsurpassed in dealing with many skeletal problems, including fractures and dislocations.

Uses of traction
The most common use of traction is in dealing with types of fracture. The purpose is to stop the fracture from moving, and thereby causing pain, and to pull the bone along its length to prevent it from shortening (see Fractures).

The fractures most often treated in this way are those of the thighbone or femur. Such fractures are unsuitable for treating in plaster, since to immobilize the femur it would be necessary to apply a bulky and uncomfortable cast, including part of the body and the whole leg. Traction may also be used in fractures of the shinbone (tibia), the pelvis, spine, and elbow.

Certain dislocations, particularly those of the hip, may also be treated with traction. This is the safest way of resting the stretched and torn tissues, and of preventing further damage (see Dislocation). Traction may also be used to relieve painful conditions of the back and the neck, such as the extremely common slipped disk, and to overcome joint deformities (see Slipped disk).

How traction works
When a bone or joint becomes painful, through injury or disease, the surrounding muscles contract in an effort to stabilize and protect the painful part. This prolonged contraction is called muscle spasm, and it is a reflex action that the individual cannot control (see Bones, and Reflexes). This may be painful in itself, and may actually be more painful than the underlying condition. Since all the muscles in the body are not equally powerful, the pull of the contracting muscles may cause a deformity in the limb (see Muscles).

The main function of traction is to overcome this painful muscle spasm by pulling steadily and firmly in the opposite direction from the contracting muscles. At the same time the deformity is improved or eliminated. In the case of a fracture, the bones are not actually pulled apart since the intact muscles, ligaments, and tendons prevent overstretching.

The technique
In order to apply a firm and steady pull along the length of a limb some form of weight is needed, and also some means of attaching it to the patient. This can be done either by attaching the weight directly to the skeleton—skeletal trac-

looks very complicated, but there is usually only one cord and weight that is actually performing the traction. Once the apparatus is established, the pull of the weights tends to draw the patient toward the end of the bed, a problem that can be overcome by elevating the foot of the bed slightly.

Another traction method is to use the patient's own weight, which is often done with children up to age two who have fractures of the femur. Both legs have skin traction bandages applied and they are tied to a beam directly overhead, with the buttocks suspended just off the bed. Thus the child's own weight provides the traction force.

Spinal problems require slightly different techniques. Simple spinal traction may be applied by means of a girdle that is placed around the pelvis or, where the neck is involved, by a halter that fits closely around the chin and the back of the neck.

For those spinal injuries where a stronger and more prolonged pull is needed, skeletal traction may be applied by means of skull tongs. The sharp ends of the tongs are actually embedded in the outer bone of the skull just above the ears, and strong traction can then be applied to the neck (see Spinal cord).

How long does it last?

Traction may be the only form of treatment used in a fracture, in which case it must be maintained until the bone is strong enough for ordinary walking, sitting, and turning. In the case of a fractured femur this may be up to three or four months.

Time spent in traction can be reduced by combining it with other forms of treatment. A fractured femur may be in traction until it is more stable, and then a type of walking cast can be applied to the limb so that the patient can start to walk with the help of crutches. Other fractures are treated with only a week or two in traction to allow the early acute swelling and any skin injuries to settle. A cast is then applied or surgery performed.

A patient with a slipped disk may have one or two weeks of continuous traction, or the traction may be applied for 30 minutes to an hour each day in conjunction with physical therapy (see Physical therapy). This can, of course, be done as an outpatient for several weeks if necessary.

Advantages and disadvantages

Traction has been used in roughly its present form since the early 19th century, so it is a tried and tested method. One great advantage is that because no exter-

Traction has been in use for centuries, so it has undeniably stood the test of time. The complicated modern apparatus (right) belies the simplicity of the principle—only one cord and weight actually perform the traction on the limb.

tion—or indirectly by sticking it to the skin (see Skeleton). Skeletal traction is applied by putting a metal pin through the appropriate bone and then attaching the necessary weights to the pin.

Skin traction is applied by means of adhesive tape that is applied to a large area of skin on the limb. The traction force is indirectly applied to the bone or joint, just as pulling on your finger pulls on the underlying bone. The disadvantage of this method is that if too much weight is applied, the adhesive tape slides or pulls off—so it cannot be used when more than about 8 lb (3.6 kg) of traction is needed.

The weights are attached to the traction pin, or tape, by cords that run over pulleys at the foot of the bed. With fractures, the limb is often rested on a splint to give further support and comfort, and other weights and pulleys may be used to suspend the splint.

The pulleys are in turn hung from a metal frame above the bed called a Balkan beam. This is why traction often

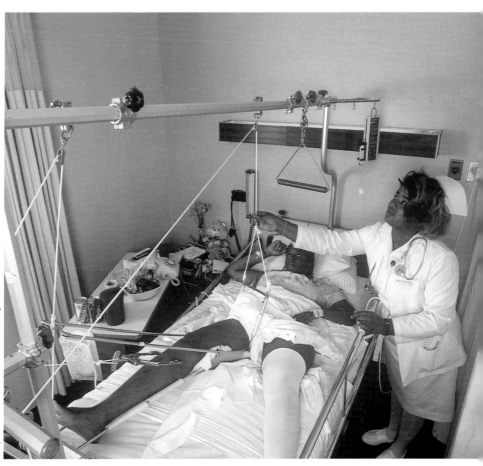

Larry Mulvehill/Science Photo Library

Q Do you always need physical therapy after traction?

A No, this depends entirely on the condition for which traction is being applied. It is often used for major fractures and dislocations, and when it is stopped, physical therapy may be needed to help strengthen muscles and to get stiff joints moving. But where there are no such problems, the patient could simply exercise by returning to normal activities.

Q Do hospitals have special floors for people in traction?

A Patients in traction need a lot of nursing care. The traction apparatus must be watched and adjusted frequently, areas of pressure must be relieved, and the patients' ordinary needs tended. This is done by a team of nurses, doctors, orthopedic technicians, and physical therapists. Larger hospitals often have an orthopedic floor where patients in traction are cared for, but this can also be done on general floors.

Q Why doesn't putting traction on a broken leg simply pull the fracture apart?

A In a fracture the bone is broken but the other tissues are largely intact. The pull of the traction is enough to keep the fractured bones at the right length for healing, and this is checked by taking X rays. It is surprisingly difficult to pull the fractured ends apart too much because of the strength of the soft tissues—the muscles, ligaments, and tendons.

Q Is it possible to move about while in traction?

A Yes, quite a lot of movement is possible in most forms of traction. The weights are suspended by pulleys that are arranged so that, whether the patient is sitting or lying, the direction of the pull is the same. Also the limb joints can be moved without disturbing the pull of the traction, and it is an important advantage of traction that the joints and muscles can be exercised while a fracture is healing.

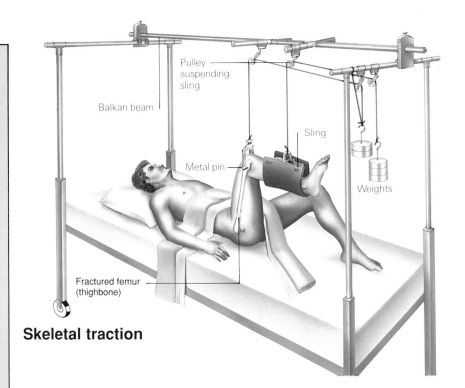

Balkan beam
Pulley suspending sling
Sling
Metal pin
Weights
Fractured femur (thighbone)

Skeletal traction

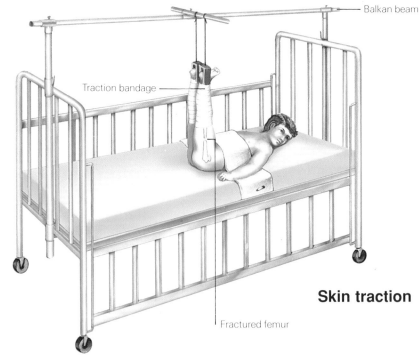

Balkan beam
Traction bandage
Fractured femur

Skin traction

Aziz Khan

nal splinting or bandaging is essential, an injured limb can be watched carefully for any sign of complications. Also because the joints are left free, early movement after an injury is possible, preventing stiffness and maintaining muscle strength. In very severe injuries of the bone itself, the length and general alignment of the limb can be maintained while the patient is awaiting any further treatment.

There are, of course, disadvantages too. Perhaps surprisingly, the traction pins give very little trouble, and most patients are comfortable once they have settled into the traction apparatus. However, lying in bed for a long period can create complications. A young patient can withstand weeks in bed without any serious problems arising, other than boredom. But the physical effects of prolonged rest in bed are more severe in the elderly. These effects include pressure sores, muscle weakening, softening of the bones, pneumonia, urinary infections, and thrombosis. These risks have led surgeons to treat fractures in the elderly by other means—such as by surgery—so that the person can get up and walk as soon as possible.

Tranquilizers

Q My doctor just prescribed tranquilizers for me. Can I become addicted to them?

A It is possible to become addicted to tranquilizers, but serious addiction is rare. Real drug addicts do not usually turn to tranquilizers when they run short of their own particular addiction. However, there is a degree of dependence in people who are taking them regularly, so that when they stop they may experience disturbed sleep or nightmares. If the dose is reduced gradually no withdrawal symptoms should occur.

Q My mother used to say that a cup of tea was the best tranquilizer when a person felt tense. Was she right?

A Strangely enough, the chemicals in tea make it a stimulant rather than a tranquilizer. But having something to drink can certainly provide a calming effect. So a cup of tea can help anyone who feels tense and anxious.

Q Is it possible to overdose on tranquilizers?

A Yes it is. Fortunately, however, tranquilizers are among the safer medicines. Taking too many in a single dose might make someone sleep deeply and wake with a hangover, but the result should not be more serious than that. Nevertheless anyone who has taken an overdose should be taken to the hospital.

Q Isn't it better to talk to people who are anxious rather than give them tranquilizers?

A It certainly is. Tranquilizers are the medical means of helping people cope with stress, and they act by reducing anxiety. But by talking about their problems, people can come to terms with their anxieties better than with any medicines. Doctors rarely have the time to help people in this way, and so may be forced to prescribe tranquilizers. A heart-to-heart talk with a sympathetic friend often helps to put our difficulties in perspective.

Although most of us seek peace and tranquillity, we often experience feelings of tension and anxiety for a variety of reasons. Tranquilizers are sometimes prescribed to restore calmness and to help us to cope.

We can all cope with some stress in our lives, and some people even thrive on it. However, there are times when we feel particularly anxious for a definite reason, and times when it's for no clear reason at all. Medical science has developed a variety of drugs to treat stress and anxiety; their general name is tranquilizers, but some of these drugs are called sedatives (see Stress, and Stress management).

Major tranquilizers

Many different types of drugs are used as tranquilizers and their actions and uses are also different. The main division is into major and minor tranquilizers. The major tranquilizers are used for the treatment of psychotic states, where the working of the mind is disturbed. They

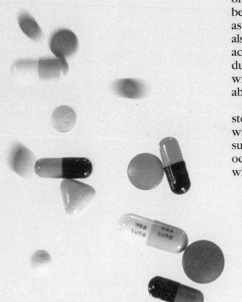

One of these highly effective tranquilizers can relieve anything from psychoses to insomnia and stress.

are of help in treating some of the major mental disorders such as schizophrenia, hallucinations, and mania (hence their name), as well as a number of other conditions including anxiety. Among the best known major tranquilizers are chlorpromazine (Largactil), and trifluoperazine (Stelazine). Most are taken by mouth, but some can be given by depot

injections. This is the term for an injection of a chemical that is actually stored in the body and remains effective for weeks (see Injections).

An important advantage of the major tranquilizers is that they do not produce dependence. Their principal side effect is muscle stiffness and shakiness, but this stops when the drug is discontinued. Muscle stiffness can also affect the face and mouth, or the eye muscles, which can be distressing if the patient does not know the cause. Often another drug is prescribed to control these unwanted effects (see Side effects).

Minor tranquilizers

The minor tranquilizers have a depressant effect on the brain and slow down its working. There are two principal types of drug in this group: the barbiturates and benzodiazepines. The barbiturates are used as antianxiety drugs, as sleeping pills, and also to control epilepsy. In small doses they act as tranquilizers, and a larger dose produces sleep. One unfortunate problem with the barbiturates is addiction or abuse (see Drug abuse).

If a person who takes them regularly stops suddenly they can produce some withdrawal symptoms; severe symptoms such as hallucinations or convulsions can occur. They can also depress respiration when taken in overdose, and overdosage

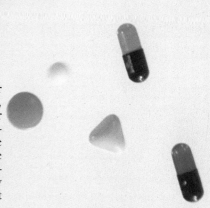

TRANQUILIZERS

Nicola Sutton

with barbiturates is frequently fatal, especially if alcohol has also been taken (see Overdose). For these reasons, barbiturate drugs are being prescribed less and less frequently, and members of this group, such as phenobarbital, amobarbital (Amytal), and butobarbitone (Soneryl) are rarely used.

The other group of drugs is the benzodiazepines. This is the family name for such well-known drugs as diazepam (Valium), nitrazepam (Mogadon), and chlordiazepoxide (Librium). These are the drugs that most people refer to when tranquilizers are mentioned. They have been in use for about 20 years, and are the most widely used drugs in the world.

They are generally given in relatively small doses during the day, and have a sedative or calming effect on the mind. This is the main reason why they are effective at relieving anxiety and tension. If the dose is too high, they will cause drowsiness or sleepiness. But this is part of their sedative effect, and if they are given in sufficiently high doses they produce sleep. Their main uses are as anti-anxiety drugs, and as sleeping pills, but their record for safety is remarkable. Taken in overdose, they can produce profound sleep or coma, but fatal overdoses are rare. Addiction is known but is uncommon. Someone taking them regularly who then suddenly stops may have a few nights of disturbed sleep or nightmares, but serious withdrawal symptoms are actually rare (see Withdrawal symptoms).

Tranquilizers should only be used as a short-term remedy. When someone is troubled by real anxiety or stress, then a course of tranquilizers for a week or two may be very helpful indeed. Similarly, if a person is unable to sleep these drugs may help to reestablish a normal sleep pattern. However, it is being increasingly recognized that these drugs are of very little use when given for long periods, since their effectiveness rapidly falls off.

Beta-blocking drugs

When a person is really anxious several things happen in the body as a result of overactivity of the sympathetic nervous system (see Autonomic nervous system). The muscles are tense and may even tremble. The heart beats rapidly, the hands become sweaty, the mouth becomes dry, and there is a feeling of butterflies in the stomach. All these feelings can develop from an acute stress, such as speaking or playing a musical instrument in front of a large audience, or taking examinations. If the stress is prolonged, the symptoms may sometimes be equally as prolonged. A person with a highly anxious personality can even focus on the very symptoms that are actually produced by anxiety, such as worrying about sweaty hands (see Anxiety, Stress, and Tension).

When stress occurs it is tempting to take a pill to control it, but getting away from it all may bring the relief we need.

Beta-blockers are a group of drugs that block these actions of the sympathetic nervous system, and are widely used in treating high blood pressure and heart disorders. However, they can also help someone faced with an acutely stressful situation, such as performing in public, to do the job without the distraction of the symptoms from his or her own body.

They can also sometimes help to break up the symptoms of chronic anxiety, but they do not possess the calming effect that tranquilizers have on the mind. Doctors quite often prescribe low doses of beta-blocking drugs for people who are troubled by anxiety symptoms or who go to pieces under stress.

Alternatives to tranquilizers

For any sudden or severe mental stress, many people recommend a cup of tea or coffee, a cigarette, or an alcoholic drink. There is nothing in the chemical composition of cigarettes or hot drinks to relieve tension or anxiety, but having someone look after you and having something to do with your hands can be reassuring. Alcohol, on the other hand, has a definite sedative effect, and may be useful in a stressful situation, but it should not be relied on regularly as a tranquilizer. People who use alcohol in this way should seek medical advice before the situation gets out of hand (see Alcoholism).

Alternatives to tranquilizers vary from herbal remedies, to jogging, and yoga. But perhaps the most important antidote is to see problems in perspective and look for solutions rather than difficulties. Keeping lines of communication open is also important, and a frank discussion may relieve tension. But if we change our way of life and our attitude, most of us should be able to cope with stress as it comes, and very rarely require drugs to control anxiety.

Prozac: the happiness drug?

Fluoxetine is the generic name for a drug that, in recent years, has aroused more public interest than almost any other. Sometimes known as the "happiness pill," this drug —best known under the name Prozac—has now been prescribed to over 11 million people in America and Europe. Many claim that it is capable of entirely altering a patient's mood and outlook, from pessimism to optimism, removing sensitivity to criticism, and totally altering his or her state of mind for the better.

Prozac is one of a group of new drugs called the serotonin re-uptake inhibitors. Serotonin, or 5-HT, is a natural chemical substance that stimulates nerves and hence brain activity, and low amounts of it are thought to cause depression. Normally serotonin is pulled back into the nerve ending that releases it, but Prozac and its sister drugs prevent this, so that serotonin is able to act for a longer period, causing greater nerve stimulation.

The drug is highly effective as a mood enhancer, and has comparatively minor obvious side effects. It does not, for example, effect noradrenaline levels and does not cause drowsiness—a criticism often aimed at other antidepressant drugs. Moreover, because it remains in the body a long time, only one capsule needs to be taken daily (usually in the morning). It can, however, cause loss of both appetite and weight, nausea, insomnia, tremors, diarrhea, and sexual dysfunction. Perhaps a more subtle effect is that people who use it need no longer make the effort to organize their lives in such a way as to bring contentment and satisfaction. A report in 1990 suggested that Prozac had caused suicidal thoughts in six patients and some deaths.

Prozac is no more effective in controlling depression than established drugs, and its popularity seems to be due to its mood-enhancing effect. Although most doctors will prescribe Prozac only to patients who are genuinely ill, there is a small but vocal school of thought that believes that the drug is justified for anyone who thinks that life is not as pleasant as it ought to be. One practitioner was said, at one stage, to have prescribed Prozac or other re-uptake inhibitors to every one of his patients. Perhaps significantly, this practitioner has been investigated by the State Board of Psychology. There are some firm guidelines when using the drug, however. Anyone considering using the drug should tell their doctor about any liver, kidney, or heart problems that they may have. The safety of using the drug during pregnancy or breast-feeding is not entirely established, so be sure to discuss these issues with your doctor. People over the age of 60 are more likely to suffer from adverse side effects, and it it likely, therefore, that a doctor will prescribe a reduced dose.

Avoid drinking alcohol, as this can greatly increase the sedative effects of the drug, and don't drive or engage in hazardous work until you are sure of how drowsy the drug is going to make you feel.

Transplants

Q Can someone who has had a heart transplant be given another one if this fails or is rejected?

A This has been attempted, but there are many problems involved. The rejection of a transplanted heart is often sudden and a further donor heart has to be available at very short notice, which is usually not the case. In addition, a second operation is much more difficult because there is always the problem that rejection can occur more quickly with the second operation. In the case of kidney replacements, however, repeated transplantation happens fairly often, since the patient can be maintained on a kidney machine until an organ becomes available.

Q My father, who is past retirement age, has bad heart trouble and his medication doesn't seem to be working well anymore. Would he be considered as a suitable candidate for a heart transplant?

A Very few people are suitable for heart transplantation. The reason for this is that after a long period of heart disease, the lungs and other organs suffer damage and this means that even replacing the heart will not be enough to cure the problem. In general, heart transplants are performed on those whose heart failure is fairly recent but so severe that it is clear that survival is not otherwise possible.

Q Is it possible to perform a brain transplant, and has this ever been tried?

A To transplant the brain really means to perform a body transplant, since it is the brain more than anything else that makes each of us an individual. Technically this is not feasible now, nor is it likely to be, since all the nerves would cease functioning irreversibly once they have been cut. In addition, the whole spinal cord would have to be transplanted as well, making this an inconceivable technical feat.

Not so long ago the idea of successfully transplanting an organ would have been considered pure science fiction. Yet today the number of people who have literally been given a new lease on life is rapidly increasing.

The idea of replacing diseased parts of the body with spares is quite old, but it has only become a reality recently. There are considerable problems that must be overcome before transplants can be done, including locating suitable replacements and resolving important ethical questions that might arise. Yet the field of transplant surgery is expanding, since it offers the hope of treating illnesses that must otherwise be disabling or fatal.

Important and valuable work also takes place in the transplanting of other body tissues. Corneal grafting (see Cornea), and bone marrow transplants (see Marrow and transplants) can be counted among some of the most successful procedures in this field of medicine.

Before any transplant surgery can be performed, vital matching of both blood group and tissue type is carried out. Tissue types are found by testing white blood cells.

In theory any organ of the body except the brain can be transplanted in surgery. However, a consistent level of success has only been achieved recently in those operations involving the kidneys and the heart. Some liver transplants have been successful for variable lengths of time, but the operation is still performed only rarely. Apart from these, and transplants of the lungs and the pancreas, which in general have not been successful, no other organs of the body have been successfully transplanted.

This young bone marrow donor, aged three, saved the life of her older sister. For both kidney or bone marrow transplants, the best donor matches are often close relatives.

Physical and ethical problems

Finding donor organs to transplant is one of the most difficult of the immediate problems that the surgeon has to face.

The organ should come from a person who was fit and preferably young at the time of death. The tragedy of modern living is that the most likely way for this to occur is through a traffic accident.

Great care must be taken to insure that the organs are removed only after death has occurred. But at the same time the organ to be used in a transplant will deteriorate quite quickly if it is no longer supplied with blood after death. Therefore it must be removed as soon as possible. It is this dilemma that has provoked most controversy in recent years because it was rapidly discovered that the exact point of death was more difficult to define than to recognize.

The solution to this problem centered on whether the brain was alive in the sense of being capable of recovering independent life support. After careful study of the survival of many victims of brain damage there have now emerged clearcut ways in which doctors can determine the point at which brain death has occurred (see Brain).

Once brain death has been confirmed, the organ for transplant can be removed immediately after the respirator has been switched off. This may sound macabre, but the reality is no more unpleasant than the death of a victim in other circumstances.

Annie Belt/Corbis

There is a crucial shortage of available organs, particularly where kidney transplants are concerned. This is because of the difficulty of coordinating the teams of surgeons doing the transplant, and the doctors caring for the trauma victim.

When an organ has been taken from a dead donor it must be preserved until it can be placed in the recipient. The organ must be placed on ice and special fluid pumped through its blood vessel system to keep the system open and free of blood clots. The technology required during this crucial period is being constantly updated and in the case of kidneys is now quite

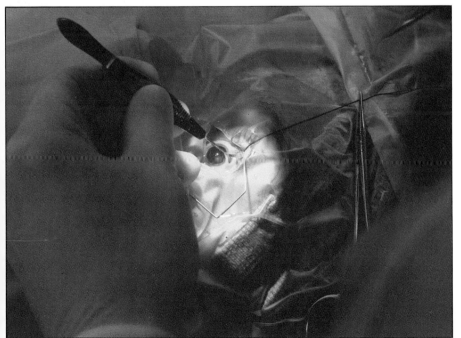

advanced. The kidney is simply flushed through to remove the blood. It is then put into a polyethylene bag that is surrounded by ice. It can be kept in this state for up to 36 hours before being used.

Living donor transplants

Transplants from living donors are common in kidney transplantation, since a normal person can easily survive in good health with only one kidney.

If a relative is prepared to give one of his or her kidneys, this is often the best match since it lessens the risk of rejection. A close relative such as a brother, sister, or parent will share many genetic characteristics of the recipient; there is thus a chance that his or her immune system will not recognize the graft as foreign and reject it. In addition the kidney for transplantation can be removed calmly without the urgency that is called for in a recently dead donor, allowing more time to plan the operation (see Donors).

Rejection of the transplant

Rejection is the main problem of transplant surgery, and directly or indirectly leads to most of the failures that occur. The body has a powerful defense system designed to repel the invasion of its domains by bacteria and viruses. The invaders are recognized because their chemicals are subtly different from those of our body. Unfortunately when a transplanted organ comes into contact with

In a corneal graft, the diseased area or scar tissue is removed and replaced by a similar sized disk from the donor eye. The graft is then sewn into place.

Q Over the past few years there has been a lot of publicity concerning transplants, particularly heart transplants, but not many such operations have actually been performed. Will transplants become more frequent in the future?

A Transplants will certainly become more common as problems such as rejection and organ preservation while awaiting transplantation are overcome. However, they are probably only a stopgap in the history of spare part surgery, since it is possible that in the future synthetic organs will be designed. These do not carry the problems of finding donors and the rather unpleasant image that is associated with this necessity.

Q If I want to donate my body to medical research, can my relatives refuse to give their permission after my death?

A No. If a person has expressed a positive wish to donate his or her organs in a will, by carrying a donor card, or by stating the intention in the presence of two witnesses during the last illness, then the relatives have no legal right to be consulted after the death. However, when death takes place in the hospital and the medical examiner wants to perform an autopsy, no part of the body can be removed without the medical examiner's permission.

Q I have heard that some people have had pancreas transplants to treat their diabetes. Is this true, and is the operation usually a success?

A Pancreas transplants have mainly been attempted in patients who have kidney failure due to diabetes. Since the pancreas lies against one of the kidneys it is technically possible to transplant the two simultaneously. But this operation has not been attempted very often. This is because patients who would benefit are usually seriously ill and, in addition, severe problems have been encountered with rejection of the transplanted organ.

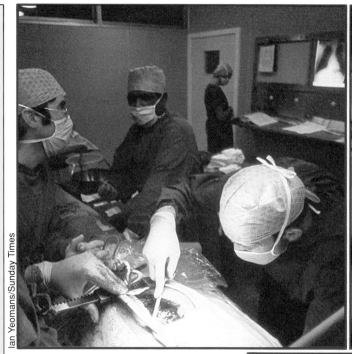

Ian Yeomans/Sunday Times

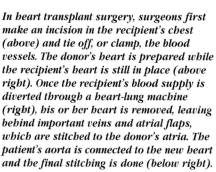

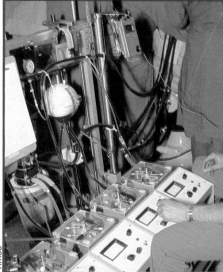

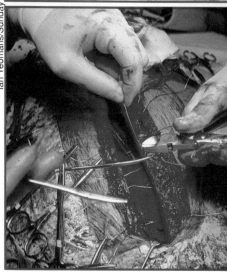

Ian Yeomans/Sunday Times

In heart transplant surgery, surgeons first make an incision in the recipient's chest (above) and tie off, or clamp, the blood vessels. The donor's heart is prepared while the recipient's heart is still in place (above right). Once the recipient's blood supply is diverted through a heart-lung machine (right), his or her heart is removed, leaving behind important veins and atrial flaps, which are stitched to the donor's atria. The patient's aorta is connected to the new heart and the final stitching is done (below right).

the body cells that act as soldiers in this defense force (see Immune system), the transplant's chemical makeup is recognized as foreign and a reaction is mounted against it as though it were a host of bacteria (see Bacteria).

For this reason attempts are made before transplant surgery to try and match the type of tissue of the donor organ and the recipient. This is similar to blood grouping, since everyone has a tissue type as well as a blood group. Tissue types are discovered by testing the white blood cells; blood groups reflect the chemical makeup of the more numerous red blood cells (see Blood, and Blood groups).

Apart from trying to match the blood group and tissue type of the donor organ with that of the patient receiving it, there are various things that can be done to stop rejection. For example, it has been discovered that the more transfusions a patient has prior to surgery, the less likely he or she is to reject the transplant (see Blood transfusion).

This preventive effect is due to the body's immune system being confronted

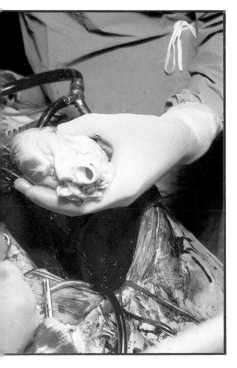

many times with foreign tissues of donated blood. It seems to become more tolerant of other invasions and less likely to reject a transplanted organ.

More deliberate prevention takes the form of using powerful drugs to control the immune system so it cannot mount its attack on the new organ. This is obviously a double-edged weapon, since the body needs some immunity to fight against infecting bacteria, viruses, or fungi. Therefore transplant patients on these drugs need to be very carefully watched for signs of infection, particularly those of an unusual type (see Infection and infectious diseases).

Other complications

Apart from the complications of the drugs used in preventing rejection, other things can go wrong. These include surgical problems related to the very considerable task of sewing the organ in place.

The blood vessels into the transplant must be carefully joined to prevent bleeding once the circulation is reestablished. Similarly, in the case of the kidney, the tubes carrying urine from the transplant must be delicately sewn into the recipient's bladder; in a liver transplant bile ducts must be implanted into the intestine.

The surgery

Usually, with kidneys or liver, the whole of the organ is transplanted into the patient's body, although segmental liver grafts can be performed from a live donor. The liver is placed similarly to its normal position, though the arteries used to supply it with blood are changed by grafting them to nearby intestinal arteries.

It is difficult to insert a new kidney in the position of the diseased one, which is usually left where it is. The new kidney is placed in the pelvis, which is conveniently spacious; this allows the new kidney's blood vessels to be joined to the large vessels to and from the legs. Also in this position the joining of its urine tube, or ureter, to the bladder of the recipient is made far easier (see Kidney transplants).

When a heart is transplanted it cannot be put in whole while the diseased heart is removed. To do this would mean that the new heart would be under the control of nerves that change its rate of pumping according to demand. In the early days of heart transplants (and still occasionally) the heart from a donor was put in the recipient in series, with his or her own heart as a backup unit. However, today almost all of the recipient's heart is removed (see Heart transplants).

Postoperative care

After surgery a patient can be vulnerable to infection, but the recipient of a transplant is at special risk. Measures are taken to shield the patient from germs, sometimes by isolating them in special rooms and/or requiring people attending them and visiting them to wear special clothing and masks.

Acute rejection is a special risk a few days after the operation, and even after this there may be a risk of chronic rejection, which is slower in causing the loss of the organ but equally dangerous. Once the drugs suppressing the rejection process have a chance to work, the person may be gradually rehabilitated to a fairly normal life. Indeed, in the case of many kidney transplants, the recipients are able to return to work, and many women who have had a kidney transplant have given birth to healthy children.

These seven men have all had successful heart transplants—a complex but ever more increasingly common operation.

Travel and health

Q I am going on vacation to Europe. Should I be worried about catching rabies?

A Although still rare, rabies is unfortunately on the increase in Europe, so you need to keep away from strays and wild animals. Rabies can be transmitted by a scratch, bite, or even a lick from an infected animal. If you are bitten, wash the wound immediately with soap and clean water and, if you can, apply alcohol. Then go to the nearest hospital or doctor as quickly as possible so that you can be given a rabies vaccination if it is considered necessary.

Q The last time I went on vacation I suffered from heat exhaustion. What causes this, and how can I avoid it?

A Heat exhaustion is a form of fatigue that can culminate in collapse. It is commonly caused by rushing about in hot weather. Try to keep out of the midday sun, drink plenty of water, and take salt tablets to replace the salt you lose when you sweat. If you ignore heat exhaustion, it may lead to heatstroke, which is a serious and potentially fatal condition.

Q I have an allergy to a particular antibiotic. How can I make sure I am not given this if I am taken seriously ill while on vacation?

A If you have an allergy or a reaction to a certain medicine you should wear a medical alert bracelet. In the event of illness or an accident where you become unconscious, this will warn anyone treating you about your allergy.

Q If I need an injection while I am abroad, how will I know whether the needle is sterile?

A In some poorer countries sterile needles are a rarity, so the best way to insure that any needle used on you is sterile is to take an emergency pack with you. These contain syringes, needles, drip needles, dressings, swabs, and suture materials. Some include a dental pack that allows you to replace crowns and fillings.

Traveling at home or abroad presents all kinds of health risks, from motion sickness to malaria. There are a number of simple measures you can take to insure that your trip is not ruined by an avoidable health problem.

Travel can all too often be ruined by people failing to take the necessary health precautions before and during the trip. Whether traveling at home or abroad, there are some basic guidelines to follow that will reduce the risk of illness and lessen the strain of long journeys.

It is a good idea to find out as much as you can about the country or place you are visiting before you go. The best sources of information are the travel agent, the embassy or tourist office, or the airline if you are flying. The Department of State publishes useful "Background Notes" on around 170 countries worldwide. These are brief factual pamphlets giving information on each country.

Packing for comfort
Once you have decided on your destination you should find out about the weather conditions you are likely to experience while you are there so that you can pack appropriate clothing. For example, if the weather is likely to be hot, then it is sensible to avoid wearing

If you are traveling overseas and need to have a course of vaccinations, you should arrange for them well in advance.

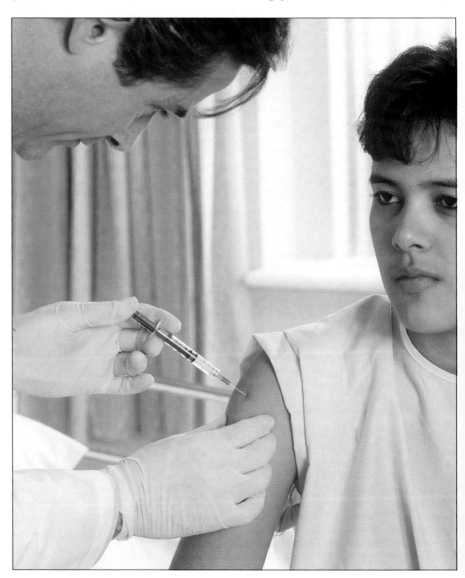

Zefa

clothes that are made of nonabsorbent materials, such as nylon or polyester, next to the skin. These synthetic materials do not soak up perspiration and will leave the skin feeling cold and clammy, which may lead to prickly heat and, in the case of footwear, athlete's foot. Natural fibers (such as cotton) are absorbent and therefore more comfortable and less likely to cause skin problems (see Athlete's foot). If you are traveling overseas to a hot climate, choose lightweight clothes in light colors that will reflect the heat, rather than clothing in dark colors that will absorb it and retain the heat.

If you are going to a very cold climate you will need to wear clothes that will prevent frostbite. These should include warm outdoor clothes, gloves, thick socks, and a hat that covers both your head and your ears (see Frostbite).

Wherever you are going it is important to wear loose, comfortable clothes for the journey so that there is nothing to impede the blood flow or the circulation of air around the body. Your feet may swell if you have to sit for a long period on an airplane, bus, automobile, or train, so it is best to travel in comfortable shoes.

Although most forms of transport are air-conditioned and comfortable, there may be a risk of dehydration, especially on long flights, so avoid consuming alcohol, and drink plenty of mineral water or soft drinks while traveling.

Motion sickness

You are unlikely to be airsick, but for some people long automobile, bus, or train journeys can lead to motion sickness. If you do suffer from motion sickness, try sitting in the front of the vehicle and keep your eyes on the route ahead. Avoid eating fatty foods or having a large meal before traveling, since these sit heavily in the stomach. Eat crystallized ginger or take ginger capsules before setting off, and suck candy or cough drops during the journey. Acupressure on the forearm, two thumb-widths above the center of the wrist, can help reduce symptoms.

If you are traveling by ship, stay on deck, especially if the sea is rough. It will help if you can keep your eyes on the horizon. A doctor will be able to recommend seasickness drugs, but these often cause drowsiness so they should be avoided if you plan to drive once you disembark. Acupressure may help to relieve nausea (see Motion sickness).

Vaccinations

Vaccinations need to be considered well in advance of any overseas travel because

Most people take out insurance to cover the theft of personal possessions while overseas, but you should also remember to take out good medical insurance.

some involve a course of treatment that has to be given at monthly intervals. Vaccinations for international travel can be grouped into three basic categories: those necessary for entry; those that all travelers have as a matter of course; and those for protection against specific diseases associated with the area you intend to visit. Under the International Health Regulations, cholera and yellow fever are the only two vaccinations that may be required on entry (see Vaccinations).

Since the current cholera vaccine is only about 50 percent effective, the World Health Organization (WHO) discourages countries from upholding policies that require cholera vaccination for entry. However, in some developing countries, especially in Africa, you may still need to show proof of cholera vaccination. This consists of a signed and validated International Certificate of Vaccination that is dated not less than six days, or more than six months, prior to your arrival in the country. This is because the vaccine's protection only lasts six months. It is sensible to have the vaccination if you are planning to make an extended visit to a high risk area where medical help may not be on hand, or if your doctor advises it for medical reasons.

Some countries will refuse you entry without an International Certificate of Vaccination for yellow fever. This is especially important if you are returning from a country that is currently infected, even if you haven't been to the actual area within the country that is affected. You may also be asked for proof of vaccination if you have visited any countries where yellow fever is known to be a problem. The vaccine needs to be given at least ten days, but not more than ten years, before traveling (see Yellow fever).

Depending on your destination and the nature and duration of your stay, your doctor may suggest that you have other vaccinations for diseases such as hepatitis A, Japanese encephalitis, meningococcal meningitis, typhoid, and rabies (see Infection and infectious diseases, Rabies, and Tropical diseases).

Malaria

In many parts of Africa, Asia, and Central and South America you can get malaria if you are bitten by an infected mosquito. You need to find out whether malaria is prevalent where you are going, and if it is you should arrange for a course of antimalarial pills.

There are different pills for different areas and to combat the many different strains of malaria. The pills need to be taken before you set off, while you are away, and for at least one month after your return. If you feel ill or just generally off-color during the immediate weeks after you have returned home, it is advisable to go to your doctor and have a medical checkup (see Malaria).

Sun sense

Although the temptation to lie in the sun may be strong, it is important to remember that ultraviolet (UV) exposure causes aging and wrinkles, and there is a possibility that overexposure can lead to skin cancer (see Skin and skin diseases). Try to avoid being out in the middle of the day when the sun's rays are at their strongest, and limit the time you do spend in the sun. Be especially careful at the start of your stay (see Sunstroke).

Protect yourself from the sun's rays by covering up and using a high factor sunscreen on any exposed skin, reapplying it frequently, especially after swimming. Cover your head with a sun hat and wear sunglasses to protect your eyes. Some drugs, including tetracyclines and tranquilizers, actually increase the skin's sensitivity to the sun, so check with your doctor if you are taking these. If you do

If you cannot resist the temptation to lie on the beach, make sure you wear plenty of sunscreen and limit your exposure time.

burn, soothe your skin with calamine lotion or calendula ointment and stay out of the sun until your skin is fully back to normal (see Sunburn).

Bites

Bites from insects, such as mosquitoes, can lead to severe itching, and because antimalarial pills are not 100 percent effective, in some countries there may also be a risk of catching malaria. Sleep under a mosquito net if possible, or protect yourself by using an insect repellent spray. Slow-burning antimosquito coils can be used at night. If you do get bitten, try not to scratch. Instead treat the bite with an antihistamine spray or cream or soothe with calamine lotion.

If you have contact with a sea urchin or jellyfish try ammonia (sold in stick form) to relieve the sting.

Diarrhea and dysentery

One of the most common illnesses experienced by travelers is diarrhea, with attacks lasting from one to three days. Dysentery, a cause of serious diarrhea, is often accompanied by vomiting, fever,

Zefa

First-aid checklist

The following items cover basic first-aid requirements if you are traveling abroad. You also need to include any regular medication you are taking.

- ● Motion sickness remedy
- ● Antidiarrhea pills
- ● Antiseptic cream
- ● Rehydration powders
- ● Salt pills
- ● Calamine lotion
- ● Insect repellent
- ● Antimalarial pills
- ● Sting relief or hydrocortisone preparation
- ● Indigestion pills
- ● Acetaminophen
- ● Water purifying tablets
- ● Scissors
- ● Band-Aids
- ● Cotton pads
- ● Bandages
- ● Contraceptives (if necessary)

diseases, including AIDS, and pregnancy (see AIDS, and Sexually transmitted diseases). You should use a condom even if you or your new partner is taking the Pill.

It is also important to remember that a prolonged bout of diarrhea or sickness can reduce the effectiveness of the contraceptive pill.

Medical insurance

The Social Security Medicare Program does not cover hospital or medical services outside the United States, so you need to take out separate medical insurance against sickness and accident if you are traveling overseas. You should always check what your coverage includes, especially for sporting activities, and read any small print before traveling.

There are a number of emergency medical assistance companies operating internationally that offer urgent medical treatment for their member travelers. Your travel agent will be able to supply you with the necessary information about these companies.

On your return

Sometimes illnesses take a few weeks to develop, so you may not become sick until after your return. If you do become sick in the first few weeks after you have arrived back from an overseas trip, be sure to tell your doctor which countries you have visited and what medication or vaccinations you had before you went or while you were there.

and abdominal pain, and this may lead to you suffering from serious dehydration (see Diarrhea, and Dysentery).

Diarrhea is usually caused by bacteria present in contaminated water, milk, or food, although the change of environment, climate, too much alcohol, and even dehydration can also cause it.

To avoid diarrhea, drink bottled water or sterilize all your drinking water, either by boiling it or with sterilizing tablets. Do not have ice in drinks, and always use sterilized water for cleaning your teeth and washing any fruit or salads. Milk should be boiled unless it has been pasteurized, and high risk foods, such as

shellfish, raw or undercooked meat, egg products, and unwashed fruits and vegetables, should be avoided. As well as these basic precautions you can take daily prophylactic pills that guard against stomach upsets.

Safe sex

The only way to have safe sex, especially if it is casual sex, is by using a condom. You should be able to buy condoms at your destination, but if you think you may be likely to need some, buy them before you set off. Do not let the sun and alcohol go to your head so that you forget this precaution against sexually transmitted

Tremor

Q I play the violin in the local orchestra and have been troubled by a tremor when performing at concerts. Can anything be done about this?

A This is a common problem among musicians and other people who have to perform in public. Often drugs that inhibit the effects of epinephrine can be used immediately before the performance. Consult your doctor because he or she will be able to advise you about this form of treatment.

Q Both my father and I have a marked shaking of the hands most of the time. Does this run in families or is it just a coincidence? For example, will my son be similarly affected?

A There is a tendency for tremor of this type to run in families and it is possible that your son will be affected. However, it is worth knowing that effective treatments are now available for this benign essential tremor.

Q I get very nervous when I am in strange surroundings and sometimes shake so badly that drinking is a problem. Is this abnormal?

A No. It is perfectly normal to tremble when nervous, but it may be that your degree of nervousness is excessive. Your doctor may feel that some form of treatment would be useful.

Q My father has been told that he has Parkinson's disease, and I have noticed that he has a tremor of the fingers that gets worse when he is anxious. Does this mean that the shaking is due to anxiety and is not part of the disease?

A It depends on what the tremor looks like. The familiar rolling of the thumb and fingers that occurs in Parkinson's disease is easy to distinguish from the regular to-and-fro tremble of pure nervousness. But even if your father's shake is due to his disease it will be much worse when he is nervous or attention is drawn to it.

We all know what it's like to tremble with fear or to feel a bit unsteady "the morning after the night before." However, sometimes a tremor can be an indication of a serious disorder of the nervous system.

The simple act of taking a drink can turn into an ordeal if you have a tremor. Using a straw can neatly overcome the problem.

We are all familiar with the involuntary shake in our hands that we get when we are nervous or have had a bad shock. This is the most common type of tremor, and is experienced by almost everyone, most commonly in the hands, feet, jaw, tongue, and head. In fact, we all have a very slight tremor, even when we are relaxed or asleep, and this can be measured by sensitive instruments. This is called physiologic tremor, and the noticeable shake that occurs under stress is simply an exaggeration of this.

The body's natural physiologic tremor is also exaggerated in certain diseases. The only difference is that it is present without any obvious anxiety. Other forms of shaking of the limbs, either when a person is at rest or in action, may look different. It is often possible to pinpoint from the characteristics of the tremor which area of the nervous system is damaged (see Nervous system).

What is tremor?
For any action to be smooth and unfaltering, or even for a hand or foot to be kept gently at rest, the muscles that move it must be balanced, each one contracting by just the right amount (see Muscles)

This synchronization of different groups of muscles is coordinated at many different levels in the nervous system, particularly in the basal ganglia deep in the cerebral hemispheres, and in the cerebellum that bulges off the back of the brain stem. This means that even holding your hands still against the force of gravity is an active process, with messages being matched in the lifting and dropping groups of muscles.

Physiologic tremor represents the minute oscillations in the different groups of muscles as they try to maintain this balance. Clearly if the functioning of the basal ganglia or cerebellum is disturbed, these main controllers of movement can no longer contribute fully to this delicate balancing act, and more pronounced movement swings occur (see Brain).

Common types of tremor
The most common tremors are those that are an exaggeration of normal physiologic tremor. The commonplace cause is anxiety or nervousness, where the tremor is caused mainly by the excess of the chemical epinephrine that courses through the blood at these times. This has the effect of increasing the swings of movement in the muscles, making them easily visible.

Other causes of this type of tremor are an overactive thyroid gland (see Thyroid) and alcohol addiction (see Alcoholism). In some families there is a tendency to an exaggeration of the normal physiologic tremor. This is called benign essential tremor, and is not an indication of any disease. Similarly, the slight persistent tremor commonly experienced by older people does not indicate any disease.

Other types of tremor
A more disabling form of tremor happens in people who have damage to their cerebellum or its major connections in the brain stem. This condition is called intention tremor, since it only appears when an intentional movement is made. The movement is broken up by increasingly wild oscillations, and is a disabling characteristic of advanced multiple sclerosis (see Multiple sclerosis).

A typical shake of the fingers when at rest occurs commonly in Parkinson's disease. This used to be called pill-rolling tremor, since the affected person seems to be always rolling a ball between the thumb and first two fingers (see Parkinson's disease). This shake disappears when a voluntary action is made, and the main disability it causes is embarrassment. Unfortunately this type of shake, as with the intention tremor, is made far worse by anxiety (see Anxiety).

A mixture of intention tremor and pill-rolling tremor occurs with damage to a particular collection (nucleus) of brain cells, and is known as red nucleus tremor. The most common cause of this type of tremor is multiple sclerosis.

A different type of shake is seen when there is failure of the kidneys or liver, with the consequent derangement of the body's metabolism. For a split second all muscle activity ceases and then returns just as quickly. Thus an outstretched hand may appear to flap if a person tries to keep it outstretched (see Kidney and kidney diseases, and Liver and liver diseases).

Tremor can also be provoked by such drugs as antidepressant and antipsychotic drugs and caffeine.

Can tremor be treated?
Depending on the type of tremor, there is often a good chance of treatment. Exaggerated physiologic tremor can be improved by drugs that suppress the nervous system. Drugs to treat Parkinson's disease can improve the tremor, but often have more effect on the other aspects of this disorder. Intention tremor, as seen in multiple sclerosis, is very difficult to treat, but the natural waxing and waning of the disease means this problem may not persist (see Side effects).

The morning shakes after a night of heavy drinking can indicate alcohol dependence, and should make the drinker seriously consider regulating his or her alcohol intake.

Shout Pictures

Trichinosis

Q Could you catch trichinosis in this country or is it only likely in the tropics?

A You certainly could get it in this country. In fact, it is wrong to think of it as a tropical disease, since it is rare in the tropics but common in Europe and America. Infection occurs through eating pork that is infected, so it is most common in those countries where a lot of pork is eaten.

Q There was evidence of trichinosis on my chest X ray, but I don't ever remember being sick. Can you have the disease without knowing it?

A Yes. It is not only possible but also common to have the disease without being aware of it. The reason why abnormalities are seen on X rays is that the larvae form cysts in the muscles that protect them for up to two years; eventually, however, the cysts become calcified (impregnated with chalk), and this calcification shows up on the X ray. In the United States studies done on muscle samples taken at autopsy have shown some evidence of infection in 20 percent of cases. The figure for the UK is nearer to 1 percent.

Q Is there an effective way to prevent trichinosis?

A Yes. One of the most effective ways of preventing it is not to eat pork. This is a method that has been practiced for centuries according to religious custom by Jews, Muslims, and Hindus. In societies where pork is eaten, preventive measures are to freeze meat before cooking, or to cook it thoroughly. Irradiation of pork using radioactive cobalt or cesium has also been used. Another preventive measure is to take proper care when raising hogs. Uncooked hog swill (feed) may contain infected raw scraps or possibly even feces from an infected animal, thereby leading to the spread of infection. The disease is fairly widespread in the animal kingdom, and rats may certainly be infected. This is another source of infection, since hogs sometimes kill rats.

Trichinosis, one of the most common worm infections in human beings, can be a serious illness. Prevention is simple, however, and consists mainly in insuring that pork, which contains the parasite, is always properly cooked.

Trichinosis is most common in Europe and in North America and is fairly uncommon in the tropics. It does not occur in Australia or in the islands of the Pacific.

Cause

The illness is caused by a small worm, called *Trichinella spiralis*, which may infest all meat-eating creatures. It lives in the intestine in its adult form, and male and female worms mate to produce huge numbers of larvae. These then spread through the bloodstream to the muscles, where they form protective cysts in which they can survive for a long period. In the meantime the adult worms in the intestines die. Each female probably lives about four to eight weeks, and during this

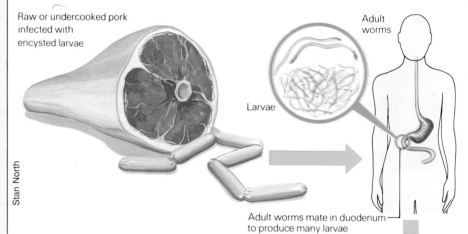

Raw or undercooked pork infected with encysted larvae

Stan North

Adult worms

Larvae

Adult worms mate in duodenum to produce many larvae

How trichinosis occurs

Hogs are the source of trichinosis in man. The larvae of the worm Trichinella spiralis *form protective cysts in the muscles of the hog, and, if infected pork is eaten, the larvae are released, mature, and breed. The new larvae circulate around the body until they reach muscles in which to lodge. Infected hog swill (feed) perpetuates the cycle.*

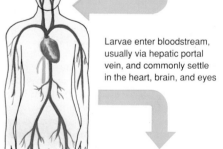

Larvae enter bloodstream, usually via hepatic portal vein, and commonly settle in the heart, brain, and eyes

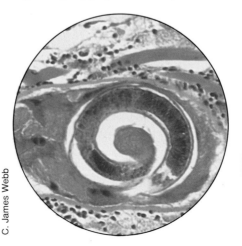

C. James Webb

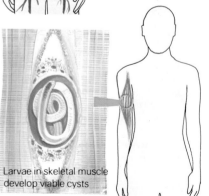

Larvae in skeletal muscle develop viable cysts

Trichinosis can be prevented by the proper care of hogs, particularly by insuring that their food is free from contamination.

time will produce about 1500 larvae. The infection of the next host will occur if the original animal is caught and eaten by a predator. The muscles are eaten, cysts around the larvae dissolve, and new adults develop in the next host.

When the infecting larvae enter the duodenum of the new host, they work their way through the wall of the intestine and pass through four developmental stages before becoming adult males or females. The mature worms then return to the lumen (central space) of the intestine. As adult worms they are just visible. The male is 0.06 in (1.6 mm) long and the female 0.16 in (4 mm). The male has a testis and the female an ovary and a coiled tubular womb. Mating takes place as soon as two adult worms are present in the lumen of the intestine, and the female then starts to produce the larvae.

Once a larva is produced it passes into the bloodstream and can come to rest in the muscles or any other part of the body. The most common sites include the heart, brain, and eye, as well as the ordinary muscles that the parasite is seeking. It is only the larvae that find muscle that form a protective cyst; the ones that find other organs soon disintegrate.

The main strain of the parasite is found in humans and in hogs, dogs, rats, and cats. The main source of infection is therefore pork, as far as human beings are concerned. The habit of eating uncooked pork sausages is particularly dangerous and infection runs very high in Germany and in countries such as the United States, which have a strong German influence.

A second important biological strain is found in Arctic regions, and here the typical hosts are whales, walruses, seals, squirrels, foxes, and dogs. Bears, particularly polar bears, are very likely to become infected, being the most powerful predators in the Arctic.

Symptoms
Most cases of trichinosis occur without showing any outward signs of infection, and they are only discovered by examining autopsy muscle samples under the microscope. There is evidence to suggest that up to 20 percent of the people in the US, and 1 percent in the UK population, have some degree of infection.

Cysts in the muscles can also be seen on X-ray film as a result of calcification after about two years.

Symptoms occur with a very heavy infection. Diarrhea and vomiting may result when the larvae invade the walls of the intestine, and this may also provoke an allergic rash on the trunk and extremities The major symptoms, of which there are four, appear when the larvae leave the intestine and start to circulate around the body. There will be fever, swelling of the eyelids and of the tissue around the eyes, pain in the muscles, which can be very severe, and a high level of eosinophils (a type of white blood cell) in the blood. Heart failure may develop if large numbers of larvae invade the heart.

By the third stage of the disease, when the larvae are forming cysts in the muscles, the patient may become very weak, and death may occur simply through exhaustion and poor nutrition. The brain can also become severely affected and various neurologic complications may also manifest themselves.

In serious infections, the fever will recede first, with the muscular pains persisting for some time. However, there is always the possibility of a secondary problem that will prove fatal.

Treatment and prevention
If the full-blown disease develops, steroid drugs are given to control the effects of the inflammation caused by the larvae. A drug called thiabendazole will kill the adult worms and this is done to prevent the production of new larvae, although the larvae themselves cannot be killed.

Prevention consists in the proper preparation of pork, particularly with adequate cooking, and in reducing the risks of hogs becoming infected.

A Jewish family drinks a toast at the festival of Purim. Orthodox Jewish meals follow strict dietary laws and never include pork.

Trichology

Q I have noticed that my hair condition changes during my period. Is this possible, or am I imagining it?

A Since hormones have a major influence on the growth and condition of hair, some women do notice fluctuations during their periods. However, in the majority of cases this is not indicative of any hormonal disturbance.

Q Should hair be dried mechanically with a hair dryer, or left to dry naturally?

A It is always better for hair to dry naturally, but with some styles this isn't possible. If you use a dryer, don't set the temperature too high and don't hold it too near your hair. When setting with rollers, use the smooth and brushless type. Spend only the minimum time that is necessary under the hair dryer. Heated rollers should not be used more than twice a week, and should be removed before the hair becomes overdried.

Q My hairdresser told me that I need a pH balanced shampoo. Is this just another sales gimmick?

A Research has shown that pH balanced shampoos (pH is the measure of acidity/alkalinity) are only beneficial after the hair has been subjected to permanent waving or straightening processes. Otherwise, there is little known advantage in using a pH balanced shampoo. Normal pH of the skin is 5.4, which is slightly acidic.

Q I have read that male pattern baldness can occur in women. Is this correct?

A Yes. Male pattern baldness, or androgenic alopecia, is an inherited condition. It involves the male sex hormones, androgens, that are secreted by the testes in men and by the adrenal glands in both men and women. An imbalance in the amounts secreted can lead to excessive hair loss. Incidentally, male pattern baldness is one of the most common causes of hair loss in men.

If your hair starts to fall out or you spread dandruff like other people throw confetti, you might benefit from a consultation with an expert in trichology, the study of problems associated with the scalp and hair.

Trichology is the study of the hair and scalp in healthy as well as diseased conditions. The people who are qualified to work in this field are called trichologists. They advise clients on all scalp and hair problems, many of which they have been trained to treat.

Trichologists often work with medical practitioners, since it is now well known that the hair can reflect the general health of an individual and may indicate internal disorders. Increased hair loss, for example, is often the first sign of a general health disorder (the normal rate of hair loss is 60 to 120 hairs per day; see Hair, and Baldness).

Hair loss and hair transplants

People who suffer hair loss due to a genetic disorder can be put under considerable psychological stress because of their problem. Many sufferers become desperate and seek out any help available, no matter how extreme. As a result they may experience far more misery when the treatment turns out to be both fruitless and expensive. In some cases even the best treatments merely prevent further deterioration. The sufferer may then resort to a wig, hair weaving, or other forms of hair replacement such as a transplant.

Well-performed hair transplants do offer a reasonable solution in some cases of genetic hair loss. However, trichologists are increasingly confronted by evidence that some operations are being performed by nonmedical people. In addition, some surgeons associated with commercial clinics have insufficient training.

Scalp massage relaxes the patient and also increases blood circulation. Trichologists may use massage as part of the treatment of hair loss or scaly conditions of the scalp.

Steve Bielschowsky

Cycle of hair growth

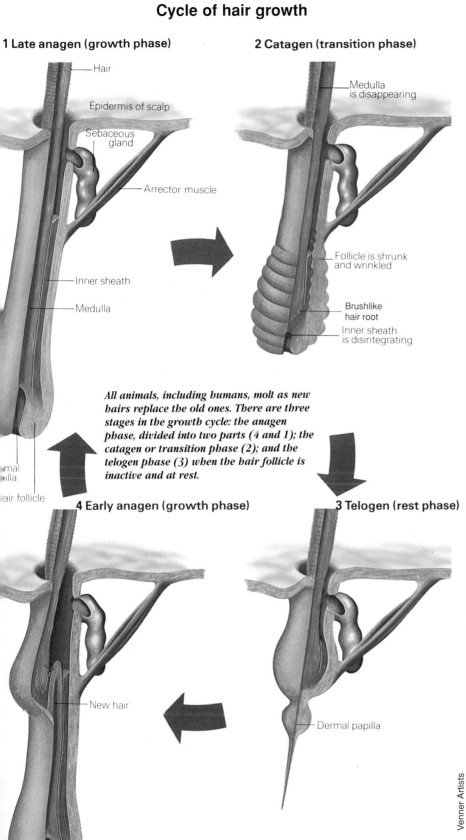

1 Late anagen (growth phase)

- Hair
- Epidermis of scalp
- Sebaceous gland
- Arrector muscle
- Inner sheath
- Medulla
- mal illa
- air follicle

2 Catagen (transition phase)

- Medulla is disappearing
- Follicle is shrunk and wrinkled
- Brushlike hair root
- Inner sheath is disintegrating

All animals, including humans, molt as new hairs replace the old ones. There are three stages in the growth cycle: the anagen phase, divided into two parts (4 and 1); the catagen or transition phase (2); and the telogen phase (3) when the hair follicle is inactive and at rest.

4 Early anagen (growth phase)

- New hair

3 Telogen (rest phase)

- Dermal papilla

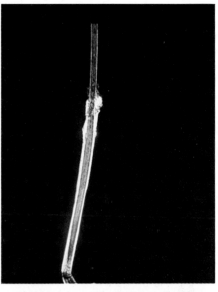

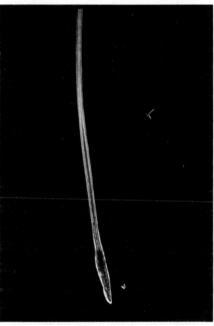

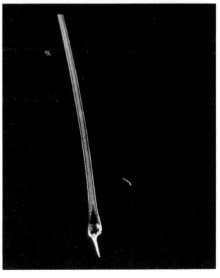

Venner Artists

Microscopic slides of a human hair during the three growth phases: anagen (top right), catagen (center right), and telogen (right).

The incidence of unsatisfactory transplants resulting from selecting the wrong type of patient, placing grafts incorrectly, and inadequate growth is also alarming. Another consideration is that additional surgery may be needed, but this may be difficult because of the limited amount of donor hair available. As a result, people considering a transplant would be advised to consult a recognized trichologist before proceeding with treatment of any kind.

The techniques used in hair transplants can be divided into three categories: flap grafting, scalp reduction, and punch grafting. Flap grafting is the rotation of a section of hair-bearing skin from the side of the head into the bald area. In scalp reduction, the thinning or bald region is surgically removed and the surrounding tissue is drawn together and sutured. The most widely used technique is punch grafting, where plugs of hair and follicle are taken from the rear of the scalp (the donor site) and inserted into the balding area (the recipient site; see Baldness).

Trichology and scalp disorders

Scaling conditions of the scalp are often dealt with by trichologists. Dandruff is the most commonly seen complaint, and a huge fortune is spent each year on preparations to combat it. The term *dandruff* is loosely applied to several different scaling conditions of the scalp. The medical definition, for example, is excessive noninflammatory scaling, and in most cases diagnosis is easy (see Dandruff).

One of the most effective antidandruff agents in current use is a compound called zinc pyrithione, which is found in some proprietary shampoos. The substance suppresses a nontransmittable bacterium that is present in the fatty deposits of the skin. The bacteria prevent normal intercellular binding (which keeps the layers of cells together) by altering the enzyme that is responsible (see Bacteria).

There is only a fine line between dandruff and other scaling conditions of the scalp, and so establishing the correct diagnosis is very important. If the dandruff persists after shampooing for a month with an antidandruff preparation on alternate days, the condition is probably not dandruff but a more complex scaling disturbance. This will require a different and more specific treatment and those who are affected should consult a qualified trichologist or a dermatologist.

The most severe example of scaling disturbance is the condition called psoriasis. This is a chronic scaling of the skin that is characterized by whitish silvery scales on a reddened base. It is not only restricted to the scalp but often also appears in other areas such as the elbows and the knees (see Psoriasis).

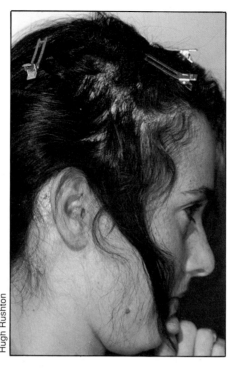

Hugh Rushton

This scalp condition is similar in its symptoms to eczema. It requires diligent and careful treatment, with washing and a daily application of coal tar.

Current developments

Improvements in the methods of measuring changes in the hair cycle, such as trichogram analysis, enable trichologists to make much more accurate assessments of hair and scalp conditions. Trichogram analysis is the removal of a small area of scalp hair for microscopic study. When taken every six months, the rate of change in growth patterns can then be calculated, and by combining these results with blood analysis, hair loss disorders can be more accurately evaluated.

The information provided is used for scientific research into effective treatment: for example, the search for a compound to control the androgens (substances acting as male sex hormones, some of which are also found in females) that initiate genetic hair loss. Recent studies in women suffering from genetic hair loss are most encouraging. Drugs are now used that can stabilize the condition.

Measuring trace elements such as iron, lead, and copper that are absorbed by the hair is one recent project. Researchers in this field believe that hair can provide clues to the nutritional state of the body, but this potentially promising line of investigation is still in its infancy.

Another area of trichological research is being undertaken by forensic scientists. They are looking for methods that enable them to identify a person from a single hair. This is not difficult if the root sheath is present, but most hairs that are found at the scene of a crime do not have a root sheath. Also the structural features of hair, such as its color, thickness, and appearance, always show considerable variation within each individual head of hair.

In the past, hair has only been of use in relatively few criminal identification cases. However, because chemical variations in the individual person are minimal, it is now possible to do a protein analysis (hair is composed of differing amounts of amino acids, which are constituents of protein) and therefore the presence of the root sheath is not required.

Perming the hair, especially if it is done frequently, can cause individual hairs to break and may also lead to hair loss.

A promising future

The major cause of hair loss in women, which is genetically determined and associated with androgens, is well on the way to being prevented, and only the side effects of treatment need to be determined. There is also hope for men, and antiandrogen treatments, without the side effects of sexual suppression, are undergoing clinical trials. Advances in the treatment of chronic scaling conditions of the scalp are also encouraging, with recent reports of safer and more effective treatments. Molecular biology is increasing our knowledge of some of the fundamental processes occurring in the skin and hair cells, and may soon help unravel the complexities of many conditions that are currently difficult to treat.

Trichomoniasis

Q I have an unpleasant vaginal discharge that has the characteristics of a trichomonas infection. Is there anything I can do, such as douching, to get rid of it myself?

A No, certain cures can only follow taking the particular drug needed for the specific germ causing your vaginitis. This depends on accurate identification of this organism from examination of a specimen of the discharge. There is no shortcut that would enable you to deal with the matter on your own. It is very unwise to try to treat yourself by douching since, if you did happen to have something more serious than trichomonas, the risk of flushing infected material up into your womb or tubes could have tragic results in spreading the infection.

Q My girlfriend has just been told that she has a trichomonas infection in her vagina. She says she hasn't been with anyone else, but since I have no symptoms myself and know that I have been only with her, surely she must be deceiving me?

A This is a situation that worries and upsets a lot of couples. But the truth is, although it seems difficult to understand how a vaginal infection can be caught other than through intercourse with an infected person, a substantial proportion of cases are not acquired in this way, but by using a toilet that was contaminated by an infected person a short time before, or unwittingly borrowing an infected friend's towel or washcloth.

Q When I had trichomoniasis, my husband was given tablets even though there was nothing wrong with him. Why?

A Though your husband may not have had trichomoniasis—it is not always sexually transmitted—there is a possibility that he may have had a mild infection without any apparent symptoms. If this was the case you might have been reinfected when you started having intercourse after your treatment.

Trichomoniasis, or trich, is a common and highly infectious condition affecting the genitals. The symptoms are both irritating and unpleasant, but fortunately this condition responds well to treatment.

Phil Babb

A case of suspected trichomoniasis can be fully investigated at a treatment center, under expert but informal medical care.

Trichomoniasis is a common condition, with at least one in five women likely to have it at some time during their lives. It can affect men, being responsible for about 4 percent of cases of nonspecific urethritis, or NSU (see Nonspecific urethritis), but more usually gives rise to disease in women, for whom it is among the most common causes of vaginal discharge (see Vagina, and Vaginal discharge).

Causes
The trichomonas organism, *Trichomonas vaginalis*, responsible for the infection is rather unusual. It is neither a bacterium nor a virus, but a single-cell, pear-shaped protozoan or parasite. Its five whiplike tentacles enable it both to swim about in the vaginal secretion and to attract particles of material on which it lives.

Although trichomoniasis can often be caught as a result of having intercourse with somebody who already has the infection, it can be contracted in other ways. Indeed, the fact that the trichomonas infection occurs in a much greater number of women than men, that it does not usually survive for long in males, and that the infection can develop in women who are not having intercourse confirms this. The answer to this apparent mystery lies in the ability of the trichomonas organism, unlike other sexually transmitted organisms such as the gonococcus, to survive outside the human body for at least 30 minutes on

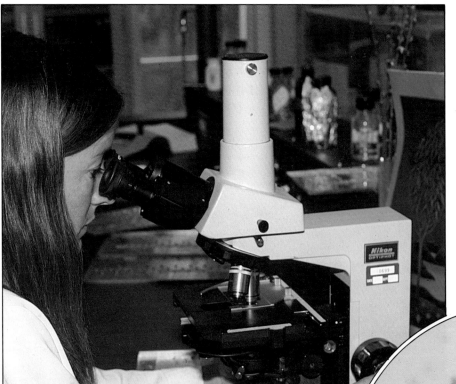

Daily Telegraph Colour Library

through casual sexual intercourse, since it is possible to have acquired other infections, such as gonorrhea or thrush, at the same time (see Gonorrhea, and Thrush). It is wise, therefore, to confirm or eliminate the presence of other infections so that appropriate additional treatment can be given if necessary. A full investigation can be carried out at a treatment center or genitourinary clinic.

Treatment

The treatment of trichomonas infection usually consists of taking oral doses of metronidazole (Flagyl) or another closely related drug. It is important that the effectiveness of the cure is checked after treatment by the examination of vaginal secretion to make sure that no organism has

objects with which the genital parts of an infected person have come in contact. It is therefore one of the few sexually transmitted diseases that can in fact be caught from a toilet seat as well as from contaminated towels, washcloths, or clothes (see Sexually transmitted diseases).

Symptoms

Fortunately almost all cases of trichomoniasis can be easily and completely cured. Usually its only manifestation is vaginitis (inflammation of the vagina), the main symptom of which is a profuse vaginal discharge. This is generally runny, yellow to green in color, and has a strong odor. The discharge is often accompanied by soreness and irritation of the genital area. It is very unusual for any organ other than the vagina, either in the pelvis or elsewhere in the body, to be affected, and the infection has virtually no complications.

Diagnosis

The diagnosis of trichomoniasis can only be made by seeing the actual trichomonas

When diagnosing trichomoniasis, a specimen of vaginal discharge is examined under a microscope. Finding the organism Trichomonas vaginalis *(inset) will clinch the diagnosis.*

organism under a microscope in a specimen of the vaginal discharge; there are no blood or other tests that will reveal it. There are a large number of diseases that can cause several different types of vaginal discharge. Even though the nature of the discharge strongly suggests trichomonas infection, this can only be proved by internal examination and microscopic analysis of the discharge.

Since trichomoniasis can only be cured completely by one particular type of drug (there is no single treatment effective for all types of vaginal discharge), it is important that the trichomonas organism is positively identified. Vaginal examination and tests are particularly advisable if the infection may have been caught

survived. Until this has been done, the patient should refrain from intercourse to avoid both the possibility of reinfection and of contaminating anyone else. Since a considerable proportion of cases are sexually transmitted, and to avoid a situation in which a couple will continually reinfect each other, the patient's partner is usually advised either to undergo the tests as well, or to take a course of metronidazole as a precaution.

However, it should be noted that medical research in the United States has shown some evidence of serious side effects in certain animals following the use of metronidazole; some doctors may therefore prefer to prescribe vaginal pessaries and gels when possible.

Tropical diseases

Q I have heard that rabies is common in India. Since I am planning a trip there soon, should I be vaccinated against rabies before I go?

A There is now a safe and effective vaccine against rabies (although it is expensive). Rabies is spread by animal bites. The risk to ordinary travelers, however, is usually so small that vaccination is not routinely recommended before a vacation.

Q Last time I went on a trip to Tunisia I had a terrible attack of diarrhea that ruined my visit. Can I take anything with me next time to prevent this from happening again?

A Your doctor may be able to give you some tablets to relieve symptoms in case it should happen again. But travelers' diarrhea is nearly always due to eating or drinking contaminated food or water, and strict hygiene is always the best preventive measure. Diarrhea is nature's way of eliminating noxious agents from the body, and treatment should focus on replacing lost fluids and salts—this is of vital importance in hot climates. If diarrhea does not get better within a short time, contains blood or mucus, or is associated with fever, consult a doctor at once. Do not try to treat it yourself.

Q I'm planning a trip to South America, and am scared of poisonous snakes. Is there anything that I should take with me in case I get bitten?

A Snakes bite in self-defense, so always wear boots when walking outdoors at any time in snake-infested areas. Snake bites are very uncommon and, usually, little or no venom is injected in the majority of cases. It is important to get to a hospital without delay, and dramatic measures such as cutting into bites or using tourniquets are unnecessary and can cause harm. Reassurance is the most important part of treatment. Antivenin can be dangerous, and should only be administered by medics.

The grim backdrop to most tropical diseases is the shocking conditions in which so many people live. Governments and medical teams are waging war against the havoc wreaked by these resilient enemies of humanity.

Alan Hutchinson Library

Errath/Explorer/Vision International

An African sign (top) promises cures for some bizarre complaints. A Peruvian herbalist displays his colorful herbal cure-alls for sale (above).

Today, in spite of all the progress that has been made in modern medicine, large numbers of people around the world still die from tropical diseases. Although we now understand a great deal about how these diseases spread, and how they can be treated, they still maim, blind, disable, and cause suffering on a massive scale.

What are tropical diseases?

Tropical diseases include not only bizarre parasitic disorders like elephantiasis, but also rare and deadly fevers like Lassa fever or Marburg fever (see Elephantiasis). Relatively few diseases occur only within the tropics. Diseases such as leprosy and plague, which most people now think of

as tropical, were once widespread in Europe. Likewise, diseases now familiar in Europe, such as measles or tuberculosis, are much more dangerous in the tropics. For example, the mortality from measles is 400 times greater among malnourished African children than among Europeans (see Infection and infectious diseases).

Fighting tropical diseases

Smallpox is the only disease totally eradicated by humans. The campaign against

Q I've heard that cholera vaccination does not always work. Is there any other treatment for cholera?

A We still need a better vaccine against cholera. At present the vaccine only protects in 50 percent of cases for only a few months. Thus, the best way to avoid cholera is to avoid food and water that might be contaminated. Cholera causes severe diarrhea, with salt and fluid loss. Prompt rehydration is vital in order to save a person's life.

Q My sister-in-law has just returned from a trip to Jamaica, where she became ill with dengue fever. What is dengue fever, and is there any chance that she could infect someone else?

A Dengue is due to a virus. It is spread by certain types of mosquito, so you could not catch it directly from her. It causes fever, painful muscles and joints, headaches, and a rash, but complete recovery usually occurs.

Q Is it true that malnutrition can be caused by worms?

A Intestinal parasites do not, on their own, cause malnutrition, although hookworms frequently cause anemia. But in the tropics worm infestation in undernourished children is common, and often leads to severe malnutrition.

Q I am going to be touring the Middle East and I have heard that there is a disease out there that causes blindness. Is there any chance that I might catch it?

A The disease you are worried about is known as trachoma, an infection of the conjunctiva and cornea of the eye. Trachoma causes blindness on a massive scale: around 500 million people have the disease, of whom 15 million are now suffering from blindness. Repeated infection is necessary for damage to occur, and transmission of the disease does require prolonged personal contact with carriers, under conditions of extreme squalor. Travelers are most unlikely to be affected by it.

smallpox began in 1967, lasted 10 years, and cost $200 million.

Unfortunately, although the World Health Organization (WHO) has a campaign to eradicate polio and leprosy from the world within a relatively short time, it is not likely that we will be able to eradicate many other tropical diseases for the

Ben Martin/Colorific!

foreseeable future, and much more money for research is necessary. However, the World Health Organization has determined that the following diseases be singled out for particular attention:

Malaria: Probably affects 200 million people each year and causes a million deaths. It is one of the world's greatest killers, and is still on the increase. There are hopes that a vaccine against malaria will be developed within the next 10 years, and a new antimalarial drug from China— Quinghaosu, developed from traditional remedies—promises to be an important weapon in the continuing struggle to control the disease.

Schistosomiasis: Also called bilharzia, this is an unpleasant and sometimes fatal disease caused by small worms in the liver, intestine, and bladder. Eggs passed out in the urine and feces hatch in water and produce organisms that infect certain types of snails. These produce other types of organisms, which penetrate human skin and then pass in the bloodstream to the liver. The disease is usually caused by contact with water that has been contaminated by human sewage.

Sleeping sickness: Spread by the tsetse fly, this has made vast areas of Africa uninhabitable. The disease is caused by a tiny, single-celled parasite that lives in the blood and the brain, and causes serious damage to the nervous system. Treatment is difficult and there is no vaccine. The disease is a risk to visitors to African game parks, who should therefore take special precautions to avoid insect bites.

Leprosy: This still affects a large number of people around the world. There are

The spectacular beauty of the Tsavo National Park attracts thousands of tourists to Kenya every year. Unfortunately such an area is home to the tsetse fly (right), which spreads sleeping sickness to both man and beast. Mosquito coils should be standard travelers' equipment because they repel such unwanted visitors.

C. James Webb

ing the lymph passages in the body. African river blindness is another form of filariasis. This can cause blindness by infestation with a worm that enters the body through a blackfly bite. There are over 250 million cases of filariasis.

Leishmaniasis: Spread by sandflies, and caused by a parasite that attacks the skin, liver, and spleen, the disease takes many forms and is not adequately understood. More research is needed.

Immunization schemes

Measles, polio, tetanus, tuberculosis, diphtheria, and whooping cough kill five million children in developing countries each year. The World Health Organiza-

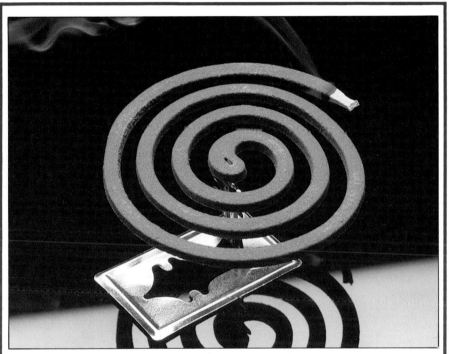

Graham Strong

probably 20 million sufferers, though no more than 3 million receive treatment. If the disease is diagnosed promptly, it can be treated effectively and disability can be prevented. But if it is neglected, blindness, paralysis, and deformity result. Almost more terrible is the social stigma of the disease due to the ancient and irrational fear of infection. This causes the sufferer to become a social outcast. More effective drugs are badly needed, as well as vaccine research (see Leprosy).

Filariasis: Caused by a variety of small worms that enter the body through the bites of mosquitoes and flies. These worms also cause elephantiasis by block-

Basic precautions

● At present many tropical diseases cannot be prevented by drugs or vaccines, so travelers should take a few basic precautions

● Biting insects spread diseases in different countries. In some parts of Africa, tsetse flies spread sleeping sickness; in others, insects spread viral diseases or filariasis. Minimize exposure to biting insects, and wear sensible clothes. Use insect repellents containing diethyltoluamide (DEET), and at night use a mosquito net or burn pyrethrum mosquito coils (above). Electronic insect repellents do not work

● Don't eat food that has been exposed to flies. Always eat food

that has been freshly cooked to kill all parasites and bacteria. Wash hands before handling food

● Check that drinking water is safe; if in doubt, drink boiled water, or use purifying tablets containing chlorine or iodine

● Wash fruit and vegetables with detergent or a dilute solution of potassium permanganate

● Never walk about barefoot

● Cleanse and dress all wounds

● Do not swim in canals or rivers

● If you develop a fever, severe diarrhea, or blood in the feces, consult a doctor

● Have a medical checkup when you return home

Q Why do babies suffering from malnutrition have such enormous abdomens when the rest of their bodies seem to be just skin and bones?

A The swollen abdomen of the malnourished child is due to wasting and weakening of the abdominal muscles, fluid collecting in the abdomen, gas distending the intestines, and an enlarged liver. This type of malnutrition, called kwashiorkor, results from a diet containing little or no protein, and carries a high mortality rate.

Q Is it true that there is now resistance to various antimalarial drugs among certain malaria strains?

A In some parts of Africa, Asia, and South America, resistance to some of the drugs used to prevent malaria is now increasing. That is why you should always check with your doctor before you travel, and tell him exactly which countries you plan to visit, so that he can select the most suitable treatment. Don't forget that even the shortest stopover in a tropical zone may expose you to malaria.

Q Is vaccination against tropical diseases dangerous during pregnancy?

A If there is a significant risk of exposure to disease, vaccination is usually the safest option. Your doctor is the best person to give you advice.

Q I thought that leprosy was only found in underdeveloped countries, but I read recently that it still occurs in Europe and the United States. Is this true?

A It is true, but it is nothing for you to worry about. Leprosy has never been eradicated completely from Europe or the United States, and there are probably as many as 20 million sufferers from the disease in the world. But contrary to commonly held beliefs, leprosy does not spread easily, and the vast majority of people are not at all susceptible to the disease.

C. James Webb

Elephantiasis (above) is common in the tropics. Blindness (top right) is a widespread tropical condition; in fact, one million people suffer from river blindness in West Africa alone. Attempts to control the spread of the disease have included the introduction of public showers in India (right), and massive vaccination programs in Africa (below).

Aspect Picture Library

Travel precautions

If you are planning to visit a country where tropical diseases are present, see your doctor well in advance to allow plenty of time for any immunizations you may need. You will probably require specific protection against the diseases listed below.

Disease	Protective measures	Dosage	Duration of protection	Effects of disease	Route of disease spread
Cholera	Immunization Hygiene	2 doses, 1–4 weeks apart	6 months	Severe diarrhea, fluid loss, and dehydration	Unhygienic food handling, and contaminated water
Hepatitis	Gammaglobulin injection Vaccine for Hepatitis B	Single dose Three doses	2–6 months Life	Fever, jaundice, viral liver infection	Contact with infected cases, unhygienic food handling, contaminated water
Malaria	Antimalarial drugs Mosquito nets Mosquito repellents	Start drug treatment before arrival, continue for at least 6 weeks after leaving	During period of exposure	Fevers and chills	Mosquito bites
Polio	Oral polio vaccine Hygiene	Single booster dose, if previously immunized	5 years	Paralysis	Unhygienic food handling, and contaminated water
Smallpox	Vaccination is no longer required or advised. The disease has been eradicated				
Tetanus	Immunization. Careful cleansing of cuts and wounds	2 doses, 4–6 weeks apart. 1st booster dose 1 year later; then every 5 years	5–10 years	Severe muscle spasms and rigidity	Contamination of a wound or wounds
Tuberculosis	BCG immunization (following skin test)	Single dose	Probably lifelong	Chronic lung disease; damage to many organs	Direct contact with infected cases; unpasteurized milk
Typhoid	Immunization Hygiene	2 doses, 4 weeks apart	3 years	Fever; intestinal infection	Unhygienic food handling, and contaminated water
Yellow fever	Immunization	Single dose	10 years	Fever, also jaundice, bleeding	Mosquito bites

tion has set itself a huge task: to immunize all children in the world against these diseases by the year 2000. The practical problems are enormous since 80 percent of the world's population live in remote areas. Even when supplies of vaccine arrive, their effectiveness cannot always be guaranteed; vaccines are quickly inactivated by tropical heat. However, the project is well under way, and good progress has already been made.

Problems
Poverty, overpopulation, overcrowding, bad housing, inadequate nutrition, poor sanitation, and lack of education are a few of the factors that facilitate the spread of

Women and children from an Ivory Coast village patiently await treatment in the local community hospital.

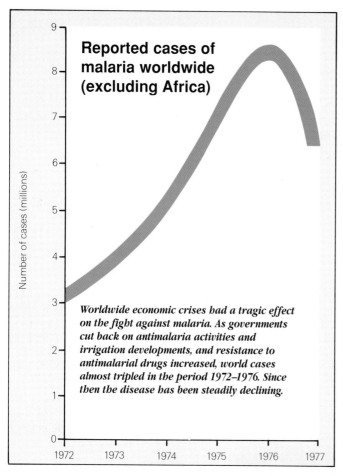

Reported cases of malaria worldwide (excluding Africa)

Number of cases (millions)

Worldwide economic crises had a tragic effect on the fight against malaria. As governments cut back on antimalaria activities and irrigation developments, and resistance to antimalarial drugs increased, world cases almost tripled in the period 1972–1976. Since then the disease has been steadily declining.

1972 1973 1974 1975 1976 1977

John Hutchinson

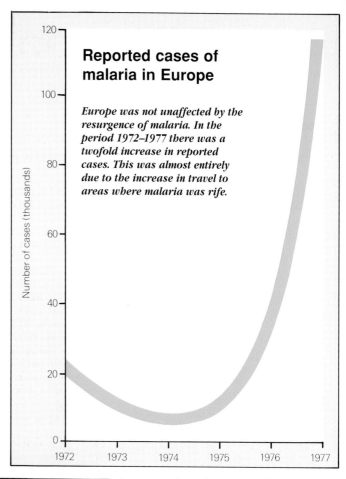

Reported cases of malaria in Europe

Number of cases (thousands)

Europe was not unaffected by the resurgence of malaria. In the period 1972–1977 there was a twofold increase in reported cases. This was almost entirely due to the increase in travel to areas where malaria was rife.

1972 1973 1974 1975 1976 1977

tropical diseases in the developing world, and make them more difficult to bring under control. A thousand million people have no access to a safe water supply within 220 yards (200 m) of their home.

Ironically many aid projects aimed at improving the quality of life have actually made things worse. In Egypt, for example, the construction of the Aswân high dam controlled the flood of the Nile and permitted much better irrigation and crop yields. While this was a benefit, unfortunately it also allowed the snails that transmit bilharzia to flourish. It is estimated that 60 percent of Egypt's population suffers from bilharzia, and that 200 million people in Southeast Asia, Africa, and South America are affected.

Sadly the countries in which tropical diseases are most common are those least able to conduct the intensive research that is essential if new drugs and vaccines to combat these diseases are to be found. They simply do not have the financial and technological resources.

It costs many millions of dollars to research and test each new drug, and developing countries can barely afford the drugs that are already available.

Travel

Jet travel has made it possible for a disease acquired in one country to produce symptoms only after the traveler has arrived in another country, often many thousands of

With the help of better health education and medical care, African children have real hope of a longer, healthier life.

Tony Stone Associates

miles away. Yellow fever, for example, which is a dangerous viral illness occurring in Africa and South America, is transmitted by mosquitoes, and the symptoms do not appear until six days after a mosquito bite. International health regulations insure that all travelers arriving in Asia from Africa or South America have

been vaccinated against yellow fever for their own safety, and to prevent the spread of the disease. There is, at present, no yellow fever in Asia, although there are plenty of mosquitoes that would be able to spread the disease rapidly.

Only a few tropical diseases can be prevented specifically by drug treatment or by vaccination, so travelers to regions where diseases are endemic must accept that they are at increased risk of picking up a disease against which they have no natural immunity.

An additional hazard is that when particular symptoms develop after a traveler has returned home, they may not be recognized immediately as symptoms of a tropical disease. In the West, over 2500 cases of malaria are imported each year, but the symptoms are easily confused with those of influenza and the diagnosis is often delayed. Travelers should, therefore, always tell their doctor where they have been when they return home, and should have a full checkup.

Outlook

Many tropical diseases are on the increase, and are a long way from eradication or control. Improved health education is one of the most urgent measures that must be taken to limit the spread of disease. New vaccines, new drugs, and more research are essential if the fight against tropical diseases is to succeed.

Tubal ligation

Q I am thinking of being sterilized. If I have tubal ligation, will I be able to have the procedure reversed later if I decide that I want another baby?

A Female or male sterilization should really only be considered if you are sure that, whatever the circumstances, you never want another child. It offers a virtually 100 percent safe form of birth control, and must be regarded as an irreversible procedure. In certain circumstances surgeons may try to reverse the procedure, but there is no guarantee that the reversal will be successful. In women, the success rate of the reversal procedure is only around 50 percent, and the pregnancy rate in the partners of men who have had vasectomies reversed is no more than 60 percent.

Q Does a woman who has had tubal ligation go through menopause after she has had this surgery?

A No. The procedure simply involves tying each of the fallopian tubes in two places and destroying the section in between to prevent sperm from reaching the eggs. The ovaries themselves are not affected and they continue to produce both eggs and sex hormones. However, some female sterilization procedures involve removing or damaging the ovaries, and after this type of surgery a woman will develop menopausal symptoms, such as hot flashes. Such a method is usually only carried out if the ovaries are already damaged or diseased.

Q My wife is planning on having tubal ligation. Will we have to use any other form of contraception after surgery?

A No. Unlike male sterilization, all types of female sterilization are effective immediately, so no form of contraception is necessary. After a vasectomy it is possible for a man to remain fertile for three months or more, and couples are advised to use some form of contraception until a sample of semen shows no sperm.

Tubal ligation is a simple sterilization procedure that is performed on a woman's fallopian tubes to prevent sperm from reaching the eggs, or on a man's vas deferens to prevent the passage of sperm from the testes.

The word *ligation* means tying off or constriction. In tubal ligation, it is the tubes that carry the eggs in a woman or the sperm in a man that are tied, and this makes the woman or man unable to reproduce—a procedure called sterilization (see Sterilization, and Vasectomy).

Why is it done?
Men or women who have completed their families or who do not want children may be sterilized so that they do not have to worry about contraception or unwanted pregnancies. Tubal ligation may be considered if a pregnancy would be a serious threat to a woman's health, or if there is a high risk of children being affected by a serious hereditary disease.

How is it done?
Tubal ligation in women is carried out through a small incision that is made in the abdomen. It is performed under local or spinal anesthesia, unless it accompanies major surgery.

Each fallopian tube is tied in two places by a tight ligature, and the segment between is removed. Sometimes a loop of the tube is tied with a tight band, but the tube is not cut so that, in theory, the sterilization procedure can be reversed. Although this procedure is more commonly carried out through the small incision in the abdomen, the procedure can also be performed vaginally, in which case the vagina is clamped open. As with abdominal tubal ligation, this process is carried out under local anesthesia.

The procedure in men can be carried out at a day clinic under local anesthesia on a day-care basis. The surgeon makes two small incisions in the scrotum (see Penis), cuts each of the two vas deferens (the extensions of the testis that run from the scrotum to join the seminal vesicle that forms the ejaculatory duct), and ties the cut ends. This procedure makes a man sterile by interrupting the route of the spermatozoa.

After surgery
Both women and men will experience some tenderness after such sterilization surgery, but any pain can be controlled with nonprescription painkillers.

After this procedure a woman becomes infertile because sperm cannot reach the egg. However, a man remains fertile after a vasectomy until any sperm already present in the vas deferens have been ejaculated or die. For this reason, alternative contraceptive measures must be used until the man has produced two consecutive sperm-free specimens.

Success rate
The failure rate of the sterilization procedure in women is about one in a thousand, and if a woman does become pregnant afterward (a very rare occurrence), there is an increased risk of an ectopic pregnancy (see Ectopic pregnancy).

In men, the two ends of the severed vas deferens may join up again over a period of time, but this occurs in less than 0.5 percent of cases. Under exceptional circumstances a surgeon may try to reverse the sterilization procedure in a man or in a woman who has not had the fallopian tubes cut, just looped. In such cases, the success rate of reversal in both sexes is about 50 percent.

In female sterilization, the vagina is clamped open and an incision is made near the cervix (at center). The fallopian tubes are drawn through the vaginal wall and ligatured, and are then pushed back into the abdominal cavity. The incision is then stitched up.

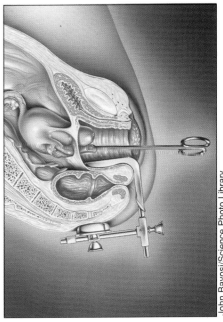

John Bavosi/Science Photo Library

Tuberculosis

Q Is it true that you can get TB from milk?

A Two strains of the TB bacterium are important causes of the disease in man. The first is the human strain, and the second is the bovine strain that can be passed on in milk. However, all cattle in the US are now tested for infection—so-called tuberculin-tested herds—so the bovine strain is no longer passed on in milk.

Q My grandfather had several ribs cut away because of TB, and he then had a very deformed chest. Why was this?

A Before antibiotics became available, surgery was one of the few ways of fighting the disease. One possibility was to cut out the parts of the lung that were affected, although this was a fairly major undertaking, and in any case the disease was likely to be widespread in both lungs. The other approach was to reduce the volume of areas of affected lung since the disease caused cavities, particularly in the upper parts of the lung. If these cavities were obliterated there seemed to be a better chance of curing the disease. This sort of surgery is no longer necessary since drugs can now cure the disease.

Q Can you be vaccinated against tuberculosis?

A Yes you can. There is a vaccine called BCG, which consists of a modified form of the TB bacterium. This is able to trigger the immune system against the disease but does not cause serious disease itself. Children are tested for evidence of previous contact with the disease (primary TB) and, if they are negative to testing, they are given BCG. Children who react are known as tuberculin positive and are immune. There are two types of tuberculin test: the Mantoux and the Heaf test. These are performed at age 13. People at risk from the disease, such as medics, are also tested and revaccinated as necessary.

Thanks to improved nutrition and living conditions tuberculosis is no longer prevalent in the developed West, although in recent years there has been a resurgence of a resistant form of the disease in inner-city areas.

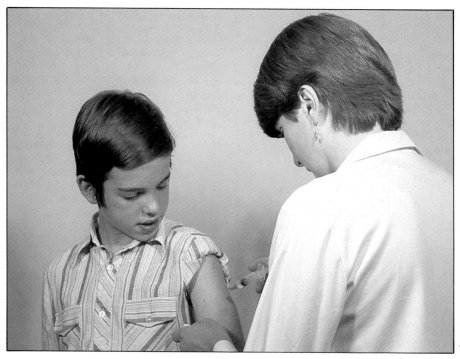

It is a routine part of preventive medicine to test older children for immunity to TB, and then to vaccinate as necessary.

Tuberculosis—or TB as it is more commonly known—remains one of the most serious infectious diseases in the world. Although the improved standards of general living conditions have made this disease relatively uncommon in the West, it remains one of the great killers among Third World communities.

TB is caused by a funguslike bacterium called *Mycobacterium tuberculosis* (see Bacteria), and there are two main strains of this particular organism that cause disease in humans: a human strain and a bovine strain, which primarily infects cattle, but which is also capable of causing human disease.

The incidence of this chronic infection and the problems it can cause vary from country to country. In the United States infection of the lungs—pulmonary TB—is the most usual form of the disease, whereas in Africa abdominal TB is very common.

How TB develops

At one time most people growing up in a country like the United States would have been in contact with tuberculosis at an early age. Such early contact with the disease leads to an infection called primary TB, which is often—but not always—without any significant symptoms. This first contact with the disease is picked up as a result of contact with someone who has sufficiently severe disease in the lungs to cough up sputum containing TB bacteria. If the amount of bacteria inhaled is relatively small, then the primary TB will be a minor infection that will help build up a partial immunity to the development of full-blown TB later on (see Immune system).

The more serious forms of the disease that occur in later life are called postprimary disease. It seems that the usual cause for these infections is that the immunity to the original infection has broken down and the TB bacteria have literally broken out of their original site. Although this is probably the usual mechanism of development of the disease, it is also likely that some people developing the disease later in life do so because they are exposed to a very high infecting dose of bacteria.

The reasons why immunity breaks down are not clear. In most cases it seems that social rather than medical factors are of greatest relevance, since there is little doubt that TB these days is a disease that is most common among vagrants and alcoholics, although it may still occur in an apparently fit person who is well fed and lives in good housing. People infected with HIV may have extrapulmonary TB, which may involve multiple organs (see AIDS).

Complications of primary TB

Although primary TB is often a relatively minor infection with no symptoms, it can develop into a serious disease in very young children or in children who have some other debilitating disease.

The site of infection is nearly always the lungs, although in some parts of the world it may be the abdomen. The original infection causes a small area of inflammation in one of the lungs, and this goes on to produce a reaction in the lymph nodes that drain lymphatic fluids from that particular part of the lung (see Lymphatic system). This patch

of inflammation and enlargement of some of the lymph nodes at the root of the lung is called the primary complex.

In most cases, the TB bacteria in the primary complex are contained by the lymph nodes and spread no further. But in a few children and adolescents with primary TB the defense mechanism breaks down soon after infection. This allows the bacteria to spread throughout the body, leading to a serious condition called miliary TB, which causes general illness, with loss of weight and a high fever. Diagnosis is by X-ray examination of the chest, which shows that both lungs are full of tiny nodules, each of which represents an area of tuberculous infection.

Sometimes the general spread of the disease soon after the primary infection leads to an infection in the nervous system called TB meningitis. Unlike the

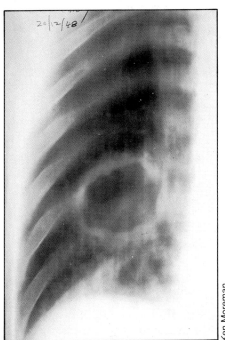

Ken Moreman

This X ray of a lung shows the large cavity created by a primary TB infection—the bacilli are still contained inside it.

The progress of pulmonary tuberculosis

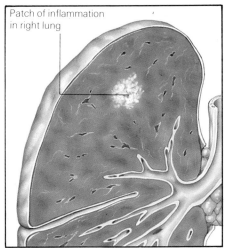

Patch of inflammation in right lung

TB begins as a small inflamed area in one lung (left), which turns into a cavity (below left). Advanced TB usually results when a dormant primary infection is reactivated

and the bacteria spread to cause extensive cavitation in both lungs (below). The blood vessels then become congested and are likely to rupture, causing hemorrhage.

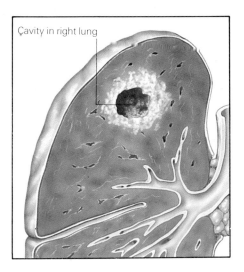

Cavity in right lung

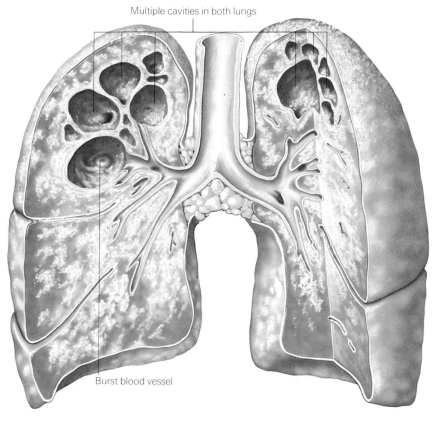

Multiple cavities in both lungs

Burst blood vessel

Frank Kennard

TUBERCULOSIS

There is a strain of the TB organism that infects cattle and can be passed on in milk— a problem overcome in the US by testing all cattle for infection. The disease in humans is diagnosed by viewing a sputum sample under the microscope. When stained, any bacteria will appear as thin red rods (below left). If the diagnosis is unclear, a bacterial culture is grown on a plate (below right) or a slope (opposite right). This will prove whether the TB bacillus is present and, if so, which strain is involved. Untreated TB can lead to infection of the pleura (the membranes encasing the lungs) and then to pleural fibrosis (opposite left). This is usually very rigid, being full of calcium, and will impede lung movement so that breathing is seriously hampered.

more common types of meningitis that develop within a day or so of infection, TB meningitis may take some weeks to develop (see Meningitis). The first symptoms are of general ill health, a slight fever, headaches (a very unusual complaint in a child), and, occasionally, fits. At a later stage the fever rises and the signs of drowsiness and neck stiffness appear. Finally the fever rises yet higher and obvious problems with individual nerves, such as those controlling the eyes, will occur. This is a very dangerous condition, and it is important to start treatment as soon as the diagnosis is

made. The diagnosis is confirmed by performing a lumbar puncture (see Lumbar puncture), which enables doctors to look at the cerebrospinal fluid that bathes the brain and spinal cord. One of the findings that indicates TB meningitis is a level of sugar in the fluid very much lower than that in the blood. This is almost unique to this condition.

Pulmonary TB

Although the primary focus of pulmonary TB occurs in the lungs, it is not

until the postprimary stage of infection that the lungs cause any trouble. In a few cases of primary TB the lymph nodes at the root of the lung may break down and liberate the bacteria into one of the main tubes (bronchi) supplying a particular lobe of the lung. This in turn will lead to a lobar pneumonia occurring soon after the original infection.

Most cases of tuberculous lung disease, however, happen many years after the original infection with the disease. The primary focus actually has a tendency to attack the lower lobes of the lungs, while the postprimary infection is much more likely to occur in the highest segments of the upper lobes of the lungs. It seems that the large amounts of oxygen that are available there, together with the relatively poor supply of blood, are particularly suitable incubators for the lung disease.

When the disease has become established in the upper part of the lungs it may cause cavities to form there. Once this has happened, large numbers of TB bacteria may be present in the sputum, and this means that the sufferer becomes a serious source of infection until he or she is treated. The sufferer is most likely to infect young children, giving them primary TB, TB meningitis, or TB bronchopneumonia. And it may well

Insets: (left) Biophoto Associates, (right) C. James Webb

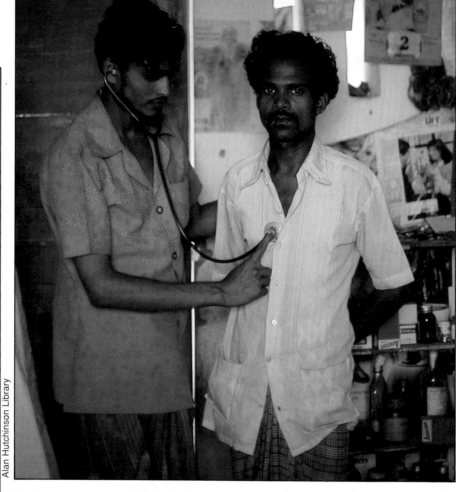
Alan Hutchinson Library

Q Is it true that you have to be hospitalized for months to be cured of TB?

A No. If you are found to have TB these days, you wouldn't necessarily have to be in the hospital at all. In the past there was no effective cure, and it was found that rest in a sanitarium was one of the most beneficial things. People who could afford it were sent away to mountain resorts where the purer air was thought to be helpful. Today the drug treatment is so efficient that you are no longer infectious with the disease after about 10 days. However, the standard length of treatment for pulmonary TB is still nine months.

Q My friend had TB which affected the liver and the rest of the abdomen. Is this common? I thought TB was a chest disease.

A You are right in thinking that the disease normally affects the chest. However, disease outside the chest certainly occurs, although it is not very common in the United States. One of the most interesting things about TB is the way it presents itself in different ways in different groups of people. Immigrants to the United States from Africa or India are much more likely to have TB outside the chest than someone who was born here. This does not seem to be a purely racial thing, however, since the children of immigrant parents who are born and raised in this country seem to get TB in the lungs if they do happen to develop it.

Q Is it true that modern drugs are so effective that TB is no longer a common problem?

A It is certainly true that the disease is much less common than it used to be, and also that the drugs available to treat the disease are very effective. However, there is little evidence that the two facts are related. TB was on the decline before the new drugs were widely available. Most people think that the combination of improved housing and improved nutrition is the main reason for the reduced incidence of TB.

be that someone spreading large numbers of TB bacteria is able to rekindle the disease in people in older age groups who have already had the primary form of the illness.

Left untreated, pulmonary TB can lead to the formation of fluid in the pleural space that surrounds the lungs, to infection of the pleura (lining membrane), and subsequently to pleural thickening and fibrosis (see Pleurisy). A particular characteristic of TB is that the fibrosis it leaves behind is often full of calcium and is therefore very rigid. Obviously, a lung surrounded by a hard wrapping of bonelike fibrosis is not going to be able to move freely, and breathing will be seriously impaired.

Sometimes the same sequence of events will happen to the pericardium—the membranous sac that surrounds the heart. This has even more serious effects since tuberculous pericarditis may restrict the activity of the heart and stop it from pumping enough blood to the rest of the body.

It is usually easy to diagnose a case of pulmonary TB. In a well-developed infection there will be marked changes on the chest X ray, particularly in the upper parts of the two upper lobes. One of the difficulties on an X ray, however, is identifying whether the changes represent new or old TB infection. The fibrosis caused by an early episode of TB

TB is a pervasive problem in India, but there are now clinics set up where people can be diagnosed and treated accordingly.

will persist for life, and will therefore leave X-ray changes for life.

In a case of suspected TB the first step is to inspect the patient's sputum under a microscope. When there is a heavy infection, the sputum will contain a lot of bacteria. These will show up as thin red rods when stained with a special TB stain called Ziehl-Neelsen stain. The presence or absence of bacteria on direct staining of the sputum is of great relevance, since if there are no bacteria the patient cannot be infectious, even if he or she does turn out to have TB at a later stage. Infection with the presence of bacteria on direct staining is called open TB, and this is the only type that can possibly be infectious.

Other forms of TB

Although pulmonary TB is the most common form of the disease, there are many other areas of the body that it may attack, such as the uterus, genitals, kidney, skin, and spine.

Abdominal TB is a common problem, particularly in Africa and India. It can be difficult to make the diagnosis since there is no convenient test, such as the chest X ray, that picks up the disease. Sufferers simply appear to be rather unwell, and will have a temperature. One of the easiest ways of making the diagnosis is by performing a liver biopsy (see Biopsy), surgically removing a small piece of liver and examining it under a microscope to see if there are any TB bacteria present.

TB may also attack the lymph glands in the neck, causing an abscess to form (see Abscess), and sometimes involving the overlying skin. This condition is called scrofula.

Treatment

Prior to the 1950s, with no effective drug treatment available, TB was often fatal. The cure for pulmonary TB, for instance, relied heavily on building up the patient's resistance with rest and nourishment. Unfortunately this care often came too late. The clarity of the air and the relative lack of oxygen at great heights were also thought to be helpful, and there were many sanitariums in mountain resorts where wealthy TB sufferers went to recover.

Surgery was also performed to remove the seriously infected parts of the lungs. This reduced the volume of the lungs and obliterated the cavities, thereby halting the spread of the disease through the lungs. However, before antibiotics were introduced as a treatment for TB (see Antibiotics), attempts to achieve a cure were frustrated by the fact that the disease was often widespread before treatment was started. This often resulted in very intense fibrous scarring of the lung tissue, which prevented it from fulfilling the function of transferring oxygen from the air into the blood. Even today, if cases of TB are left untreated for too long, fibrosis will occur and cannot be helped by antibiotics.

With modern treatment, however, it is possible to stop the progress of TB within a few days of starting treatment, although it takes many months to achieve a complete cure. There are now a selection of drugs that can be used to treat the TB infection. The first of these was streptomycin and, although still used, it is somewhat limited by the fact that it has to be given by injection. The usual drugs used today are rifampicin, isoniazid, and ethambutol. To prevent the organism from becoming resistant to the use of any one drug, it is customary to use a combination of these drugs during the early stages of the infection. Once the organism has grown—and this may take three months—it is possible to show that it is sensitive to at least two of the drugs and one is then left out.

The length of time it takes to cure TB varies depending on the particular type

TB was not only once a great killer, its victims were often tragically young, like the poet John Keats who died at age 26.

of infection. For instance, treatment has to continue for at least nine months in the case of pulmonary TB, but much longer in the case of abdominal TB.

Prevention

It is possible to test the population for immunity to TB using a preparation of TB-derived protein called tuberculin (see Protein). People with a partial immunity to the disease as a result of a primary TB infection in the past will show a reaction when tuberculin is injected into the skin. In cases of established postprimary TB the extent of the reaction will be greater.

If a child between the ages of 11 and 13 has not yet come into contact with the disease, then it is well worth him or her being vaccinated with BCG (bacille Calmette-Guérin), a vaccine that consists of a modified form of the TB bacterium (see Vaccinations). The vaccine produces the same effect as a minor primary infection, and gives a certain amount of immunity against the disease. It is also worthwhile having younger children vaccinated where there is a risk of contact with the disease.

However, the main element of prevention is the social element. It has, after all, been the social rather than the medical advances of the last hundred years that have reduced the incidence of TB in countries like the United States. Although the introduction of curative drugs was undoubtedly important, the number of people suffering from the disease had actually started to decline before these drugs became available. Today, TB is very uncommon in well-nourished, well-housed communities, and it is likely that it would disappear altogether if everyone lived under such circumstances.

Incidence of tuberculosis in the United States

In 1994 a total of 24,361 cases of tuberculosis (TB) were reported to the Centers for Disease Control and Prevention (CDC) from the 50 states, the District of Columbia, and New York City. This represented a 3.7 percent decrease from 1993. However, the number of cases reported in 1994 represented a 9.7 percent increase over 1985, the year with the lowest number of reported TB cases since national reporting began in 1953.

Tumors

Q What is the difference between a cancer and a tumor?

A The term *cancer* is used to describe any malignant tumor. The medical terms for cancer are *carcinoma* and *sarcoma*. A carcinoma is a tumor arising from a lining membrane, while a sarcoma arises in connective tissue, like fat or muscle. When doctors use the words *growth* or *tumor* they could be referring to one that is either benign or malignant.

Q My doctor thinks that I may have an abdominal tumor, and he has referred me to a surgeon at the hospital. What will happen next?

A The surgeon will ask you a number of questions and examine your abdomen to help locate the tumor. He or she will then arrange for you to have some special X rays to support the diagnosis. Any subsequent treatment will depend on the type of tumor and its location.

Q My father just had a malignant tumor removed from his colon. Is it possible to tell whether or not it may recur?

A Yes, the surgeon should have a good idea. He or she will have some information about the tumor's spread after the operation itself. There may also be evidence of any secondary tumors from X rays and other tests. In addition the surgeon will have examined a piece of tissue from the tumor under the microscope, and this will tell him or her something more about the growth's malignancy.

Q Do malignant tumors develop quickly, and are they always likely to be fatal?

A By no means. Some types of malignant tumor are so slow-growing that they are unlikely to spread at all. Many other tumors can be treated very successfully with surgery, radiotherapy, or with a course of chemotherapy. To a large extent successful treatment depends on early diagnosis.

It can be very alarming to discover a growth or swelling, which a doctor would describe as a tumor. But, in fact, some tumors are harmless, and many others respond to treatment—especially if diagnosed early.

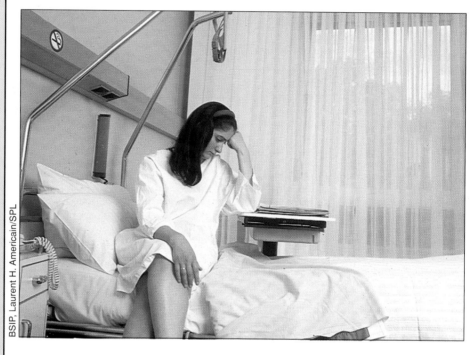

BSIP, Laurent H. Americain/SPL

A patient who is waiting for the diagnosis of a tumor is understandably apprehensive and anxious about the future.

Strictly speaking, any type of abnormal growth should be called a tumor. This can cause distressing misunderstandings, since medical staff tend to use the term accurately, while laypeople often mistakenly think that all tumors are malignant or cancerous growths.

The body's normal cells are subject to controls that insure that new cells are made at the same rate at which the old cells are lost. For example, as skin cells are destroyed by friction and abrasion on the surface, equal numbers of new cells form. This means that the skin is roughly the same thickness throughout life.

The details of this control mechanism are not understood. But if it breaks down, cells are formed at an unchecked rate and a tumor is formed.

Types of tumor

There are two basic types of tumor; benign and malignant. Benign tumors are localized growths of tissue that produce swellings. There is no tendency for these extra cells to spread or grow into other parts of the body. However, these tumors can have serious consequences as a result of their location.

A benign tumor of the nerve tissue in the spinal canal can put pressure on the spinal cord, causing paralysis (see Paralysis). Similarly, an organ may be damaged if pressure is put on one of the blood vessels that supply it.

The major identifying characteristic of malignant tumors is that they have a tendency to spread to other parts of the body. However, it can still be extremely difficult to identify a tumor as being malignant, since some tumors are, in fact, very slow-growing.

Malignant tumors are separated into two further groups; primary and secondary. The original tumor is known as the primary one. As this grows, fragments of the tissue may break off and settle in other parts of the body. These then multiply and the cells that make up the fragments form secondary tumors.

Secondary tumor cells can usually be identified under a microscope because they consist of cells that are normally found in another part of the body. For instance, a primary tumor of the thyroid gland may spread to the bones, so that a secondary tumor formed of abnormal thyroid cells is found in a bone.

How tumors spread

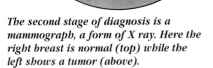

The second stage of diagnosis is a mammograph, a form of X ray. Here the right breast is normal (top) while the left shows a tumor (above).

The portal veins carry nutrients from the stomach to the liver. But fragments of a malignant tumor may also be transported to the liver and secondaries may grow here.

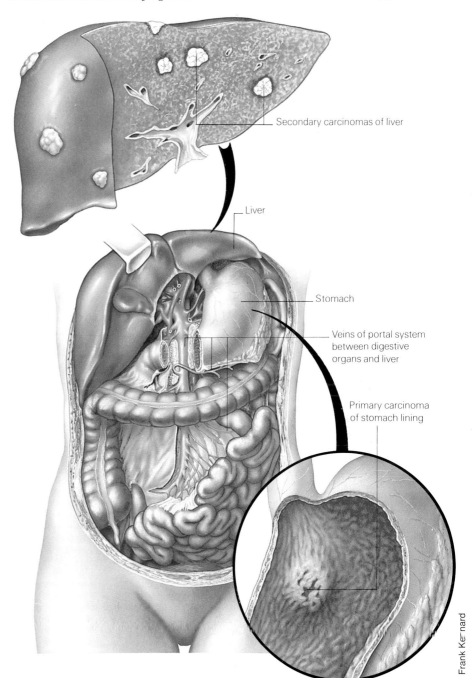

Secondary carcinomas of liver

Liver

Stomach

Veins of portal system between digestive organs and liver

Primary carcinoma of stomach lining

Frank Kennard

How malignant tumors spread

Malignant tumors can spread in many ways: through blood vessels or lymphatic channels, by direct extension into organs, or by growing across body cavities.

Small clumps of cells can break off from a primary tumor and enter the veins that drain the tissue around the tumor. The fragments are carried back to the heart and on to the lungs, where the cells can lodge and grow.

The body has a system of tiny channels that carry lymph to and from the lymph glands. Tumor cells can enter this system and cause secondary tumors in the lymph glands. The secondaries are sometimes quite some distance from the primary tumor. For example, a tumor in one of the testes can sometimes lead to a secondary tumor appearing in the neck.

Tumors can also spread when affected cells extend into adjacent tissues. This can make treatment particularly difficult, since completely removing the tumor may involve cutting away a vital part of a neighboring organ.

Finally, tumors can spread across spaces in the body such as the abdominal or chest cavities. A malignant stomach tumor may sometimes spread across the peritoneum (the membrane that lines the abdomen) so that secondaries occur in the pelvis (see Peritoneum).

Treatment

The treatment for tumors varies enormously. Benign tumors are usually removed, unless their location makes them unlikely to cause any problem. Malignant tumors can be treated by surgical removal, a course of radiotherapy, or one of chemotherapy. Surgery is the preferred treatment. However, sometimes it is not possible to operate; for example, the patient may not be sufficiently strong enough to undergo a surgical procedure. Radiotherapy and chemotherapy (see Cancer, and Radiotherapy) both destroy the rapidly dividing cells that are found in a malignant tumor.

Each type of treatment has side effects, particularly chemotherapy, which can also damage normal body cells. However, the benefits of these treatments can vastly outweigh these effects.

Twitches and tics

Q When I am tired I get a twitching in the corner of my eye. Does this mean that there is anything wrong?

A No. This happens to people when they are tired or irritated, and it is quite normal. Occasionally such a twitch may become ingrained and happen more frequently; it is then called a tic.

Q My young daughter has suddenly started grimacing for no apparent reason. Is this a tic, and what should be done about it?

A This may well be a tic and these are frequent in the five- to ten-year-old age group. If the matter is not made into a major issue and your daughter is not made aware of it, the tic will probably disappear. Other tics may show themselves from time to time, but they need not cause concern.

Q Sometimes, just as I am going to sleep, I have a sudden large-scale twitching in my arms and legs. What is this?

A This is known as a myoclonic jerk, and it is not unusual in the early stages of sleep. It is harmless, and there is nothing to worry about. It is, in fact, one of the most common forms of twitches, and can sometimes be so violent that it shakes the person back into a state of full consciousness.

Q My son has a mild form of epilepsy and I have noticed recently that, in addition to his occasional seizures, he sometimes has sudden twitching of his muscles, particularly when he is using them. Does this mean his epilepsy is getting progressively worse.

A Probably not. This is another form of myoclonus and is a common feature of epilepsy, especially in children. Although it can be associated with serious brain damage, it is usually just a symptom of the electrical instability of the brain that goes along with your son's tendency to have epileptic seizures.

The thought that you might not be in full control of all your body's actions may be rather alarming. However, most unconscious movements are simply twitches or tics.

Shout

Occasional twitches of our muscles happen to all of us from time to time, but in some disorders of the nervous system these involuntary movements may become numerous and troublesome.

Sometimes a repeated twitch in a particular group of muscles, particularly in the face, may take on a stereotyped pattern, and it is then referred to as a tic. Larger scale jumps of the muscle, called myoclonic jerks, are also common.

The sufferer from the rare condition called Tourette's syndrome is subject to involuntary grimaces and tics and, in more extreme cases, to episodes of barking, grunting, and obscene language.

What causes twitching?
When operating normally, muscles contract smoothly and evenly, and work together to produce coordinated movements (see Muscles). However, a twitch

in a group of muscles happens in isolation and obviously does not result in any planned action. The body has a complex movement control system designed to eliminate such wasteful actions, so a twitch usually indicates some minor breakdown in the system.

The most common time for motor control to be upset and a twitch to occur is when we are tired (see Tiredness). It is usual for the odd twitch to occur around the eyelids, for example, when feeling drowsy. More severe disturbances can occur when the metabolic systems of the body are upset. In kidney or liver disease, muscle twitching may eventually become quite pronounced (see Kidneys and kidney disease, and Liver and liver disease).

Tics

Most tics are simply coordinated twitches that occur in groups of muscles, usually in the face and especially around the eyes. Basically a tic differs from a twitch in that it is a repeated, coordinated but purposeless twitch that often occurs in bursts. A tic is common in children between the ages of five and ten, and normally only lasts for a week or two. Usually, though, the tic only causes parental anxiety or teasing from other children. If, however, the child begins to worry about it then this can cause the tic to get worse.

The most common types of tic involve muscles around the eyes and mouth. The tic takes the form of a grimace or frown that transiently distorts the face and quickly disappears. The same pattern of movement, or expression, is repeated many times, often more frequently in stressful situations. Most people with tics have just one repetitive movement; however, occasionally people suffer from multiple tics, which may have completely different patterns.

Gilles de la Tourette's syndrome

On rare occasions multiple tics may develop into a more serious syndrome named after the doctor who first described it, Gilles de la Tourette. It is not common, although it probably occurs in a mild form where it is often not diagnosed. It usually starts in the teens with the development of multiple tics and the appearance of odd grunts and shouts. The person's intelligence is usually normal, but the full-blown syndrome can give the sufferer a very strange appearance, and the multiple tics can often be seriously disabling when they occur.

What causes tics?

The precise reason why some people develop persistent tics is not yet known. Although many psychological theories have been advanced to explain these abnormalities, in terms of anxiety and stress, few have been accepted. It is believed that there is probably some electrical problem in the movement control centers of the brain, particularly those of the face, which have to control a large range of very sensitive muscle groups. There never appears to be any damage to these areas and a tic is never a symptom of a serious disease, so any abnormality in these control centers is probably only a temporary disturbance that eventually rights itself. Where a tic becomes permanent or prolonged it is thought that the movement becomes an ingrained habit.

Myoclonus

Myoclonus is a sudden, large-scale twitch that we all sometimes get, especially when about to go to sleep. Severe persistent myoclonus can indicate brain degeneration, although this is rare and occurs with other signs of serious brain disease (see Brain damage and disease).

Treatment

In most cases no treatment, other than an explanation and reassurance, is needed for those who have a twitch or tic. When there are multiple tics, these may need to be suppressed, and there are several drugs that can help. Myoclonus can be controlled since drugs used against epilepsy seem to be effective (see Epilepsy).

Facial tics can be distressing, but are momentary. However, severe twitching can be a symptom of liver or kidney disease.

Shout

CLARKSTON

WITHDRAWN

CLARKSTON